Writing Test Items to Evaluate Higher Order Thinking

Related Titles of Interest

How to Make Achievement Tests and Assessments, Fifth Edition
Norman E. Gronlund
ISBN: 0–205–14799–2

Test Scores and What They Mean, Fifth Edition
Howard B. Lyman
ISBN: 0–13–904178–8

Classroom Assessment: What Teachers Need to Know
W. James Popham
ISBN: 0–205–15429–8

Writing Test Items to Evaluate Higher Order Thinking

THOMAS M. HALADYNA
Arizona State University West

Allyn and Bacon
Boston   London   Toronto   Sydney   Tokyo   Singapore

Copyright © 1997 by Allyn & Bacon
A Viacom Company
Needham Heights, MA 02194

Library of Congress Cataloging-in-Publication Data

Haladyna, Thomas M.
  Writing test items to evaluate higher order thinking / Thomas M. Haladyna.
    p.   cm.
  Includes bibliographical references and index.
  ISBN 0–205–17875–8
    1. Examinations—Design and construction.   2. Critical thinking—
Evaluation.   I. Title.
LB3060.65.H35 1997
371.2′61—dc20   96–19255
                                                              CIP

Printed in the United States of America
10 9 8 7 6 5 4 3   00 99

Contents

Preface

THIS BOOK INTENDS TO BE A COMPREHENSIVE GUIDE TO WRITING TEST items that will measure important higher level student outcomes at all educational levels. The book also addresses ways to improve test items once they are written.

Many comprehensive textbooks exist on educational measurement and evaluation, and these books cover many topics in the related fields of measurement and evaluation. Although this book provides more information about item writing than is found in a traditional textbook, it is not a comprehensive textbook on educational measurement and evaluation.

This book is intended for the professional development of teachers or teachers-in-training. Persons involved in other settings, such as training, may also benefit from this material.

A book like this one is an ambitious project in this decade of educational reform. Currently, performance testing has become a focus of the reform movement. Because educators typically have failed to define adequately, teach, and measure the most desirable outcomes of schooling—namely, various types of higher level thinking such as problem solving, critical thinking, and creative thinking—we face an enormous challenge. The most important outcomes of a good education are the abilities to solve problems, to think critically, and to create. In writing this book, I have had to define these different types of higher level thinking before I could write test items that reflected each type. Although this book may not provide adequate answers to the century-old problem of defining types of higher level thinking, it does attempt to synthesize current thinking and research and to meld together various suggestions for defining types of higher level thinking. The result is a relatively simple typology of mental and physical behaviors, which guides the chapters in this book.

The focus of this book is not on a particular orientation, such as performance testing or authentic assessment. I have tried to achieve a balance between traditional practices and newer ones, to recognize the strengths and limitations of both. For the most part, effective teaching involves the clear statement of what students are supposed to learn, an atmosphere that is conducive to learning, engaging and interesting activities that provide opportunities to learn, and dependable measures of student outcomes. These outcomes provide information that enables us to guide students in remedial or corrective activities and to satisfy the need for accountability and credit for grading and promotion.

How Is This Book Organized?

Part One, Foundations for Item Writing, provides a context for test-item writing. Chapter 1 offers an overview of the book and defines basic concepts, principles, and terminology. It tries to maintain a consistency in language and to avoid confusing jargon. Chapter 2 integrates the vast literature on the organization of content and types of higher level thinking. The resulting simple typology of student behavior is used consistently in the other chapters in the book. Chapter 3 presents item formats and argues that some formats are better than others for measuring certain types of student behavior.

Part Two, Writing Test Items, is the core of this book. It represents the most complete and comprehensive treatment of the subject of item development for practitioners to date. Chapter 4 focuses on multiple-choice formats for measuring knowledge and some mental skills and abilities. Chapter 5 deals with student outcomes that require expert judgment in using a rating scale. I refer to this kind of behavior as *high-inference* to reflect the judgment that a teacher makes when viewing a student response and classifying that behavior into three to seven descriptive categories that represent a developmental continuum. Other terms used to describe this approach to student testing are *authentic assessment* and *performance testing*. The topic is significant enough to be divided into two parts: 5A and 5B. Chapter 5A deals with issues in performance testing and how to design items. Chapter 5B addresses the important and complex issue of scoring student performance.

Chapter 6 complements Chapters 5A and 5B and discusses *low-inference* student behavior. In this chapter, we examine right/wrong scoring, checklists, simple observation, or observation with a measuring instrument such as a scale, clock, or ruler. Chapter 7 deals with collections of performances that we call a *portfolio*. Collections can form a type of super-item, a template for a well-planned series of activities that provides a unique view of student performance. Chapter 8 discusses the writing of *affective* items that can be used in student surveys to find out if affective outcomes are being achieved in the classroom. These affective outcomes may include motivation, attitude, self-confidence in learning, self-concept, locus of control (fatalism), and class climate, among other worthwhile outcomes.

Part Three, Evaluating Test Items, consists of two chapters that provide guidance on examining and improving items. Chapter 9 includes a series of item reviews that are painstaking but necessary to polish these items. Teachers do not have enough time to do all reviews, but if the stakes for the tests are high enough, item reviews can accomplish many good things. Chapter 10, the only technical chapter in the book, deals with student responses. Statistical methods are emphasized, but qualitative methods are also included. Following the suggestions in Chapter 10, as in Chapter 9, requires much time and effort. But who ever said that writing good test items is easy?

Like any other valued creative act, writing a test item requires both creativity and hard work before the item can be used effectively to measure the extent of student learning. Although this book contains many ideas about item writing, we have no shortcuts or easy ways out. Your personal creativity has much to do with writing good items. However, the concepts, principles, and procedures in this book should help you to develop items that will serve you well as you try to develop various types of higher level thinking abilities in your students.

Acknowledgments

First, and most importantly, I wish to thank Nancy Forsyth, who suggested this book and got me started. Also a special thanks to Del Hammond and Ron Carriveau, who provided thoughtful feedback and encouragement. Sharon and David Moore provided me with some excellent assistance in the area of reading assessment, and Bill Cobern did the same in science assessment. Two anonymous reviewers also provided constructive criticism and encouragement. Many students in the past wrote brilliant items, criticized my items, and provided me with many insights into the creative process of writing and responding to items.

Part One
Foundations for
Item Writing

These three chapters provide a foundation for thinking about item writing for various types of higher level thinking. Chapter 1 introduces terminology and makes some basic distinctions. Chapter 2 defines classes of student behavior and gives an organizational system for matching test items to teaching. Chapter 3 presents a wide variety of item formats useful for measuring the types of higher level thinking described in Chapter 2.

1 Overview of the Book

IN THIS CHAPTER, BASIC CONCEPTS AND PRINCIPLES OF EDUCATIONAL testing are briefly introduced and defined. In other chapters, these concepts and principles are extended and refined. Therefore, this chapter connects to all other chapters. In recognition of the developmental nature of item-writing ability, the main idea in this book is to help each reader acquire item-writing knowledge, skills, and ability to meet the challenges of testing what is taught by teachers and learned by students.

What Is Teaching and Learning?

The reason for schools, training programs, and courses is to promote student learning.

Learning is defined here as any change in mental behavior that is lasting and the product of experience. Learning is intellectual in nature. Learning is probably the joint result of (1) our natural ability to learn, (2) teaching, and (3) experiences outside of the classroom.

Teaching is a formal process for helping students learn. Teaching is a coordinated set of activities that require measuring student behavior reflecting our instructional intent. A synonym for teaching in this book is *instructing*. We know that learning can happen without teaching. We also know that even with effective teaching, learning may not occur. Our goals are to see that teaching results in student learning and that students use what they learn to deal with life's challenges.

What Are the Three Domains of Student Behavior?

We classify student behavior according to three domains. This section will briefly introduce each domain. Item writing applies to student behavior in all three domains.

Cognitive Domain

The cognitive domain consists of all intellectual behavior. This domain includes two major categories of behavior, *achievement* and *ability*, but it is often difficult to distinguish between the two.

Achievement refers to cognitive behavior that is easily changeable. In other words, achievement is short-term learning. Teachers tend to influence achievement. We generally classify achievement as either specific or general.

Specific achievement includes statements of student/learner outcomes that tell both student and teacher what kind of behavior is being sought. Teacher-made classroom tests are intended to measure these specific outcomes.

General measures of school learning are found in published standardized achievement tests, such as the Iowa Test of Basic Skills. These tests measure such general achievement as reading comprehension, mathematical reasoning, and study skills. Published standardized achievement tests are not designed to reflect a specific school curriculum but, rather, to reflect what a school curriculum generally represents. You might think of a published standardized test as measuring a student's achievement over a lifetime. One has to be careful in interpreting and using test scores based on classroom-specific learning and general lifelong learning. Although classroom tests and general educational achievement tests are related, the connection is hardly strong, clear, or well conceived. One is *never* a replacement for the other; the two have completely different interpretations and uses.

Ability refers to cognitive behavior that is harder to change than achievement. Ability is long-term learning. In fact, we might conceptualize ability and achievement on a continuum, where achievement is something that is learned in a shorter period of time when compared to ability. The following example shows this distinction in terms of salad-making ability. Using a packaged dressing is a simple skill that can be learned in a short period of time, whereas designing a new salad requires much knowledge and skill and a good deal of creativity.

Achievement	Ability
Learned in a short time period	Learned in a long time period
Making salad dressing from a packaged mix	Designing a new salad

Some typical abilities are *verbal* and *quantitative*. The word **aptitude** is often used synonymously with ability. Sometimes, we call this **scholastic aptitude**, because students seem to develop this ability in school. Some educational psychologists have noticed a decline in scholastic aptitude when formal schooling ends. In this century, educational and cognitive psychologists have struggled with defining the term *ability* (Lohman, 1993; Royer, Cisero, & Carlo, 1993). Is it one factor or many factors? If it is many factors, what are various human cognitive abilities? Theorists like Robert Sternberg and Howard Gardner take this multifactor view, much as J. P. Guilford did in the 1950s and 1960s with his Structure-of-the-Intellect model of human intelligence; before him, there was the primary mental abilities theory of Louis Thurstone. The alternative view championed by Arthur Jensen argues that general intelligence exists and that specific abilities are secondary in nature. How we measure and develop these abilities continues to be a major challenge to us.

A growing realization is that abilities can be developed, but very slowly (Lohman, 1993). Some educational psychologists, like Lohman, believe that the development of ability is the most important goal of schooling. Some student cognitive behaviors that qualify to be called an ability are (1) critical thinking, (2) problem solving, and (3) creativity, including creative thinking and artistic and scientific creative production. In this book, I take the position that no clear-cut line of demarcation exists between achievement and ability. The main difference is that achievement is something that can develop in a relatively short time period in school, whereas ability develops more slowly and more unpredictably. We have considerable experience in teaching and testing for lower forms of achievement, such as recall of facts and understanding, and practically no experience or success with developing students' mental abilities, such as critical thinking, problem solving, and creative thinking and production. That is the challenge for you: writing test items that measure mental abilities.

Affective Domain

Affective student behavior is largely emotional in nature and includes such important concepts as attitude, interest, motivation, self-confidence, self-esteem, self-concept, learning environment (class climate), learning style, and personality or temperament. We have an increasing understanding and appreciation of the role of the affective domain in teaching and learning. In fact, many affective outcomes of schooling are almost as important as cognitive outcomes. Most educators would agree that the affective domain is importantly related to the cognitive domain. We appreciate the roles of attitude, motivation, self-concept, self-esteem, and self-confidence in cognitive development. Teachers today do not ignore or underrate the effects of affective behavior on cognitive behavior. Chapter 8 provides some guidance on writing items for student surveys of affective traits.

Psychomotor Domain

Psychomotor behavior is largely physical and includes such activities as running, writing, computer keyboarding, skateboarding, pulling weeds in the yard, or speaking. Again, we do not want to underrate the importance of psychomotor outcomes in schooling or in life. All psychomotor behavior contains an element of cognitive behavior in it, but the psychomotor domain mainly focuses on the physical acts of performing rather than the cognitive basis for performing. For instance, we can learn how to skateboard by reading about it (acquiring knowledge), but performing it mainly involves physical ability (and courage, or perhaps stupidity). It takes a long time to be proficient on a skateboard.

> Considering the relative importance of all three domains, the main focus of teaching is cognitive development. But we should recognize that affective and psychomotor student outcomes are also important and should be part of many instructional programs because these types of student behavior are connected to cognitive student learning in important ways. Affective behavior is important in and of itself.

Need to Specify Clearly Each Learner Outcome

The theory of human behavior developed by the famous psychologist B. F. Skinner, often referred to as *behavioral learning theory,* has greatly influenced American education. One feature of this theory is the development of behavioral objectives, which were renamed *instructional objectives* to soften the image. More recently, cognitive psychology has replaced behavioral learning theory as the mainstream way of studying human behavior. Nonetheless, a legacy of behavioral learning theory is that students must have a clear idea of what they are to learn. In this book, we use the following structure:

1. TSW (The Student Will)
2. Verb and conditions
3. Some explicit standard

> The student will skateboard off a flat surface at least 4 feet above the ground and land on the pavement without damaging anyone or anything. (Three successful, successive trials are proof enough.)

Although this point has been made several times, it is important enough to repeat here again:

> Effective instruction is based on the identification of content that is worthy of instruction and the communication of this instructional intent to the students.

There is a consensus of both thinking and research that points to the need to specify carefully what students need to learn. An extreme position is that if that is all you do, you may succeed with many of your students without even teaching. Of course, the teacher wants all students to succeed, and this will take considerably more effort than simply presenting students with clear-cut statements of desired learner outcomes.

Knowledge and Skills

At this point, it is time to make some useful distinctions that we will continue to refine in Chapters 2 and 3 and will use for item writing in Chapters 4 through 8. Earlier in this chapter, *achievement* and *ability* were defined as being at opposite ends of a continuum. Achievement can be thought of as consisting of two aspects: *knowledge* and *skills*. Let us imagine that achievement (the acquisition of knowledge and skills) eventually leads to the development of ability, as Figure 1.1 illustrates.

Knowledge

Acquiring knowledge is a fundamental goal in life and in school. Psychologists call this *declarative knowledge*. These theorists often view knowledge as being content- or domain-specific and in need of organization in one's mind. The next chapter provides a more comprehensive treatment of knowledge. One popular position is that acquiring knowledge is less important than using knowledge. This might be a reaction to the long-standing overemphasis on testing for knowledge on well-known, published standardized achievement tests. This kind of thinking is behind the current trend to downgrade testing for knowledge in favor of performance testing, as we see in state testing programs in Arizona, Connecticut, Kentucky, and Vermont.

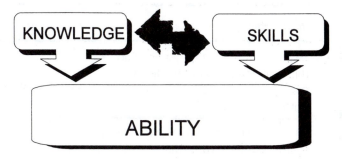

FIGURE 1.1
Relation of Knowledge and Skills to Ability

Another fallacy is that knowledge involves simply memorizing facts, concepts, principles, and procedures. In the past we have been expert at teaching students to memorize isolated facts. In other words, we can test for memory, but when it comes to higher level knowledge, we have difficulty asking the right questions. Chapter 2 will give you a better idea of the dimensions of knowledge that are worth testing. Chapter 3 aims to help you become a better tester of knowledge by selecting better item formats.

Testing for knowledge is crucial in building a foundation for higher level thinking. Therefore, we should *never* underestimate the importance of learning knowledge. But the exclusive testing of knowledge is pointless unless this knowledge is intelligently applied to solve problems, to think critically in meaningful settings, and to think creatively.

Skills

Skills are complex acts that require knowledge and involve performance. We have mental and physical skills, some that are easily visible and others that are less visible but must be inferred through student behavior.

This is the heart of the difference between achievement and ability. Achievement consists of knowledge and skills that are readily learned. Ability, too, is based on knowledge and skills but is considerably more complex and more difficult to learn. This difference comes into sharp focus here because both knowledge and skill are easily taught and learned in a short time period, whereas the correlated ability emerges much later and is much more complicated.

The connection between knowledge, skills, and abilities can be illustrated with reference to a familiar student ability: writing. The federal government, through the National Assessment of Educational Progress, has defined *writing* as written expression that may accomplish any one of three purposes: declarative, narrative, and persuasive.

Writing Achievement	Writing Abilities
Knowledge: Knowing about spelling rules, punctuation conventions, capitalization rules, subject–verb agreement, etc.	Ability to write declarative, persuasive, and narrative passages
Skills: Spelling, punctuation, capitalization, subject–verb agreement	

We can ask students to show their knowledge by looking at examples and choosing correct or incorrect spelling, punctuation, capitalization, subject–verb agreement, and the like. Or we can analyze their writing to determine their achievement of these skills. However, persuasive writing ability is the bigger entity that takes longer to learn. Knowledge and skills are the everyday kind of learning in elementary school. A complex combination of this knowledge and these skills makes up what we call *writing ability*. A good writer has acquired the knowledge and the mastered writing skills that lead to writing ability, as Figure 1.1 implies.

Another example to illustrate this distinction comes from a physical ability, baseball.

Willy Mays is considered to have exceptional baseball playing ability, which is why he is in the Baseball Hall of Fame in Cooperstown, New York. Baseball ability contains many skills, both teachable and natural. The learning of baseball skills occurs rapidly in boys and girls. But the development of baseball ability unfolds very slowly over many years. Some of these skills (base running, throwing, hitting, fielding) are easy to learn initially. Many cognitive strategies are involved in baseball ability. Also, learning the rules of baseball is part of this ability. Finally, baseball has an affective component based on poise, courage, motivation, hustle, teamwork, and attitude. We can see with baseball ability that knowledge and skills are related to ability in a complex way. While knowledge and skills are important in developing baseball ability, they are never sufficient. And baseball ability develops slowly over many years.

Whereas physical ability may be easily defined in terms of knowledge and skills, mental abilities are numerous and often ill defined (Cole, 1989). Critical thinking is one ability that has a positive history of study and use (Marzano, 1992). We will develop this idea of critical thinking in Chapter 2 and show how we can write items for some types of critical thinking in Chapters 4, 5A, 5B, and 6.

High-Inference and Low-Inference Behavior

Some student outcomes are abstractly defined. A student makes a response, and the teacher or some other judge must decide where that response fits into a list of categories called a *rating scale* or *scoring rubric*. Much of current-day performance testing emphasizing meaningful complex student learning requires the judgment of two or more experts using these rating scales. Chapter 2 defines high-inference student behavior more completely; Chapter 3 presents high-inference item formats, and Chapter 5A provides a comprehensive treatment of how to write test items. Chapter 5B discusses the high-inference scoring of student responses.

Some student outcomes are clearly seen and are termed *low-inference*. This term applies to student performance that is plainly visible and easily observed, sometimes using a checklist or a measuring instrument. In some instances, the student provides a right or wrong answer. Low-inference testing has very desirable characteristics, but few student outcomes can be measured with low-inference items. Chapter 2 expands this idea of low-inference behavior, Chapter 3 presents item formats used for low-inference testing, and Chapter 6 provides a complete treatment of how to write low-inference items.

Defining the Test Item

Because this book is about writing test items, it might be a good idea of define the term *test item*:

> A test item is an instruction or question that requires a student response and a rule for scoring the response.

This simple definition is not really useful, because, on closer review, we might recognize that not all items are alike. As Chapter 3 shows, an incredible variety exists. Let us make some basic distinctions here. Then, in Chapter 3, we will further examine further these distinctions. Chapters 4 through 8 offer advice on writing good items of each type.

The basic difference in items depends on whether a student *chooses* an answer or *constructs* an answer. Let us examine the anatomy of these two types:

Constructed-Response Item	Selected-Response Item
Instruction or question is written.	Instruction or question is written.
Student gives a response.	Teacher constructs choices.
Teacher develops a scoring system.	Student selects among choices.
Teacher uses scoring system.	Objective scoring is used.

Theorists, reformers, practitioners, and others have argued the merits and differences of constructed-response versus selected-response test items (Bennett, 1993; Bennett, Rock, & Wang, 1990; Haladyna, 1994; Snow, 1993). Their analyses and arguments are very complex. As used in this book, the structural differences between the two are noted here, and research seems clear about some generalizations:

1. When measuring knowledge (declarative knowledge), whether one uses multiple-choice formats (as presented in Chapter 4) or constructed-response formats (as presented in Chapters 5A and 6), the resulting test scores are highly comparable.
2. When measuring mental skills or abilities where there is a right answer, selected-response and constructed-response items provide comparable information.
3. When measuring mental skills or abilities where students generate multiple answers of a creative nature, the constructed-response format appears appropriate.
4. When measuring physical skills or abilities, the constructed-response performance format is the only reasonable choice.

In Chapter 2, we will sharpen our understanding of these generalizations. In Chapter 3 we will link item formats to student outcomes in a manner compatible with these four generalizations. The following table summarizes the kinds of student outcomes and the chapters addressing how to write items for each type:

Student Behavior	Inference	Item Type	Chapter
Knowledge/ mental skill/ability	High	Multiple-choice	4
Mental skill/ability	High	Performance	5A
Mental skill/ability	Low	Performance	6
Physical skill/ability	High	Performance	5A
Physical skill/ability	Low	Performance	6

Summary

In this chapter, you have studied basic definitions of aspects of student learning that can be tested. The chapter provided a link to other chapters in this book to help you develop knowledge, skills, and abilities to write test items that reflect complex and important outcomes of teaching. A central idea in this chapter is that the most important outcome of schooling is the development of abilities, and that this takes a long time. In the past we have avoided defining, developing, and testing for abilities. In the future, we need to concentrate on ability development because our students need these abilities to function in this increasingly complex, diverse world. Items in this book will focus more on abilities and less on the knowledge and skills needed to develop abilities.

References

Bennett, R. E. (1993). On the meaning of constructed response. In R. E. Bennett & W. C. Ward (Eds.) *Construction versus choice in cognitive measurement: Issues in constructed response, performance testing, and portfolio assessment* (pp. 1–27). Hillsdale, NJ: Lawrence Erlbaum Associates.

Bennett, R. E., Rock, D. A., & Wang, M. (1990). Equivalence of free-response and multiple-choice items. *Journal of Educational Measurement, 28*, 77–92.

Cole, N. S. (1990). Conceptions of educational achievement. *Educational Researcher, 19*, 2–7.

Haladyna, T. M. (1994). *Developing and validating multiple-choice test items*. Hillsdale, NJ: Lawrence Erlbaum Associates.

Lohman, D. F. (1993). Teaching and testing to develop fluid abilities. *Educational Researcher, 22*, 12–23.

Marzano, R. J. (1992). *A different kind of classroom*. Alexandria, VA: Association for Supervision and Curriculum Development.

Royer, J. M., Cisero, C. A., & Carlo, M. S. (1993). Techniques and procedures for assessing cognitive skills. *Review of Educational Research, 63*, 201–243.

2 What We Measure with Test Items

A FUNDAMENTAL ASSUMPTION IN WRITING ANY TEST ITEM IS THAT WE know what we are testing. In this chapter we will think about a problem that has troubled educators and psychologists for most of this century: defining different types of cognitive behavior that we want to develop and measure. To satisfy this need to know what we are testing, that *something* for which we want to write the test item must be defined. Once we have defined or identified that something, we need to consider whether that something is a high-inference or low-inference behavior. That decision influences the kind of item format we use and how we score a student's response to that item. The tasks ahead in this chapter are by no means easy.

This chapter contains a synthesis of recent thinking about cognitive behavior. When it comes time to write the test item, each item addresses two dimensions at the same time:

1. The type of content on which the item is based
2. The type of cognitive behavior needed to respond

These two dimensions form the basis of an organizational system for helping you think about what you want to teach and test. The emphasis is clearly on forms of thinking that are higher level instead of recall (memory).

Introduction

Good tests consist of good test items. Just as atoms make up a molecule, so every test item is a building block for every test. A good test gives us dependable information about something important we want to know about our students. As part of teaching, good test information tells us about our students' knowledge, skills, or abilities. But the most fundamental step in item writing is knowing what you want to test. In this chapter, we will first review the concepts of achievement and ability, examine the content of test items, and then study some basic types of mental behavior. The chapter includes many examples to give you a better understanding of the types of content and mental behaviors that test items can measure.

What Is the Difference between Achievement and Ability?

To review and extend some ideas introduced and briefly explained in Chapter 1, we need to differentiate between achievement and ability. (As you may have guessed, like most teachers, I often repeat myself. I often repeat myself.)

Achievement

Achievement refers to cognitive behavior that varies from simple memory of facts to more complex types of thinking where a right answer exists. Achievement happens in a short period, such as after a lesson or a class unit, over a semester, or during a course. As a rule, the mental behaviors falling into this category are less complex than abilities.

We have two basic types of achievement: knowledge and skills. *Knowledge* represents course content that is memorized or understood. Educational psychologists prefer the term *declarative knowledge*. A *skill* is a sequential set of behaviors leading to a result. Educational psychologists often use the term *procedural knowledge*, but I find this term puzzling. Anyone can have knowledge about how to do something, such as how to make bread using my new electric bread maker. But knowledge of a skill is declarative knowledge. In other words, knowing something is one thing, and doing it is something else. That is why I prefer the terms *knowledge* and *skills*.

Ability

Ability refers to behaviors that resemble skills but are usually more complex and therefore take longer to develop. These abilities may be complex combinations of what we have called knowledge and skills, but they also include affective components like motivation and attitude. We have mental and physical abilities, although most abilities consist of odd mixtures of mental and physical performance. Some psychologists believe that teachers should help students develop their mental abilities (Lohman, 1993). This is why there is such a strong push to encourage higher level thinking in the schools, to develop student mental abilities. Unfortunately, we have very little knowledge or experience of how to define and help students develop these mental abilities.

We can define, develop, and measure physical abilities. We do an outstanding job in such fields as sports (baseball, figure skating, swimming, running), industry (training employees to do the job), public administration (city workers, street repair, garbage collectors, public utilities employees, firefighters, postal workers, police), and military personnel (training soldiers to do their various jobs).

Mental abilities will be defined in this chapter, but with caution, because the defining, teaching, and measuring of mental abilities is still a developing science.

One goal of teaching is to transform student achievement into ability, as suggested by the examples that follow:

Achievement	Ability
Describing the elements of good performance in a movie (knowledge)	Becoming a great film critic
Learning how to wash lettuce for a salad (skill)	Becoming an expert salad maker
Writing sentences in the active voice (skill)	Developing narrative writing ability
Memorizing characteristics of vegetarian dinosaurs (knowledge)	Becoming a paleontologist

The activities on the left are teachable and learnable in a short period of time. These represent potential classroom learning activities that are somewhat easy to develop, which we commonly call knowledge or skills. The activities on the right are more complex and involved, take longer to develop, and may be considered abilities. As you can see, achievement may be conceived as simpler than ability. These examples illustrate that an ability is probably the elusive *higher level thinking* that we prize and wish to help students develop. The emphasis in this book is on the development of abilities reflecting these desirable types of higher level thinking.

To help us understand the basis for writing a test item, we will look at two dimensions that are represented in every test item: content and type of mental behavior. Most elementary textbooks on testing recommend using a two-way grid or test blueprint that contains these two dimensions.

For my seminar on making salad, I have constructed a test specification table as shown in Table 2.1.

I teach according to the weights in the blueprint, and the test is designed to reflect these weights. As I have said repeatedly, my tendency will be to teach and test in the direction of higher level mental behaviors instead of recall.

Content

In this section, we will study four basic types of content and illustrate each using the familiar item formats. The next section will address the five types of mental behaviors.

TABLE 2.1
Test Specifications for Salad-Making Seminar

	TYPES OF LEARNING BEHAVIOR		
	Knowledge	*Skill*	*Ability*
Planning	10%	10%	10%
Buying	5%	5%	10%
Preparing	5%	10%	5%
Serving	10%	10%	10%

Facts

Facts are basic knowledge that is not disputed:

The sum of 4 and 8 is 12.
The capital of Illinois is Springfield.
Water boils at 212 degrees Fahrenheit at standard atmospheric pressure.
Sentences begin with a capital letter and end with punctuation.
Lima beans are yucky.

Most educators would agree that learning facts provides an important foundation for other types of learning. One could hardly operate in our world without knowing many facts, such as your address, phone number, social security number, and the birthdays of favorite relatives and friends.

On the other hand, excessive learning of facts or exclusive teaching of facts without application to some problem seems to be a negative influence in education. Although factual learning is necessary, it is only a small piece of the puzzle when developing a student's mental abilities.

Concepts

Concepts are classes of objects or events that share a common set of defining traits. For instance, a tree has the following characteristics:

plant; needs water; takes in carbon dioxide; emits oxygen; often green; grows; has a root system in earth; has a trunk, branches, and leaves or needles; sheds its leaves or needles periodically; propagates; dies

We probably can list more traits, and we probably can identify some trees that are exceptions in some odd way. But generally a concept has enough defining traits to separate it from all its rivals—in this case plants that are not trees.

Concepts can be abstract or intangible; we define such a concept and then rate the extent to which a student's response to a test item exemplifies it. Concepts can be concrete; we define such concepts in ways that are factual and without question. Examples of abstract and concrete concepts follow and represent a major distinction that we made in Chapter 1 about high-inference and low-inference student behavior. The column on the left represents those abstract, high-inference things we may want to evaluate. With high-inference student performance, we make an inference about the level of performance using a rating scale. We use high-inference items and rating scales (scoring rubrics) that are discussed in Chapters 5A and 5B.

The concepts at the right represent low-inference behaviors, where we can simply observe or use a measuring instrument or checklist. This is what Chapter 6 is about.

Abstract and Concrete Concepts

ABSTRACT HIGH-INFERENCE	CONCRETE LOW-INFERENCE
Ambience	Income
Artistic expression	Cost
Attractiveness	Volume
Effectiveness	Tardiness
Clarity	Attendance
Aroma	Weight
Beauty	Height
Thoroughness	Speed
Originality	Distance
Appropriateness	Time

We have a well-organized science for testing the learning of concepts. We can have a student (1) choose the best definition of a concept, (2) identify examples and nonexamples of a concept, or (3) pick characteristics or noncharacteristics of a concept. Students also can generate definitions, examples, and nonexamples, or characteristics or noncharacteristics of a concept. Testing for concept learning is well developed in Chapters 4, 5A, and 6.

Principles

There are four kinds of principles that explain relationships between concepts. Each will be briefly described and examples will be given.

1. *Cause and effect:* This is the easiest to understand and forms the basis of much higher level thinking, especially critical thinking, which we will discuss later in this chapter. Cause-and-effect principles can be absolute or relative. An absolute principle might involve a statement that driving your car will eventually result in your having an empty gas tank. A principle about cigarette smoking would be relative: Cigarette smoking is not guaranteed to shorten one's life span, but it usually does so.

2. *Relationship between two concepts:* On the basis of a correlation, we can predict with a certain degree of confidence. For example, it is true that tall people tend to weigh more than short people, and that lima bean lovers tend to like okra as well. The accuracy of our predictions depends on the correlation between the two (height and weight; liking lima beans and liking okra).

3. *Laws of probability:* Theoretical probability distributions can be used to make predictions. Drawing from our examples, survival in an auto accident depends on safety features. Highway safety statistics provide probabilities of survival based on actual data. (We all know that the odds of winning a state lottery are very, very close to zero—that's why we keep trying, right?)

4. *Axiom:* An axiom is any universally accepted truth, like a law or a rule. Most axioms in school apply to science and to writing skills (e.g., spelling, punctuation, grammar). Our examples deal with a physical change (from liquid to vapor) and a real-life phenomenon dealing with cable television, as shown in the following examples:

Examples of Principles

Principle	Type
Cigarette smoking shortens life.	Cause-and-effect (relative)
Driving your car will eventually lead to an empty gas tank.	Cause-and-effect (absolute)
Tall people tend to weigh more than short people.	Relationship
Lima bean lovers tend to like okra.	Relationship
Your chance of survival in a head-on crash at 45 mph with an air bag and your seat belt fastened is very high.	Probable
Your chance of winning the state lottery is very low.	Probable
When water boils, it changes from liquid to gas.	Axiomatic
Cable TV always goes out during the most exciting time in a movie or a sporting event. (That's a joke.)	Axiomatic

Procedures

A procedure consists of a sequence of mental and/or physical acts leading to a result. In every subject matter or profession, or in everyday life, we have procedures. We teach and learn procedures and practice, polish, and perfect them. As in the examples, procedures can be simple or complex, involving considerable mental or physical abilities. Procedures dominate our lives every day in many ways. Teaching and learning a procedure is usually a complex activity. The simplest procedure may be called a skill; a more complex procedure may be called an ability. Generally we see a connection between the two: The learning of a skill leads to the development of an ability. For instance, learning to play the game of tennis requires mastery of much knowledge and skill; the integration of these two areas; and lots of time, energy, motivation, and patience. One skill is volleying the ball (hitting it in the air without letting it bounce). Another skill is saying, "Nice game, you really played great!" when you are thinking "You creep! I could have beaten you left-handed if I wasn't playing so badly." The many skills of tennis can be mastered individually, but the integration of all of these skills, in addition to the knowledge and other qualities needed to play, constitutes tennis ability.

In writing our test items to determine whether a procedure has been learned, do we want to study the steps involved or are we more concerned about the outcome? This is the distinction between *process* and *product*. Most procedures are tangible, sequential, and observable. For these reasons, a procedure is best measured using techniques presented in Chapter 6, because these are low-inference activities.

In this book, as in life, procedures can be thought of as either mental or physical. Sharpening a pencil is a physical procedure. Performing a lobotomy on yourself may involve both mental and physical procedures. Solving a complex mathematical problem involves a mental procedure. Some examples of procedures follow:

Examples of Procedures

Making a Cobb salad	Changing a tire on a car
Performing a lobotomy	Planning a long vacation
Sharpening a pencil	Steps in writing a book
Mowing the lawn	Washing dishes
Planning your retirement	Making bread
Buying a new car	Going out for lunch with a friend

Summary

Facts, concepts, principles, and procedures provide the core of content as we know it. While variation exists within these four content categories, we can simplify content by considering just these four groups. What we do with facts, concepts, principles, and procedures is the subject of the next section. Most experts on item writing suggest that you concentrate on testing only one thing at a time. If you choose to test a fact, don't test any other type of content. Save that for another item.

Types of Mental Behavior

Up to now, you have been exposed to just one of two dimensions: content. This section deals with the second dimension: types of mental behavior. This section will be very challenging to read and understand. One reason is that, collectively, those of us in cognitive psychology and classroom testing are not all that knowledgeable about these types. The venerable Bloom taxonomy has been the standard for types of mental behavior (Bloom, Engelhart, Furst, Hill, & Krathwohl, 1956). But this system was intended for the classification of objectives and has not enjoyed widespread acceptance in terms of research and practice.

This second dimension in item writing is the more important consideration when writing the test item. What type of mental behavior will be developed and tested with a specific item? Mental behavior ranges from simple recall to the very complex behavior that we label *ability*. Because we want a simple, workable system for classifying mental behavior, we will keep the list of types of mental behavior short. The system presented here draws from other systems. For instance, Robert Marzano and his colleagues have developed a complex description of higher level thinking that has achieved much recognition (Marzano, 1992; Marzano, Brandt, Hughes, Jones, Presseisen, Rankin, & Suhor, 1988; Marzano, Pickering, & McTighe, 1993). Much of this chapter rests on this excellent work, but the system has been simplified. Some significant compromises have been made here in the hope that what remains will work for you.

Understanding

This type of learning is more complex than memorization but is not in the same league as those that follow. Understanding, like *comprehension* in Bloom's taxonomy, applies to facts, concepts, principles, and procedures. Understanding is related to three specific types of student behavior:

1. Can the student define the fact, concept, principle, or procedure without using the verbatim definition given? To show understanding, the student should either generate a paraphrased correct definition, or select a paraphrased correct definition from a list.
2. Can the student generate or select the relevant characteristics of the fact, concept, principle, or procedure? To show understanding, the student must generate or select a set of characteristics that are not memorized.
3. Can the student select or identify examples of the fact, concept, principle, or procedure being understood? To show understanding, the examples must not be previously encountered, or else the testing would involve memory.

Definitions and characteristics are probably susceptible to memorization, but the use of previously unencountered examples is a good way to test for understanding. The student can generate these examples or select from a list via a multiple-choice item. In Chapter 4, we will provide good examples of ways to test for understanding using the multiple-choice format. This format is excellent for measuring this kind of mental behavior. Some examples of understanding behavior are taken from my salad-making seminar:

> **Examples of Understanding**
>
> Describing the following salads in your own words: Cobb, taco, chicken
>   Caesar, honeymoon (lettuce alone), spinach
> Identifying examples of salad fixings (e.g., tomatoes, zucchini, cucumbers,
>   mushrooms, carrots) from nonexamples (e.g., potatoes, lima beans,
>   chocolate syrup, bananas)
> Identifying nutritional characteristics of salad dressings

Problem Solving

Problem solving is not really well defined. In a review by Zambo and Follman (1994), a number of contrasting definitions are proposed, and many have common elements, but it is interesting to note the diversity of definitions and lack of consensus that now exists. The Curriculum and Evaluation Standards for School Mathematics developed by the National Council of Teachers of Mathematics fails to provide a clear-cut definition, but it includes problem solving as one of the main activities in the reformed mathematics education.

In this section, problem solving is described as a set of mental steps leading to the realization of a goal, usually an answer. Problem solving can also involve physical steps or a combination of mental and physical steps; it may also involve other types of mental behavior, like memorizing, understanding, and critical thinking. Creativity may also be involved. In some problem solving, several right answers might exist.

As a general class of behavior, problem solving is probably an ability because it is complex and develops slowly over a long period. We need to identify the steps we follow in solving a problem and ensure that the student has learned these steps and can apply them to *any* problem of the same kind.

Problems have several elements, as Table 2.2 shows. Each element might be tested with a specific item, or one item might holistically address the goal of problem solving: the solution. It depends on whether we are interested in knowing the student's ability to follow the steps in the process or the student's ability to arrive at a correct solution.

Table 2.2 outlines the steps in problem solving. In their textbook on teaching mathematics, Troutman and Lichtenberg (1994) provide a detailed treatment of problem solving that resembles the process illustrated in Table 2.2.

Let's examine each element and use Table 2.2 to understand the process of problem solving better.

Problem identification.   The very first step, and maybe the most obvious one, is to know that you have a problem. Thus, we will identify the fact that we have a problem that requires a solution.

TABLE 2.2
Illustration of a Problem Solving-Process Applied to a Gardening Problem

ELEMENTS	EXAMPLE
Problem identification	I have an unsightly area in the front of my house.
Problem definition	The plot of ground in front of my dining room window, facing south, located under an overhang, does not support plant life very well. I would like to improve the appearance in the front of the house.
Analysis	Consider the water supply and source of water, the condition of the soil, the light by the seasons, temperature extremes in that area, and the history of plant life in the past ten years there.
Proposed solutions	1. Call in a landscaper and follow advice and pay a small fortune. 2. Go to Home Depot and get some plants and plant them. 3. Consult with a nurseryman or nurserywoman or nurseryperson and get some good advice and follow it. 4. Read *Sunset's Western Gardening Guide* and take appropriate action. 5. Ignore the problem and get a life.
Experiment	Among proposed solutions, choose the cheapest approach and try it. Then try the next cheapest approach.
Conclusion (problem solution)	A landscaper came in and planted four flowering shrubs after adding peat moss to the soil. He charged me a small fortune, but, you know, the dang things are actually growing and have covered up the ugly pipes and stuff below the dining room window.

Problem definition. What is the problem? What are aspects of the problem? What information do you need to understand the problem? This step seeks to understand characteristics of the problem.

Analysis. Create models (processes) that attempt to solve the problem. You might consider this to be a series of competing hypotheses about the problem solution. You analyze and evaluate these models before using them, mentally testing to see which ones will work and not work. Some models might work more effectively than others. This gives rise to the idea that we may have more than one right answer and that some answers are "righter" than others.

Propose solution(s).   From your analysis, you might reach one or more proposed solutions. Then, set up an experiment to formally test these models.

Experiment.   Conduct experiments to test your models. See which models work. Evaluate your results. This will help lead you to a conclusion.

Conclusion.   Draw a conclusion based on your experiment. Select the model that works. In other words, provide the problem solution.

Two Basic Kinds of Problems

In life we encounter well-structured and ill-structured problems. Well-structured problems have a well-defined structure with replacement sets. For instance, in simple arithmetic problems, a well-defined structure is $A + B = C$, where A and B can be any numbers from zero to 100. Each replacement set is a variable, with several variations. Our numerical example has two replacement sets. Well-structured problems fit nicely in mathematics and other fields that have quantitative aspects, such as many sciences, but this kind of problem solving also applies to other problems (see Haladyna, 1991).

The following example shows a problem with several facets, each of which can be varied. By varying the percentage, day of the week, purchase price, and sales tax, a large number of similar items can be produced.

We have a coupon for _____% off the purchase price of a food item. On Tuesday, the coupon is worth double. Today is _____. The purchase price is _____. Tax is _____. What is the cost of the food item?

Well-structured problems have enormous implications for good teaching. If a replacement set like the one above represents some very desirable student learning, then students could be given problems from the replacement set for practice. When they learn the process, a new problem from the replacement set gives the teacher a valid way to test achievement of this kind of problem solving. Because we can teach this problem solving in a relatively short period, we might call it a skill instead of an ability. Mathematical problem-solving ability might consist of the knowledge and skills required to solve a host of different types of problems.

Ill-structured problems usually lack this replacement-set thinking:

Your lawn sprinkling system is not working. Fix it.

Ill-structured problems occupy significant parts of our lives. Most persons who study problem solving recommend that both kinds of problem solving be taught and tested (e.g., Marzano et al., 1988).

How should we teach problem solving? Should we teach it as a general approach to the many problems we may encounter, or does each type of problem require a specific problem-solving technique? This question cannot yet be answered. You may want to consider specific approaches until you acquire an effective strategy for general problem solving.

Whether the problem is well structured or ill structured, and whether you use general or specific strategies to teach problem solving, you will want to consider the *process* of problem solving versus the *result* of problem solving.

If it is process you want, then a checklist is probably warranted. I discuss this in the material on low-inference testing in Chapter 6. The steps on the checklist are observable, and the student needs to show how these steps were followed.

If it is a product you want, then most problems have a right answer, which makes them objectively scorable. For this reason, we might use a short-answer format, featured in Chapter 6, or a multiple-choice format, featured in Chapter 4. Some problems have more than one answer. In that event, you might consider using a performance test that acknowledges that there is more than one right answer. You will need to assess your resources, time, costs, and other factors when making a decision about item format. Chapter 3 helps you on this point.

Finally, some processes and outcomes are high-inference in nature and require the judgment of an expert or two, using a rating scale. Chapters 5A and 5B address the kinds of problems in which high-inference ratings are needed.

Here are some examples of important ill-structured problems to be solved:

Examples of Problems to Be Solved

Determining why your car doesn't start in the morning
Figuring out where your money goes each week
Trying to use grocery coupons to get the best food values
Finding out how to get your azaleas to grow better
Finding a shortcut to work
Figuring out how to get your son to clean his room
Finding uses for lima beans

Critical Thinking

Critical thinking has a long history, dating back to the ancient Greek scholars. Critical thinking has us reflecting, comparing, evaluating, and then making a judgment. Critical thinking is not easy to characterize. It is often thought of as a collection of mental skills that can be taught. Although the richness of this detail cannot be adequately condensed into this section of the chapter, this section provides several major elements in critical thinking and tries to help you construct strategies for writing test items of each aspect of critical thinking. Interested readers should consult more basic references on critical thinking for more information about it, such as Ennis (1985) or Marzano et al. (1988).

In this section, we will study two aspects of critical thinking for which we can prepare test items: evaluating and predicting. We also will briefly address deductive and inductive reasoning; but, as mentioned previously, reasoning is not well developed enough here for very effective item writing.

Evaluating.   All evaluating behavior involves judging and choice. To be more specific, we have three distinctly different aspects of evaluating:

1. We can evaluate criteria to use for a judgment.
2. We can simply assign the criterion or criteria and then ask students to judge using the criterion or criteria we have assigned.
3. We can ask students to choose criteria and also use them, which is quite a bit harder and more complex.

We can evaluate facts, concepts, principles, or procedures, or things that are more complex, such as solutions to problems or even creative processes or production. As you can see, evaluating is a very powerful, broad category within what we have called *critical thinking*. Following are three examples of evaluating behavior, one for each type discussed.

Examples of Evaluating Behavior

Selecting a criterion	Which factor would you use to select a used car for your college-age son? (Select a criterion, such as reliability, cost, style, speed, insurance costs, or *Consumer Reports* rating.)
Using a criterion	Which action is most effective for reducing utility costs in the home? (The criterion is utility costs.)
Selecting and using a criterion	Which type of roof is most effective when building a home in a four-season climate? (Choose among various criteria and apply them to the problem encountered.)

Predicting.   This kind of behavior provides a situation and involves the use of an absolute or probable principle to anticipate the outcome. It is very much like evaluating, except that the criterion is a principle that must be applied. The student is given a situation and is asked to tell what will happen, what will happen next, or what caused something to happen. This requires a knowledge of cause–effect relationships in a probabilistic or absolute sense and the application of this knowledge to a unique situation unencountered in the past. Predicting is inextricably linked to what we call *causal reasoning*. Predicting also must involve principles, because principles involve relationships among concepts. Therefore, the examples we saw in the section on principles apply very well to this section, if students are required to use principles to make predictions or recognize cause–effect relationships.

Examples of Predicting Behavior

Is it going to rain tomorrow?
Will I find true happiness?
What happens when I pour water in a hot frying pan?
Where does fire go when it goes out?
What are the causes of lung cancer?

Deductive and inductive thinking.   Drawing a conclusion is often necessary. Both deductive and inductive thinking are mental behaviors that lead to a conclusion. These two types of thinking are complementary.

Deductive thinking operates from a premise and leads the thinker to a conclusion that is absolutely true. This is part of what we generally refer to as logical thinking. Deductive thinking is characteristic in mathematics but applies widely to school and other situations. According to Marzano (1992), deductive thinking generally has three categories: categorical, conditional, and linear.

We might demonstrate categorical deductive thinking in the following way:

All categorical deductive thinking has two premises and a conclusion. If a premise is used incorrectly, then the conclusion is incorrect. For instance, with the foregoing deduction, the two premises are correct, but the conclusion is wrong because other types of music might be loud, too.

All heavy metal rock music is loud.
This music is loud.
Therefore, this is heavy metal rock music.

Marzano (1992) presents an extensive discussion of deductive thinking with many varieties and examples. Interested readers should read his Chapter 3 (pp. 67–105) for a more complete discussion of deductive thinking. For our purposes, we will merely mention it and illustrate it occasionally in various chapters.

Inductive thinking is similar. It starts with a premise or two. Students are given data and draw a conclusion that is probable. This is typical of the researcher, who begins with a premise or hypothesis, collects and analyzes data, and draws a conclusion. In a court of law, the same process holds true. Evidence dictates the consensual judgment of the jury in an absolute verdict.

Marzano (1992) presents four categories of behavior subsumed under induction: (1) constatives, (2) directives, (3) commissives, and (4) acknowledgments. We will focus on constatives because they are the core of the kind of inductive thinking that we may want to develop and test. With constatives, you start with a proposition. Table 2.3 contains propositions of various types surrounding a personal belief system. Basically, lima beans are not very tasty; I have my doubts about the goodness of anyone who loves lima beans. Table 2.3 contains a series of propositions about lima bean lovers and lima bean eaters. These propositions can form the basis of questioning strategies and provide a basis for debate, argumentation, analysis, reasoning, and a host of other mental activities that fall under the rubric *inductive thinking* and are given in this table using the situation about lima bean lovers.

The dilemma for you, the teacher, is how to use the idea of inductive thinking to ask questions if you want to develop each student's inductive thinking ability. Some examples are provided in Chapters 4–8.

Creativity

Creativity has been one of the most elusive of human traits studied. We know what creativity is, but teaching and testing it still pose a problem. We might think about what creative behavior is and then see if it is possible to nurture creativity and test for it effectively.

There are two aspects of creativity: creative thinking and creative production. The latter also has two aspects: scientific and artistic.

In school settings, we might think of creativity not so much as a formal part of the curriculum but as a natural aspect of our humanness. If schools nurture creativity, we may be privileged to observe it and help it along in each student. Words associated with creativity are *innovative*, *original*, *novel*, and *unique*. However, creativity involves new combinations of familiar elements. Experts on creativity often associate creativity with a proliferation of ideas, intense motivation to create, and a profusion of creative acts. Creativity requires tremendous energy, commitment, discipline, dedication, hard work, and motivation. While creative ability may be innate, teaching and testing for creativity involves creating situations where creativity can be expressed, providing resources for creative expression, and evaluating the result (the test item). Table 2.4 gives some examples of creative activity in different media.

This listing is limited, but it exemplifies the range of situations that can nurture creativity. A challenge to you, the teacher/item writer, is to develop activities that nurture creative behavior and simultaneously to construct items that allow you to evaluate your students' creative behavior.

TABLE 2.3
Proposition: Lima Bean Eaters Are Generally Healthier Than Non–Lima Bean Eaters

ACTIONS	EXAMPLE
Assert	Lima bean lovers are healthier than non–lima bean lovers.
Predict	I predict that a change in diet from whatever to lima beans will improve your health.
Recount	My studies have shown that lima bean lovers are healthier than non–lima bean lovers.
Describe	The characteristics of lima bean lovers . . .
Ascribe	A characteristic of lima bean lovers is good health.
Inform	I would like to announce that I believe a link exists between good health and lima bean consumption.
Confirm	The data show a link between good health and love for lima beans.
Concede	The data show that there is no connection between health and love for lima beans.
Retract	I have discovered that lima bean lovers are sick people, both mentally and physically.
Assent	I believe that lima lovers are basically mentally and physically healthy people.
Dissent	I don't believe that lima lovers are basically mentally and physically healthy people.
Dispute	I dispute the allegation that I own three huge lima bean farms.
Respond	I suggest that Professor Ham Burger's hypothesis about my proposition is totally without merit.
Suggest	I suggest that school cafeterias serve boiled lima beans every day.
Suppose	Suppose we began infants on a steady diet of lima beans for three years . . .

Source: Adapted from Cooper (1984).

TABLE 2.4
Situations Where Creative Behavior Can Be Demonstrated

Writing	Novels, books, short stories, essays, speeches, poems, skits, plays, scripts, screenplays, laws, policies, plans, newspaper or magazine articles, narratives, technical reports
Speaking	Speeches, oral essays, oral performance, readings
Artistic	Paintings, sketches, water colors, sculpture
Scientific	Explorations, inventions, ideas, innovations, modeling, proposals, research, solutions
Theatrical	Play writing, performing, directing, stage design, advertising, marketing, production
Musical	Composing, performing, directing, production
Business	Entrepreneur, inventions, product development, manufacturing, marketing, bookkeeping, income tax returns, sales

Other Types of Mental Behavior

We intentionally ignore a variety of terms that reflect the richness and complexity of higher level thinking, for the very reason that this chapter started out to avoid: having a system that is too complex to follow and using terms that are not well defined. Because cognitive science is somewhat new and still developing, lack of clear understanding of the variety of types of higher level thinking has forced us to limit this chapter to several of the best defined, most easily established, and most readily tested.

A danger here is to ignore the others because of their complexity, lack of familiarity, or lack of development, among other factors. This action does not suggest that you ignore these, but understand that in the past part of the failure to test certain types of higher level thinking has been due to the lack of development of adequate definitions, teaching strategies, and clear-cut item-writing methods representing these types of higher level thinking. It might be useful to mention these types briefly for the sake of completeness. But I do not suggest that these other types of higher level thinking are easy to define, teach, or test. And no reference will be made to them subsequently in this book.

Metacognition.   This somewhat new area of research reflects students' abilities to change their thought processes to benefit themselves. In a real sense, students acquire the ability to teach themselves to learn. To do so requires students to study their thinking processes and develop strategies for better learning. Teaching metacognitive learning strategies helps students redirect themselves from less productive prevailing habits and attitudes to more productive habits and attitudes. Formal methods of teaching metacognitive strategies can lead to effective item writing and testing, but not yet. In the future, we will need to know more about how to develop metacognitive abilities in students, and then we might learn how to write test items that measure these abilities.

Strategic knowledge.   Some cognitive psychologists categorize knowledge as *declarative* and *procedural*, roughly approximating *knowledge* and *skills*, respectively. Strategic knowledge is a category of behavior that is higher and more complex than declarative and procedural knowledge.

Abstract thinking.   Abstract thinking is a method of discourse that generally applies to many instances. In this book, much student learning has an abstract quality and is viewed as high-inference, requiring a definition of the abstraction via a rating scale. An inference is required, linking observable behavior to an abstract thing, often referred to as a *construct*.

Reasoning.   This term is so broadly applied that it often encompasses a variety of other terms. For example, Snow and Lohman (1989, pp. 279–293) treat the topic of reasoning generally as opposed to specifically. But they do state that reasoning is a general term for types of mental abilities.

Self-regulation.   This is a new field of study that involves students' reflections about their own well-being. Students think about their mental habits, make plans, consider resources, seek and use feedback, and continually adjust after evaluating results. This is like a sensible, logical self-guided tour through life. Highly successful people are said to have self-regulated thinking patterns. They guide themselves systematically. In Chapter 8, with the portfolio, we will visit this idea and apply it to the development of a student portfolio.

Crystallizing Our Understanding of Higher Level Thinking

Previous sections have tried to develop some basic categories of student behavior that begin with recall and end with several significant types of higher level thinking. Table 2.5 lists these categories and key verbs we can use in student learning outcomes that relate to each category. These key verbs also can be used to phrase test items. We will use some of them to test mental behaviors in Chapters 4–7.

TABLE 2.5
Types of Mental Behaviors and Key Verbs We Use in Teaching and Test Item Writing

MENTAL BEHAVIOR	KEY VERBS IN STUDENT OUTCOMES AND TEST ITEMS
Understanding	Define, demonstrate, describe, find, exemplify, illustrate, list, listen, provide, show, tell
Problem solving	Answer, compute, conclude, determine, find, figure out, locate, solve
Critical thinking	Anticipate, appraise, attack, analyze, classify, compare, contrast, critique, defend, distinguish, expect, evaluate, hypothesize, infer, judge, predict, relate, value
Creativity	Build, construct, create, design, invent, make, perform, plan, redesign, write

Student Outcomes

As a means for organizing what we have learned in this chapter, this final section of this chapter provides some meaningful student behaviors and discusses how they are classified by the types of higher level thinking we have presented, defined, and discussed. Table 2.6 lists student outcomes for the ensuing discussion.

Table 2.6 provides a variety of types of mental and physical knowledge, skills, and abilities related to a single meaningful life experience that virtually everyone has encountered (except bachelor men).

Summary

This chapter started with the presentation of two dimensions of student behavior: types of content and types of mental behavior. Content was represented by four categories: facts, concepts, principles, and procedures. The use of this content constitutes what we call mental behavior. I characterized the higher forms of mental behavior as (1) understanding, (2) problem solving, (3) critical thinking, and (4) creativity. Recall is the lowest and most familiar type of mental behavior. Other forms of higher level thinking have been presented and discussed in various sources, but there is no well-established taxonomy or typology of these from which to draw. The organization of mental behavior used here draws from well-established ideas and is simple in structure. Examples provided the connection between the abstract descriptions and concrete student outcomes and testing

TABLE 2.6
Examples of Student Outcomes of Various Types for a Single Instructional Program

TYPE	THE STUDENT WILL (TSW)	TYPE OF INFERENCE	PROCESS PRODUCT
Knowledge	Evaluate different solid and liquid dishwashing soaps in terms of cost.	Low	Product
Physical skill	Load the dishwasher[a]	Low	Process
Mental ability	Design a new system for washing dishes that saves time and money. (Creative)	High	Product
Knowledge	Identify the parts of a dishwasher.	Low	Product
Mental skill	Predict the life span of a budget dishwasher.	Low	Product
Physical ability	Win the dishwashing Olympics speed loading competition.	Low[a]	Product
Mental skill	Estimate the cost of washing dishes.	Low	Process
Physical skill	Load the dishwasher[a]	High[a]	Process

[a]How could we have two physical skills, both representing process but with different types of inferences? The first, a low-inference, refers to following steps stated on a checklist. The second, a high-inference, refers to a rating of an abstract trait, "loading style."

strategies. The next chapter will link these types of higher level thinking to the rich variety of item formats that you can use.

References

Bloom B. S., Engelhart, M. D., Furst, E. J., Hill, W. H., & Krathwohl, D. R. (1956). *Taxonomy of educational objectives.* New York: Longmans Green.

Cooper, M. M. (1984). The pragmatics of form: How do writers discover what to do when? In R. Beach & L. S. Bridwell (Eds.), *New directions in composition research.* New York: Guilford Press.

Ennis, R. H. (1985). A logical basis for measuring critical thinking skills. *Educational Leadership, 72,* 45–48.

Haladyna, T. M. (1991). Generic questioning strategies for linking teaching and testing. *Educational Technology: Research and Development, 39,* 73–81.

Lohman, D. F. (1993). Teaching and testing to develop fluid abilities. *Educational Researcher, 22,* 12–23.

Marzano, R. J. (1992). *A different kind of classroom.* Alexandria, VA: Association for Supervision and Curriculum Development.

Marzano, R. J., Brandt, R. S., Hughes, C. S., Jones, B. F., Presseisen, B. Z., Rankin, S. C., & Suhor, C. (1988). *Dimensions of thinking: A framework for curriculum and instruction.* Alexandria, VA: Association for Supervision and Curriculum Development.

Marzano, R. J., Pickering, D., & McTighe, J. (1993). *Assessing student outcomes.* Alexandria, VA: Association for Supervision and Curriculum Development.

Snow, R. E., & Lohman, D. F. (1989). Implications of cognitive psychology for educational measurement. In R. L. Linn (Ed.), *Educational measurement,* 3rd ed. (pp. 263–332). New York: American Council on Education and Macmillan.

Troutman, A. P., & Lichtenberg, B. K. (1994). *Mathematics: A good beginning.* Pacific Grove, CA: Brooks/Cole.

Zambo, R., & Follman, J. (1994). Gender-related differences in problem solving at the sixth and eighth grade levels. *Focus on Learning Problems in Mathematics, 16,* 20–38.

3 Item Formats

THIS CHAPTER EXPANDS THE DEFINITION OF A TEST ITEM GIVEN IN Chapter 1. A typology of item formats is presented that is based on a major factor: whether the student *creates* a response or simply *selects* a response to the test item. These item formats can be used to test any of the variety of student outcomes discussed in the previous chapter. These formats are more adequately discussed in Chapters 4, 5A, 6, 7, and 8. Each chapter also provides specific guidelines about how to write these items.

The considerations in choosing an item format are complex and interrelated. Sometimes, you have several choices. Your choice is influenced by such factors as cost, time, effort, and fidelity to the *something* you are trying to measure. *Fidelity* refers to the extent that the test item matches exactly what you are teaching and wanting to test. Often we compromise because the item that has the greatest fidelity may be too expensive to administer and score or too demanding. For instance, if you were in a class on designing skyscrapers, it would be difficult to build skyscrapers to test your designing ability. In that class, we would use a low-fidelity test, such as a project portfolio containing designs, cost estimates, and the like. Chapter 2 gave us some ideas about that *something*, and we concluded that understanding, problem solving, critical thinking, and creating were major mental activities that we wanted to teach, see developed in students, and test effectively.

Introduction

Because one of our objectives is to write test items that reflect types of higher level thinking we intend to teach, we will need to choose a test item format that matches our instructional intent. Therefore, we will try to develop a strategy for linking each student outcome to an appropriate item format. Sometimes, several formats might work, so your job is a little more complex. You will need to decide which of a set of competing formats is the best choice. We will refer frequently to other chapters where more attention is given to a specific type of item format. For instance, for measuring knowledge and some mental skills and abilities, the multiple-choice format is appropriate (Chapter 4). For measuring high-inference mental skills or abilities and some physical skills and abilities where you want the student to construct an answer, refer to Chapter 5A. For measuring low-inference mental skills or abilities or physical abilities, refer to Chapter 6. Chapter 7 concentrates on developing a collection of student performances called the *portfolio*. Chapter 8 concerns the writing of student surveys that tap affective characteristics.

What Is a Test Item?

A test item is an instruction or question that requires a student response under certain conditions and specific scoring rules. All test items begin with the same first element, a command or question, but the subsequent elements vary somewhat.

A Comparison among Item Formats

Multiple-Choice	High-Inference Constructed-Response	Low-Inference Constructed-Response
Chapter 4	Chapters 5A and 5B	Chapter 6
Command or question	Command or question	Command or question
Judge-based construction of choices	Student response	Student response
Student choice	Judge-based construction of rating scale categories	Development of scoring system using right–wrong scoring, observation, or a checklist
Objective scoring	Judge-based classification of student response	Objective scoring

---

As presented here, the multiple-choice format provides choices for students to select. Scoring is objective because two or more scorers should get the same result for a set of items. For high-inference testing, where what is tested is considered to be abstract, a rating scale is customarily used. The teacher/judge constructs the categories and then decides in which category the student response belongs. For low-inference items, where the student outcome is plainly visible, the teacher/judge must decide whether the performance has been completed as directed. The judging of a low-inference performance is objective, like the multiple-choice response.

The more common term for selected response is *multiple choice*, and we will use this latter term throughout this book.

Much has been written on the underlying mental processes required in constructing versus selecting answers (Bennett, 1993; Haladyna, 1994; Snow, 1993; Traub, 1993).

The research and theory on this issue are far too complex and unresolved to discuss adequately here. We have much to learn about this topic. As a teacher who needs to write a few good test items, you can select any format based on certain assumptions and intents, which are also affected by practical matters—resources, time, personnel, and the like. Some simple guidelines are offered here to help you decide which kind of format, constructed-response or multiple-choice, is appropriate.

Table 3.1 lists student behaviors connected to the possible formats that you might use. Research evidence suggests certain types of formats for certain outcomes, although these guidelines are flexible enough to permit variation in your choices.

The purpose of any test item is to obtain a student response so that you can make an inference about the status of a student's knowledge or a mental or physical skill or ability. Table 3.1 contains the five basic categories of student behavior described in Chapter 2. For knowledge, you have two alternative item formats: multiple-choice and extended-answer or short-answer constructed-response essay. For many reasons presented in Chapter 4, the multiple-choice is preferable. The information obtained from a multiple-choice test is very comparable to information obtained via the essay. Multiple-choice data is often more dependable (reliable), easier to score, and free from problems of interjudge consistency of scoring and bias. On the other hand, an essay response gives you a sample of student writing that can be independently evaluated. Your time, resources, and interest in gaining extra information should affect your decision about how to measure knowledge. Some test reformers argue that involving students in writing is a more natural way to elicit what they know. Detractors of the essay claim that writing ability influences students' test scores, and, therefore, is a major contaminant in measuring what they have learned. Chapter 4 provides guidance on multiple-choice item writing; Chapters 5A and 6 provide guidance on writing essay items for high-inference and low-inference student behaviors.

Knowledge Outcomes

Declarative knowledge can be measured using familiar multiple-choice or essay formats. High-inference knowledge and mental and physical skills and abilities can be measured using various formats, but all require rating scales (scoring rubrics). Low-inference knowledge and mental and physical skills and abilities can be measured using a variety of formats, but these outcomes require simple observation, a checklist, or a right answer.

Constructed-Response and Multiple-Choice Formats

The next two sections introduce you to the rich array of item formats that you can choose to measure the important *something* your students are learning (understanding, problem solving, critical thinking, and creating). Table 3.2 lists the

TABLE 3.1
Types of Student Behaviors and Suggested Item Formats

BEHAVIOR DOMAIN	POSSIBLE FORMATS (CHAPTER)	EVIDENCE SUGGESTS
Knowledge (declarative knowledge)	Multiple-choice (4) or essay (5A or 6)	Multiple-choice be used instead of essay because the former provides more reliable test scores at a lower cost without the risk of bias in scoring.
High-inference cognitive skills or abilities (procedural knowledge)	Multiple-choice (4) or performance (5A)	Multiple-choice would work well here for problem solving and critical thinking, but a constructed response may be more universally acceptable.
High-inference psychomotor skills or abilities	Performance (5A)	Constructed-response items are the only viable choice.
Low-inference cognitive skills or abilities	Multiple-choice (4) or performance (6)	Multiple-choice or constructed-response gives you highly correlated results, so either one will work. Both are objectively scorable.
Low-inference psychomotor skills or abilities	Performance (6)	Constructed-response items are the only viable choice.

To make this table more user-friendly, let us define some student outcomes that resemble the kinds of behaviors above.

Declarative knowledge is simply what most students routinely are taught and learn. They memorize or understand things. For example we might ask them if they understand how a dishwasher works. Explain its workings. List the parts. How much water does it use? This listing shows that knowledge mainly consists of memorizing and understanding facts, concepts, principles, and procedures.

High-inference cognitive skills or abilities represent more complex, and not-easy-to-observe behavior that may have to be judged in terms of a graded response (rating scale). We may want to rate the student on their efficiency in loading the dishwasher or the thoroughness of the cleaning process or the cleanliness of the plates, dinnerware, and glasses. These traits are abstract and have to be judged by an expert.

High-inference physical skills or abilities represent more complex and not-easy-to-observe behavior that may be judged in terms of a checklist, simple observation, or instrument-aided observation. For example, we might observe the student scraping and rinsing dishes before loading into the dishwasher. The question is: How clean are the dishes going in? Since this is largely a physical act, a rating scale will be used.

Low-inference cognitive skills or abilities represent simple, easy-to-observe student behavior reflecting some type of higher level thinking. Using our dish washing example, a student who fixes a dishwasher is demonstrating a problem-solving process that leads to an observable result: It works.

Low-inference physical skills or abilities represent simple, easy-to-observe activities that do not have a strong mental component but have a large physical component. For example, we might observe if a dishwasher was loaded in a certain time limit without the breaking of any dishes.

TABLE 3.2
A Typology of Constructed-Response and Multiple-Choice Item Formats

CONSTRUCTED-RESPONSE	CHAPTER	MULTIPLE-CHOICE	CHAPTER
Anecdotal	5A	Conventional	4
Cloze[a]	5A	Alternate-Choice	4
Demonstration	5A,6	Matching	4
Discussion	5A,6	Complex Multiple-Choice[a]	4
Essay	5A,6	True-False[a]	4
Exhibition	5A,6	Multiple True-False	4
Experiment	5A,6	Comprehension Item Set	4
Fill-in-the-blank[a]	5A,6	Pictorial Item-Set	4
Writing Sample	5A,6	Problem-Solving Item Set	4
Interview/Observation	5A,6	Interlinear Item Set	4
Instrument-Aided Observation	6		
Interactive Videodisc	5A, 6		
Oral Report	6		
Performance	5A,6		
Portfolio	7		
Project	5A,6		
Research Papers	5A,6		
Review	5A,6		
Self/Peer Assessment	5A,6		
Short Answer (Completion)	5A,6		
Visual Observation	6		

[a]Not recommended.

choices available to you and references the chapters where more information is presented. This chapter provides examples and analysis of various types of test item formats by the basic distinction shown in Table 3.1. Table 3.2 is loosely based on a proposed taxonomy of constructed-response format suggested by Osterlind and Merz (1994). Most of these items are not as highly polished as those you will see in later chapters. These illustrative items are not intentionally brief and are intended to give you an idea of the variety of formats from which you can choose. In the next part of this book, you will learn how to write very high quality test items that contain the "bells and whistles" that characterize professionally developed items.

Constructed-Response Formats

This section features the left half of Table 3.2. In subsequent chapters, items will be presented in greater detail. The main idea of this section is to acquaint you with a variety of formats to use in the classroom.

Anecdotal

Anecdotal methods have been a favorite of teachers as a data collection method for student problems. Strictly speaking, an anecdotal record is a brief written report about student behavior that goes into the student's file. This information can be used with other information to draw conclusions about achievement and make educational decisions affecting students. Strictly speaking, this technique is a type of high-inference testing, but it could also apply to testing in the affective domain. Anecdotal reports are recommended, but only with considerable caution and with other sources of information. Some teachers like to use anecdotal reports to collect "evidence" on students for referral to a school psychologist or for special education consideration. Such a collection can help school psychologists, counselors, or other personnel make good decisions about plans and treatments for troubled students. Chapter 5A includes a brief section on anecdotal reports.

> Elise has made rapid improvement in reading this term. She has read three unassigned books and has expressed interest in sea life. She appears to be very motivated to increase her breadth of reading and might be interested in periodicals on these topics other than *Ranger Rick Magazine.*

Cloze

This technique is included in the list but is *not* recommended. Cloze involves lifting printed material from a text and then testing to see if the student can supply a missing word, phrase, or sentence. Cloze has had a long history in research on reading, but it is not a good testing tool. A main criticism is that it seems designed to tap memory. Until research demonstrates its utility as a test item format, it is suggested that the cloze item format *not* be used.

> This technique is known as _____.
> Answer: *cloze*
> If you answered *clothes*, it is not *close* enough.

Demonstration

This type of item requires students to show a physical skill or ability. The demonstration would typically be subject to scoring, using a rating scale (Chapter 5A) or checklist (Chapter 6).

> Demonstrate how to load the dishwasher, using the method we learned in class.

In this example, we probably would want to use a checklist that contained all the important steps in performing the task. A more suitable item would contain some conditions for performance and a standard. If we were interested in style, which is abstract, we could design a rating scale for a judge to use.

Discussion

This format is best for types of critical thinking. Students would be asked to discuss, orally or in writing, an issue that requires evaluation or prediction.

> Discuss the benefits of a dishwasher over hand washing. Indicate what criteria you are using. (Evaluation)
> Predict what would happen if large pieces of fish were stuck to plates when loaded into the dishwasher. (Prediction)

This item format is very much like the next format, essay, but it requires the development and use of criteria, which is the mainstay of critical thinking or the use of a principle on which to base the prediction. The format requires more than just knowledge. Sometimes, there might be NO one right answer. Scoring might be a problem with this format.

Essay

This word can be taken in one of two ways. The first meaning refers to an item format that is used as an alternative to multiple choice for measuring knowledge. For instance:

How should dishes be loaded into the dishwasher?   (Essay)

How should dishes be loaded into the dishwasher?   (Multiple-Choice)
A. Glasses first, silverware second, and larger items last
B. Silverware first, and everything else next
C. Large items, glassware, silverware

The essay item asks students for a right answer to a question that reveals their knowledge. Scoring is done with a rating scale or checklist unless there is a specific right or wrong answer.

The essay item has enormous popularity and is widely used in testing around the world. Historically, it was the predominant method of questioning; it is very natural to ask a question and have the answer written out for inspection. Multiple-choice items were invented to make the scoring process easier, objective, and unbiased. In Chapters 5A and 6, we will spend more time on the essay.

A second meaning of *essay* is a declaration of an opinion or stand on an issue with supporting rationale. This second meaning involves more than just asking for knowledge; it also requires critical thinking. This item can be scored with a rating scale or a checklist. It is probably more important to evaluate the process followed than the worthiness of the opinion expressed. This process involves evaluating the clarity of the arguments and the logic of the rationale supporting the opinion, among other desirable characteristics associated with critical thinking.

Develop an argument supporting the purchase of a top-of-the-line dishwasher for your family residence.

Exhibition

This format is most useful for those in the creative or performing arts, where a collection of student work can be exhibited. Such work is also subject to evaluation using a high-inference technique (Chapter 5A) or a low-inference technique (Chapter 6).

The most common form of exhibition is student art. Students in the performing arts want to exhibit their work. Juries (collections of experts) evaluate this work using rating scales or checklists.

> Using the Rubbermaid dish rack, prepare an exhibition of correctly washed dinner dishes. Include a representative sampling of silverware (forks, knives, and spoons), dinnerware (plates and bowls), and glasses. You will be judged on cleanliness.

Experiment

This format requires the student to set up and complete an experiment and record observations. Then the student must draw a conclusion. Generally, an outline is used that follows the reasoning process in problem solving.

> Set up and complete a study on the cleanliness of milk-stained glassware using at least four cleaning methods: (1) cold rinse, (2) dishwasher with regular liquid, (3) dishwasher with regular liquid and one of the special additives for clean glassware, and (4) hand washing using liquid dishwashing soap. Collect data and draw a conclusion.

Fill-in-the-Blank

This format is expressly designed for measuring knowledge. It is simple and direct, and it probably is best suited for simple memory. This format also resembles the cloze technique, except that the latter is based on a theory and requires that material be taken verbatim from written material, such as a textbook. The fill-in-the-blank item does not have these conditions. Like the cloze, this format is *not* recommended for several reasons. First, we have decided to avoid memory-type questioning. Second, the blank format has some undesirable qualities that a direct questioning format avoids (Haladyna, 1994).

> _____ is the main ingredient of dish washing detergent.

Interview

The student interview is *not* a widely recognized or often used item format, but it is a promising one. Another term for interviewing here is *conferencing*. Innovative approaches to obtaining qualitative information from students about their achievement may enhance or supplement information obtained from other sources. Stiggins (1994) supports the interview as an *informal* method of obtaining information from and about students. In his view, interviews may be structured or unstructured. With a grade at stake, interviews should be structured so that all students have the same opportunity to perform. Stiggins states that this method helps build trust between teacher and students, with the idea that students take more responsibility for their achievement.

Self-regulation and self-analysis are recurring themes in modern teaching. Getting students to assess their own achievement and reflect on where they want to be with respect to the abilities being developed may be the objective of the interview. Eventually, the idea is to get students to assume responsibility for developing their abilities.

Instrument-Aided Observation

The instrument-aided observation is a popular technique in content areas where a visible outcome is noted that can be timed, weighed, or measured for length, width, height, or color. Science classes come to mind as the most obvious application. In some applications, speed is important, and timing is essential. Weighing objects can be an observation.

> Given the dishes from a meal for six people, load the dishwasher correctly in less than five minutes. One minute deduction for every broken glass or dish or for any error from the error checklist. (Timing instrument is a wristwatch.)

Interactive Video

This method involves high technology. Students might be exposed to CD-ROM, videodisc displays, or other forms of information and be questioned on the spot. The present technology allows for student responses and may even score the students. There is little doubt that this emerging technology will increase our ability to simulate performance for students and allow them to interact in a meaningful way as they learn.

Oral Report/Examination

The oral report is used in various settings, including speaking, certification testing in professions, language instruction, and language arts, among many others. It is different from oral discussion presented earlier in this chapter, because the purpose of the oral report or examination is to obtain information from the student, whereas the oral discussion is more of a vehicle for obtaining information about critical thinking. Public speaking is often evaluated by peers or the teacher using a rating scale or checklist, and points are awarded that lead up to the assignment of a grade. Therefore, the oral report is a viable item format both for collecting information about recall and understanding, and for public speaking.

> Give a report on the recent state law that mandates the use of helmets for motorcycle riders. Summarize the supporting and refuting arguments. Keep your report under three minutes in length. Make the report clear and interesting to your audience.

Even problem solving can be measured with this format. For instance, the oral examination is often used for certification in a profession, where a candidate is questioned by an examining board member or panel on questions pertaining to professional practice. In medicine, a patient problem is presented as a stimulus for a series of questions dealing with the physician's problem-solving ability. The panel member then uses a rating scale to judge the level of performance. Oral examinations add an important element to the testing process: the pressure of performing in the public and of oral presentation. Both factors could increase test anxiety. On the other hand, public speaking is a desirable ability to develop.

Performance

Performance is a general term for a variety of student activities that may be evaluated as part of teaching and testing. The most obvious performance activity comes in the visual and performing arts, for example at musical recitals, concerts, skits, or plays.

> Perform the skit *Three Strikes and You're Out* for videotaping. Allow five minutes for the skit. You will be evaluated on the following criteria: . . .

All performance testing is time-consuming, but this is the ultimate test in many fields of study and the most faithful to the ability that is being developed. In these fields, performance is the only reasonable choice. Chapter 5A and 6 contain examples.

Portfolio

A portfolio is an organized collection of student work that is subject to grading standards. This definition deviates from a more general definition of a portfolio as simply a loose-leaf collection of student work. For testing, the portfolio must be organized along specific assignments and subject to uniform standards. Chapter 7 is devoted to the portfolio because this continues be an important way to reflect various types of higher level behavior. However, scoring the contents of portfolios still poses major problems and gets considerable attention in Chapter 7.

Portfolios are popular in various professions and in the visual and performing arts. Architects, poets, painters, and photographers, among others, often place examples of their best work in a portfolio. One difficulty with the portfolio is that it represents the student's best effort, not a typical effort. It would be difficult to require that students include examples of both good and bad work so that we could judge the effort in the context of "true" performance. This may be one limitation of the portfolio. The other limitation is that it takes considerable time to read a portfolio, and scoring it using a rating scale may introduce inconsistency or bias. Using a checklist may be more objective but also very time-consuming. You will have to decide if this is worth the effort.

> During the semester, you will have 12 writing assignments. All should be neatly organized in your portfolio (folder) using the checklist I have given you. This portfolio will constitute 80% of your grade. All writing assignments should be done on the computer using your spell checker and grammar checker. You are responsible for the quality of your work, but you are welcome to get help from parents, other students, or me as you polish your writing.

If a portfolio is going to be used to make a high-stakes decision, like graduation or a grade, a threat exists that students may tamper with their portfolios by adding material that is not theirs but might increase their score. Because their use invites cheating, portfolios probably should not be used in a high-stakes setting

As noted here and in Chapter 7, many of us are exploring the potential of portfolios in teaching and testing, and we are learning along the way. Research will help us better understand the benefits and limitations of portfolios, but much of what we are currently doing is groping for a better way to teach and test. The portfolio seems to be a very promising approach, but let us not overrate its potential until we know more about it and have more personal experience.

Projects

Projects are the mainstay of most good classroom teachers. It is hard to imagine teaching without projects. Projects often provide opportunities for students to do significant work, individually or collectively. Projects vary considerably from written reports to actual activities, such as performing community service as part of fulfilling a high school social studies requirement. Projects involve complex directions and scoring standards. They require considerable commitment from teachers and effort from students.

You have been assigned to evaluate, purchase, and install a new dishwasher in your home. You have a budget of $450. You want the best that money can buy. Refer to *Consumer Reports* for evaluation information. Select a store from which you buy the dishwasher. Ensure its deliver. Go to Home Depot to get connecting parts. Install it so that it works perfectly. Do this without any whining, noise, or fuss.

Now, that's a project!

Research Paper

The research paper has been the mainstay of colleges and universities and is found in high schools, junior high schools, and elementary schools as well. With the coming of the information highway, CD-ROM encyclopedias, and the like, access to more information makes research easier and more extensive than ever before. The availability of word-processing programs with spelling and grammar checkers and laser printers makes the quality of research papers much as you would see it in books and journals. Therefore, the research paper gains viability as a performance item.

Write a research paper on any one of the following topics:
1. Energy use of various dishwashers
2. Reliability of dishwashers
3. The extra-quiet dishwasher: Is it really quieter?
4. How a dishwasher works
5. The history of dishwashers

You may choose a related topic, but consult with me first. The research paper should be no more than 5,000 words. All words should be spelled correctly. Grammar and punctuation should be correct. Your paper should show good organization and clear writing. References should be at the end of the paper and count toward the 5,000-word limit. You may develop a strategy for where you will obtain information. You may survey or interview people. Consult with me or your parents or classmates, or with the librarian. Write a draft. Have it reviewed by me, your parents, classmates, or the librarian. Develop your report in typeset quality, suitable for publication. Make your report interesting. Use illustrations, charts, graphs, or other pictorial aids.

Review/Critique

Critical thinking involves evaluating or predicting. One effective way to test for critical thinking is to teach students how to review or critique events, actions, policies, laws, or performances. The review/critique requires students to write a short piece that analyzes and evaluates a movie, play, book, poem, story, new building, park, new TV program, trend, social problems, new law, new car, housing development, business activities, your new mother-in-law, or a new product, among other things.

Review/critiques are performance-oriented. They require considerable ability to think critically and express one's views clearly and persuasively. The major limitation of the review/critique as a type of test item is that it requires extensive analysis by the teacher using a set of rating scales or a checklist. Each teacher has to ascertain whether assigning a review/critique is worth the effort required to score the result properly, as is the case with many other types of performance.

> Visit Circuit City and evaluate the new Dishitronic Silent Dishwasher. Write a review for the *Dish Washer News*. The review should be no more than 500 words and should address such factors as (1) noise level, (2) effectiveness, and (3) cost.

Peer/Self-Assessment

This format is not very popular and may not survive. Asking students to evaluate one another can be fraught with difficulties and can introduce bias that may make the assessment counterproductive. If the peer assessment is being used in grading, then, indeed, it is a testing process, and evaluation constitutes one of our item types. Confidentiality becomes an issue because students are entitled to privacy. Public disclosure of their test performance is *not* appropriate.

Self-assessment requires students to evaluate their schoolwork with respect to an important learning outcome in terms of how they think they did. This kind of test item has its pros and cons. In general, the issue of bias comes up in having students provide their own scoring of their performances.

On the other hand, an emerging trend in U.S. education is to have students keep journals detailing their learning processes and their successes and failures. This kind of activity promotes self-regulation and the development of metacognitive abilities that were discussed in Chapter 2. But this kind of activity is *not* recommended as part of student testing but, rather, as a part of effective teaching.

It seems advisable to reject both peer and self-assessment as formats for collecting information about student performance for the many reasons listed here, primarily the issues of confidentiality and bias.

Short-Answer (Completion)

This format is useful for measuring knowledge and nothing else. It can be used instead of multiple choice, as was discussed earlier. Chapters 5A and 6 provide some guidance on writing short-answer essays or completions. Many teachers favor short-answer essays because they force students to write and to express their understanding of what they have learned. Too often this format is used to measure memory of things learned in class. Generally, you can use this format or multiple choice to measure recall, understanding, and other types of knowledge.

> Briefly, describe two differences between liquid and powder dishwashing soap. (6 points)

Visual Observation

Early childhood development and special education rely on simple observation of events to verify that a student outcome has been achieved. In later grades, this observation may simply mean checking that homework has been done or that some simple activity has been completed. Visual observation is easy and not time-consuming. Unfortunately, few important outcomes of student learning fall into this category.

> Using the fifty-cent double bonus coupon, purchase a twenty-four-ounce container of Sunlight dishwashing liquid.

Writing Sample

The purpose of obtaining a writing sample is to measure a student's writing ability. The writing sample is the dominant type of performance test item format in the United States. Students are asked to write in either an informative, persuasive, or narrative style, anywhere from a paragraph to a much longer passage. Writing is an ability because it is developed over a long period and requires considerable knowledge about writing as well as identifiable skills such as correct usage of grammar, writing and style conventions, punctuation, spelling, and capitalization.

Writing can be scored in two ways: holistically or analytically. Holistic scoring involves rating scales of a general nature (Chapter 5A). Analytical scoring is more detailed but also employs rating scales.

The writing sample also may be interpreted in many other categories in this section, such as the critique/review, essay, discussion, research paper, and project. Almost any student-written response can be subjected to additional analysis to assess writing ability or one of the many writing skills.

> Tell about a favorite story you have read, heard, or seen on television or at the movies. Include interesting details about ideas. (Grade 4) (Applebee, Langer, Mullis, Latham, & Gentile, 1994, p. 26).

Summary

This section has introduced you to the variety of performance item formats from which to choose. As you can see in Table 3.2, the list is impressive. The formats are linked to Chapters 5A, 6, and 7.

Multiple-Choice Formats

In this section, we review the multiple-choice formats presented in the right-hand side of Table 3.2 in this chapter. These formats consist of old-timers and some new ones that research has supported. Two of these formats are *not* recommended, but the others are. Certainly we would not use multiple choice to test creativity or writing ability. But for aspects of critical thinking and problem solving, some of these formats are useful and appropriate.

Conventional Multiple Choice

This format is the mainstay of a multiple-choice test. Typically, there is a stem and three to five options. Haladyna and Downing (1993) provide evidence that most item writers seem to have a natural limit of three options. Writing more than three options is very difficult. As it is good to have more than three options, try to write as many good options as you can, but don't be disappointed if you come up with only three good ones.

Conventional multiple choice comes in three formats: (1) question, (2) completion, and (3) best-answer. Statman (1988) and others recommend against the completion format for several reasons. In the example on the next page, notice that the reader of the completion item has to read the stem and then combine the stem and each option each time. That means storing each image in short-term memory, which puts a lot of stress on the student. Because many students already have test anxiety, the completion format is viewed as increasing stress. Asking a question and providing correct and incorrect answers seems to be a more direct and less stressful way to get to the point of the item.

The best-answer format is desirable because it provides all right answers with one being perceptibly better than the others. This format is recommended as a useful way to test for simple forms of critical thinking, such as evaluating.

Correct Answer Question (RECOMMENDED)

Which cycle is recommended for milk-stained glasses?

   A. Rinse and hold
   B. Energy saver
   C. Potscrubber

Correct Answer Completion (NOT RECOMMENDED)

The cycle recommended for milk-stained glasses is

   A. potscrubber.
   B. heavy.
   C. normal.

Best Answer (RECOMMENDED FOR CRITICAL THINKING)

Which product is most effective for cleaning glassware?

   A. Glow-and-Dry
   B. Jet Shine
   C. Spots-Be-Gone

Alternate Choice

This format resembles the conventional multiple choice except it offers only two options: correct and incorrect. The incorrect choice should be plausible but clearly incorrect. Research shows that highly discriminating students can narrow most conventional multiple-choice items down to just two choices (Downing, 1992; Haladyna & Downing, 1993). So the alternate-choice format saves time and trouble. Alternate-choice items are easy to write and easy to answer, so testing time is minimized. Alternate choice does not take up a lot of space, and scoring is simple. A score of 50 percent, of course, is very low, so you have to take this into account when developing a grading standard.

Which is the most effective for producing crystal clear glasses?

   A. Glow-and-Dry
   B. Spots-Be-Gone

Matching

The matching format is used when the same set of options can be applied to two or more items. This format is very effective for measuring students' understanding of concepts, principles, and procedures as discussed and presented in Chapter 2. We generally try to have an unequal number of options and items, because students tend to try to match up the items and options if they are the same number.

Match the options on the right to the items on the left.
Indicate the proper place in the dishwasher to load the following items.

1. Bowls	A. Top
2. Large kitchen utensils	B. Back-bottom
3. Pots	C. Center-bottom
4. Fine china	D. Front-bottom
5. Glasses	
6. Silverware	

Complex Multiple Choice

This format was developed to test situations where more than one right answer existed for an item stem. The item writer lists possible answers and then forms combinations of right and wrong answers where only one combination contains right answers. This format is *not* recommended. It is too complex, it is more difficult than conventional multiple-choice items, and it has other deficits that argue against its use (see Haladyna, 1994).

Which of the following are examples of metaphors?

1. It's kistimary to cuss the bride.
2. That giraffe is taller than a building.
3. She gave 110 percent in effort.

A. 1 and 3
B. 1 and 2
C. 2 and 3
D. 1, 2, and 3

True–False

This familiar format offers a statement that is judged by the teacher (item writer) to be correct or incorrect. Much advice exists on how to write true–false items. Some critics recommend against this format because wrong answers tend to be more reliable than right answers and bias may exist in answering these questions (Grosse & Wright, 1985). Therefore, it is recommended that this format *not* be used.

> Generally speaking, a two-stage dishwasher is more efficient than a one-stage dishwasher.

Item Sets

Item sets are groups of items arranged around a stimulus, which provides a basis for testing the students' understanding, critical thinking, or problem solving. Therefore, the item set is a highly recommended item format. In many instances, the item set can take the place of the more expensive constructed-response item to test one of these types of higher level thinking. Strictly speaking, however, the item set can consist of items of any format, including the performance formats presented in this chapter, but multiple choice is the most commonly used. Following pages will present four kinds of item sets, each with a specific purpose. One of the major problems with the item set format is that an answer to one item may be connected to answers to other items, especially in problem solving. Another limitation is that these items are very hard to write. However, research on item sets shows this to be a very promising item format with a long history of use (Haladyna, 1992b).

Comprehension Item Set

The main purpose of the comprehension item set is understanding. The item set in the example on page 54 shows the use of the item set to test reading comprehension. The item set comes from the Carriveau Individual Profile Reading Assessment (Carriveau & Carriveau, 1994). Their approach to measuring reading comprehension is to use short stories that contain all the elements of a short story. They then use a set of eight generic questions for each story:

1. Identify the main idea, theme, or main concept of the story.
2. Identify traits or attitude of a main character.
3. Identify a conflict or problem.
4. Identify a detail important to the meaning of the story.
5. Recognize a sequence or ordering of events.

A Story

Today was apple day for Tanya and her friends. They had talked about Farmer Jackson's apples all week, and they had finally decided to risk picking a few. Tanya led her friends to the fence by the south orchard. Hanging over the fence, they could almost touch those apples. Farmer Jackson's apples were famous for their taste.

Of course, they had to be careful of Farmer Jackson's watchdogs. The dogs were fast, and they were mean. As the desire for those apples became stronger, the children's fear of the dogs grew less. They decided to risk picking some of the apples anyway. Carefully they began to climb over the fence. They would be back over that fence in a hurry if those dogs saw them in the orchard.

Tanya was the first to reach the closest apple tree. She waved to her friends to follow. As she reached up, ready to pick a large red apple, she heard the sound of barking dogs. Tanya froze. The dogs were coming! She left the apple hanging on its branch and started running toward the fence. Her friends had already scrambled back over the top of the fence by the time she reached it. As Tanya tried to climb over the top, one of the dogs caught her by the pant leg. The other dog went for a bite somewhere else. With the help of her friends, Tanya finally made it back over the fence to safety.

Tanya and her friends watched through the fence as the dogs played tug-of-war with the seat of her pants. The children looked sadly at the apples. Kicking at the dirt as they walked away, they wondered what they should do next for fun. They decided Farmer Jackson should keep all of his beautiful apples this year.

1. What does this story mostly tell about?
   A. A farmer and his orchard of apples.
   B. Children who wanted to eat some apples.
   C. Unfriendly dogs.
2. What were Tanya and her friends like?
   A. They put their desire for apples before their safety.
   B. They were troublemakers.
   C. They did things without thinking about it.
3. What was one big problem in the story?
   A. The apples were famous.
   B. The children could not run fast enough.
   C. The dogs were not friendly.
4. Where were the apples?
   A. Almost within the reach of the children.
   B. Close enough for the children to reach from the fence.
   C. Falling off the trees near the fence.
5. What did Tanya do right after she went over the fence?
   A. She told her friends to stay back because of the dogs.
   B. She told her friends to come over too.
   C. She reached for an apple.
6. What made the children want to pick the apples?
   A. The farmer was going to pick the apples anyway.
   B. The apples were famous for their taste.
   C. They had been talking about it.
7. How did the story end?
   A. The children had to get new clothes.
   B. The children watched the dogs.
   C. The children decided to give up.
8. What probably was Tanya like?
   A. She could get others to follow her.
   B. She waited for others to make decisions for her.
   C. She was afraid to take chances.

Source: Reprinted with permission of Ron Carriveau.

   6. Recognize a causal relationship.
   7. Make a decision about how the story ended.
   8. Make a prediction or give a reason for a past action or event based on the story.

Each story was written at an appropriate grade level and checked with text analyzers for grade-level appropriateness and vocabulary. The test also features a student's written retelling of the story to provide a performance accompaniment to the multiple-choice exercises.

The comprehension item set format has a long history of effective use. Yet research continues on the construct of reading comprehension as one of our most essential language arts. This format will continue to be used both in this research and in testing reading comprehension.

Pictorial Item Set

The pictorial item set features a graph, chart, photograph, work of art, or other visual presentation as the stimulus, followed by a correlated set of items. You can be very imaginative with this format. The important thing is that the item set consists of items that are relatively independent but tap various types of higher level thinking that involve understanding and critical thinking.

The example in Table 3.3 draws questions from the graph to emphasize a student's skills at reading a graph. The set of items in the example is limited in measuring just two aspects of graph reading. On the basis of the data presented in the graph, you might ask for extrapolation, such as what percentage you would expect for older age groups, or what is the total percentage represented in this graph, taking all age groups into account (100 percent). The pictorial item set has tremendous potential but depends on your own creativity and ingenuity. Newspapers and magazines provide good sources of tables, charts, cartoons, and other pictorial stimuli for item sets.

Interlinear Item Set

This type of item set seems appropriate for measuring an aspect of writing skills dealing with choices among homonyms, the correct use of grammar, or spelling ability. This peculiar format is objectively scored. It gets students to correct writing that contains errors by using a multiple-choice format. While the interlinear item set is *not* a substitute for measuring writing, it does address writing skills in this simple, scorable format. Therefore, it is recommended for lessons and units where specific writing skills are being practiced.

TABLE 3.3
Example of a Pictorial Item Set: Hooked on Tobacco—The Teen Epidemic

Read the article in *Consumer Reports* (March 1995) on teenage smoking. Referring to the graph below, answer the following questions.

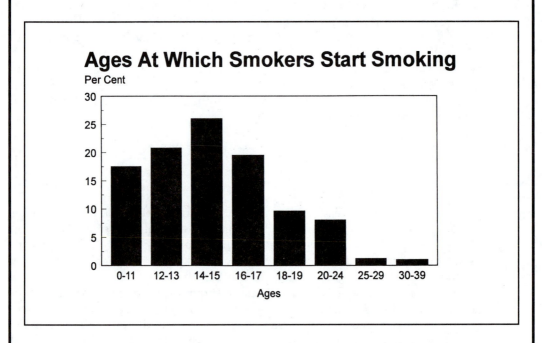

Ages At Which Smokers Start Smoking

1. At what age do most persons begin smoking?
   A. 0–11
   B. 12–13
   C. 14–15
   D. 16–17
   E. Older than 17
2. At what age is a person least likely to start?
   A. 11
   B. 15
   C. 19
   D. 27
   E. 33
3. About what percentage of persons begin to smoke between ages 0 and 11?
   A. 11%
   B. 16%
   C. 20%
   D. More than 20%
4. Which age group is most likely to choose to smoke?
   A. Preteenagers
   B. Teenagers
   C. Postteenagers

Jen Jen Goes to the State Fair

Jen Jen and her (1. A. *friends* or B. *fiends*) went (2. A. *to*, B. *two*, C. *too*) the state fair. They used discounts to get in for (3. A. *half*, B. *have*) price. They visited the animal exhibits, went on some rides, and (4. A. *buyed*, B. *bought*, C. *brought*) interesting food from the many booths there.

Problem-Solving Item Set

This item set (see Table 3.4) is one of the best ways to measure problem-solving skills or abilities with a multiple-choice format instead of a performance format. Like the other three types of item sets, the stimulus prepares the student for answering the questions. The questions should systematically probe into the problem-solving process, using the guidelines we established for problem solving in Chapter 2. The example that follows gives some of those guidelines for a mathematics problem in the elementary school. Notice that the problem simulates real life. Another observation here is that this item set contains 8 items, but it could have contained 12 items. Generally, item sets take a long time to complete, so teachers should always allow sufficient time. This is problem solving, and it is not easy.

Warning

Much has been said in the previous two chapters about the beauty and wonder of higher level thinking. Writing such items may seem attractive and promising. Although you may write incredibly good items that test critical thinking, problem solving, and creative thinking, your students will fail miserably and suffer if they have *not* received appropriate instruction. None of these kinds of items should be used in the classroom without adequate preparation of the students. In my own teaching at the undergraduate and graduate levels, I use items similar to those that will be found on a test in everyday exercises, so that when students do encounter these items on the test, the shock of being tested on problem solving or critical thinking is not so great.

TABLE 3.4
Example of a Problem-Solving Item Set: Throwing a Party

Mom said I could have a slumber party for seven friends on Friday night, but that I would be responsible for pizza and soft drinks, and the friends would be responsible for cleanup. Mom suggested using the coupons in Wednesday's paper to shop for the goodies. Below is some information about coupons.

Store-brand cola	$1.19 per six pack
Double coupon on soft drinks	$0.35 (store doubles the value of the coupon)
Frozen pizzas (8 pieces per pizza)	2 for $5.00

You estimate that each friend will have two and a half drinks (on the average) and eat three pieces of pizza. Answer the following questions:

1. What is the cost of store-brand cola using the double coupon?
    A. 49 cents
    B. 84 cents
    C. $1.19
2. What is the cost of each piece of pizza?
    A. $5.00
    B. About 62 cents
    C. About 31 cents
3. How many pizza pieces do you need?
    A. 21
    B. 24
    C. More than 24
4. How many six-packs of soft drink will you buy?
    A. 3
    B. 4
    C. 5
5. How many pizzas will you buy?
    A. 2
    B. 3
    C. More than 3
6. What is the total cost of this party?
    A. About $10.00
    B. Much less than $10.00
    C. Much more than $10.00
7. Pizza is 2 for $5.00. How much does the store charge for one pizza?
    A. More than $2.50
    B. $2.50
8. How much did you save by shopping on Wednesday instead of Tuesday?
    A. About $1.00
    B. About $2.00
    C. About $3.00

Summary

This chapter has introduced many test item formats linked to the kinds of student outcomes for which these formats are well suited. Table 3.2 provides a useful, one-page summary of these formats. Sometimes you have choices among item formats. For example, for some high-inference cognitive skills and abilities, you can use multiple-choice or constructed response. For measuring writing and physical skills and abilities, performance-item formats seem most suitable. For creative activities, too, performance-item formats are appropriate.

This large array of item formats should motivate you to choose formats that bring life to your teaching, formats that get students thinking and working on school learning that goes well beyond just memorizing answers to questions. But these formats are not enough. You will need the spark and inspiration of your creativity to think of good items. The next five chapters provide specific guidance on how to write items of various types for higher level student outcomes.

References

Applebee, A. N., Langer, J. A., Mullis, I. V. S., Latham, A. S., & Gentile, C. A. (1994). *NAEP 1992 Writing Report Card.* Washington, DC: U.S. Department of Education.

Bennett, R. E. (1993). On the meaning of constructed response. In R. E. Bennett & W. C. Ward (Eds.), *Construction versus choice in cognitive measurement: Issues in constructed response, performance testing, and portfolio assessment* (pp. 1–27). Hillsdale, NJ: Lawrence Erlbaum Associates.

Carriveau, R., & Carriveau, T. (1994). *Carriveau Individual Profile Reading Assessment (CIPRA).* Phoenix: Impact Educational Services.

Downing, S. M. (1992). True–false and alternate-choice item formats: A review of research. *Educational Measurement: Issues and Practices, 11*, 27–30.

Grosse, M., & Wright, B. D. (1985). Validity and reliability of true-false tests. *Educational and Psychological Measurement, 45*, 1–13.

Haladyna, T. M. (1992a). The effectiveness of several multiple-choice formats. *Applied Measurement in Education, 5A*, 73–88.

Haladyna, T. M. (1992b). Context dependent item sets. *Educational Measurement: Issues and Practices, 11*, 21–25.

Haladyna, T. M. (1994). *Developing and validating multiple-choice test items.* Hillsdale, NJ: Lawrence Erlbaum Associates.

Haladyna, T. M. (1995). *The instrumentality of test item formats.* Submitted for publication.

Haladyna, T. M., & Downing, S. M. (1993). How many options is enough for a multiple-choice test item? *Educational and Psychological Measurement, 53*, 999–1010.

Osterlind, S. J., & Merz, W. R. (1994). Building a taxonomy for constructed-response test items. *Educational Assessment, 2*, 133–147.

Snow, R. E. (1993). Construct validity and constructed-response tests. In R. E. Bennett & W. C. Ward (Eds.), *Construction versus choice in cognitive measurement: Issues in constructed response, performance testing, and portfolio assessment* (pp. 45A–60). Hillsdale, NJ: Lawrence Erlbaum Associates.

Statman, S. (1988). Ask a clear question and get a clear answer: An enquiry into the question/answer and the sentence completion formats of multiple-choice items. *System, 16,* 367–376.

Stiggins, R. J. (1994). *Student-centered classroom assessment.* New York: Merrill.

Traub, R. E. (1993). On the equivalence of traits assessed by multiple-choice and constructed-response tests. In R. E. Bennett & W. C. Ward (Eds.), *Construction versus choice in cognitive measurement: Issues in constructed response, performance testing, and portfolio assessment* (pp. 1–27). Hillsdale, NJ: Lawrence Erlbaum Associates.

Part Two
Writing Test
Items

This part contains five chapters that form the core of this book. Chapter 4 deals with measuring knowledge and some mental skills and abilities using the multiple-choice format. Chapter 5 deals with measuring knowledge and mental and physical skills and abilities that require an inference to be made by a judge about each student response—hence the term high-inference. This inference is made with the use of a rating scale, often called a rubric after its inventor, Rube Goldberg (just kidding). Chapter 6 deals with measuring knowledge and mental and physical skills and abilities that require simple observation or a series of observations using a checklist (named after a famous Czech psychologist—oops, there I go again!). Thus, the term low-inference is used because the observers all see the same student response, and objectivity in scoring is realized. Chapter 7 deals with an old format that has enjoyed a revival, the portfolio (not named after anyone). Chapter 7 provides guidance on how to design and score a student portfolio, as well as a realistic appraisal of the portfolio's strengths and weaknesses. Chapter 8 deals with designing items for student surveys of affective traits such as self-concept, self-esteem, attitude, motivation, self-confidence, and learning environment, among others.

4 Multiple-Choice Formats

IN CHAPTER 2, YOU STUDIED SEVERAL TYPES OF MENTAL BEHAVIOR—
namely understanding, critical thinking, problem solving, and creativity. In Chapter 3, you studied item formats that could be used to measure these types of mental behavior. Chapter 4 is devoted entirely to the multiple-choice format. This chapter is long but leaves no stone unturned. After reading this chapter, you should be well informed about many aspects of multiple-choice item writing.

This chapter contains the following sections:

- Anatomy of a multiple-choice test item
- Kinds of learning outcomes usually measured by multiple-choice testing
- The rationale for using a multiple-choice item format instead of a constructed-response item format for certain types of student mental behavior
- How to write multiple-choice items
- Some do's and don'ts for writing multiple-choice test items

Anatomy

The conventional multiple choice you met in Chapter 3 has three main parts: stem, correct answer, and several distractors.

The *stem* is usually a question. The *correct answer* is a word, phrase, or sentence that answers the question. The *distractors* are plausible wrong answers to the question. Some writers call distractors *foils* or *misleads*. (Some students call distractors something else, but that can't be repeated here.) Among three basic multiple-choice formats presented in Chapter 3, my recommendations are as follows:

1. The conventional multiple choice is recommended.
2. The completion format is *not* recommended.
3. The best-option format is recommended.

Kinds of Student Outcomes Measured by Multiple-Choice Test Items

The multiple-choice test format is mainly intended to measure knowledge and mental skills and abilities. This format is *never* used to measure physical skills or abilities. Table 4.1 provides a summary of how a multiple-choice format might be used; the table provides only the stem for each item.

A recall item is easy to design and use. We agreed not to bother with this kind of item in this book because most of us are already experts at this. The understanding item usually requires evidence that the student understands a fact, concept, principle, or procedure. We use a questioning strategy that asks students to

TABLE 4.1
Examples of Uses of Multiple Choice

TYPE OF STUDENT BEHAVIOR[a]	SAMPLE ITEM STEM
Recall	What is a typical growth rate of the azalea?
Understanding	What is distinctive about the azalea compared to other spring-flowering shrubs?
Critical thinking (prediction)	What happens if an azalea receives a plant food high in alkaline and low in acid?
Critical thinking (evaluation)	Given highly acidic soil and an annual rainfall of about 40 inches, what is the most effective plant food for an azalea?
Problem solving	Your azalea is planted in full shade under the eaves of your house. Leaves are yellowing, and the plant has shown little growth in two years. What is the best treatment of this problem?

[a]Any item may really test recall if teaching is aimed at having student memorize responses to questions that may otherwise appear to test something other than recall. This is the difference between teaching the test and teaching so that test performance is good. The latter is what's being emphasized here.

identify a correct definition (nonverbatim), identify characteristics or noncharacteristics, or identify examples or nonexamples. With the critical thinking prediction, we expect the student to anticipate or predict what will happen or what caused something to happen. With critical thinking evaluation, we ask students to select a criterion or criteria, use a criterion or criteria, or both select and use a criterion or criteria. Evaluation and prediction often involve principles. Problem solving involves multiple steps. No single item is sufficient for measuring problem solving. The item set is recommended because it usually allows the item writer the ability to study student responses to each step in the problem-solving process.

Which Type of Format Should We Use—Multiple-Choice or Essay?

When measuring knowledge and some mental skills and abilities, you have two choices: multiple choice or essay. Chapters 5 and 6 show how to construct essay items and score student responses. This section discusses the pros and cons of multiple choice over the essay format.

Reasons for Using Multiple Choice

1. Better content domain sampling. A test is supposed to represent a fair sample from a well-defined content domain. To get the most representative sample from the test blueprint requires many items. The multiple-choice item format permits a broader sampling from the domain of desired student behaviors when compared to the essay. In other words, the sampling of the content domain that occurs when using a multiple-choice format is more representative simply because one can ask more multiple-choice items in a one-hour test compared to what is accomplished with the essay format in that same hour. Because adequacy of sampling from the domain is an important piece of evidence in test score validation, the multiple choice is the better choice.

2. Higher reliability. The consistency or dependability of test scores over time is its reliability. Every test score has some degree of random error, which can be minimized by using a more reliable test. Generally speaking, for multiple-choice and essay tests covering the same content, multiple choice will have higher reliability. Because reliability is essential evidence in validating a test use, the argument is strong for multiple choice when it is a viable option.

3. Greater efficiency. The effort you put into writing test items for a test as well as the time spent administering and scoring the test is part of efficiency. If items can be reused later, this is still another factor in the consideration of relative efficiency of these two rival formats for measuring knowledge. Cost is another consideration. For most classroom situations, preparing an essay test is more efficient than preparing a multiple-choice test, but scoring an essay test is less efficient than scoring a multiple-choice test. Taking the two considerations together, writing the test and scoring the test, multiple choice is probably more efficient because multiple-choice tests takes less time to score and good items can be saved and reused in future tests, reducing test preparation time in the future.

4. Objectivity. Objectivity is the ability to obtain the same results when the test results are rescored or scored by different people. Multiple-choice tests provide identical scores when a key or scoring template is used and one or more persons score the test. With an essay test, this claim cannot be supported, because scoring is subjective, even with the help of a checklist or rating scale. Objectivity/subjectivity relates to reliability. The more subjective the scoring process, the larger the error component in test scores is likely to be.

5. Measurability. Some critics of multiple-choice testing claim that this format is best suited for memory learning, recall, verbatim or rote learning, and trivial knowledge, whereas essay formats are better suited for testing higher level thinking, which is the more important outcome in schooling. Although it is easier to write essay items that measure critical thinking and problem-solving abilities, this chapter contains many examples of multiple-choice items that measure higher level thinking.

6. Mechanical scoring. Multiple-choice test results can be rapidly and accurately machine-scored. The low cost of this scoring, the ease of obtaining computerized item analysis results, and the rapid feedback afforded to students are attractive features. Scanning equipment is now affordable and common in many school buildings at most educational levels. Hand-scoring templates also provide the ability to give rapid feedback to students with machinelike accuracy. I use hand-scoring templates to give student feedback right after the test, so we can discuss and debate results, which is always fun. With essay testing, quick feedback is rare—you have to spend your weekend reading the essays.

Reasons against Multiple Choice

1. Trivial learning and testing. Multiple-choice testing leads to multiple-choice teaching, which emphasizes trivial learning of isolated facts. Although it is true that much of multiple-choice testing focuses on the lowest level of learning, this is not the fault of the format but the fault of those who teach and test this way. Multiple-choice formats can be used for better purposes than just testing recall, as this chapter shows.

2. Inappropriate for some purposes. Abilities like writing and creative thinking should not be measured with a multiple-choice format. At times, it may be convenient to measure isolated skills that lead to such performance-oriented abilities, but generally you should not use multiple choice for something for which it was never intended.

3. Lack of student writing. A multiple-choice test does not give students an opportunity to write. The development of writing ability is important, but this criticism of the multiple-choice format is very misguided. Both multiple-choice and essay formats are intended to measure student knowledge and some mental skills and abilities, but not writing ability. However, if an essay test also provides a scorable sample of writing ability, this is a strong argument in favor of such a test because you test two things: knowledge and writing ability.

Summary. Given the pros and cons for the multiple-choice format, it seems that if you are interested in measuring student recall or understanding or some mental skills or abilities, then the multiple choice is very desirable. But sometimes the multiple-choice format is not appropriate, as with measuring writing ability.

How to Write the Multiple-Choice Item

Writing items is very difficult. Writer's block is a common ailment among item writers. The item writer knows what to test but has difficulty in phrasing the item. In training item writers in such fields as pharmacy, medicine, nursing, and education, we have concluded that everyone needs an item-writing crutch. We use *item shells* (Haladyna & Shindoll, 1989). These are stripped-down items that have the content removed but retain a tried-and-true structure to help you write the item. Table 4.2 provides a list of item shells for conventional multiple-choice, alternate-choice, or multiple true–false formats. Some of these item shells suggest a scenario for the item set. As you can see, item shells are sketchy and totally without content. They are only skeletal. You can add the substance to the item and vary them to write good items to measure understanding, critical thinking, or problem solving. Item shells are strongly recommended to get you started and build confidence in your item-writing ability. Once you develop your ability, you should wean yourself from item shells. If you use only item shells, your items will start to look alike and will not be very interesting.

Table 4.3 is a template to help you write an item. It provides a checklist that will help guide you from idea to fruition. First, you need to decide if you are simply testing knowledge or a mental skill or a mental ability. There is a fine line between skill and ability. Both require performance, but skill is more easily developed than ability. Many abilities are more easily or appropriately tested using the open-ended for-

---

TABLE 4.2
Item Shells

Understanding:

Which best defines _____?
Which is (un)characteristic of _____?
Which of the following is an example of _____?

Critical thinking (evaluating):

What is most effective (appropriate) for _____?
Which is better (worse) _____?
What is the most effective method for _____?
What is the most critical step in this procedure?
Which is (un)necessary in a procedure?

Critical thinking (predicting):

What would happen if . . . ?
If this happens, what should you do?
On the basis of . . . , what should you do?
Given . . . , what is the primary cause of . . . ?

Problem solving (given a scenario):

What is the nature of the problem?
What do you need to solve this problem?
What is a possible solution?
Which is a solution?
Which is the most effective (efficient) solution?
Why is _____ the most effective (efficient) solution?

---

mats featured in the next three chapters. Critical thinking and evaluating usually involve principles and a procedure. Critical thinking and predicting involve concepts and principles. Problem solving involves most types of content and a combination of mental behaviors. That is why problem solving is so hard to teach and test.

The choice of a format is yours. Conventional multiple choice serves a variety of purposes, including critical thinking and problem solving. Matching and alternate choice are good for items testing recall and understanding. Multiple true–false is especially good for understanding.

TABLE 4.3
A Template for Developing a Multiple-Choice Test Item

Choose the type of student outcome:

Knowledge	Mental Skill	Mental Ability

What content are you teaching/measuring?

Fact	Concept	Principle	Procedure

What type of mental behavior are you developing?

Recall	Understanding	Critical Thinking	Problem Solving

What format will you use?

Convention MC	Alternate-Choice	Matching	Multiple TF

Stem:

Correct Answer:

Distractor 1:

Distractor 2:

Distractor 3:

Notes: If matching, write at least five stems.
If alternate choice, write only one distractor.
If multiple true–false, the stem is the stimulus and the choices become the test items.
If an item set is designed, use the item set template in Table 4.4.
Notice that the complex multiple-choice and true–false formats are not recommended and therefore are not listed as choices.

TABLE 4.4
Item Set Template

Choose the type of student outcome to be tested:

Knowledge	Mental Skill	Mental Ability

What kind of content are you teaching/measuring?

Fact	Concept	Principle	Procedure

What type of mental behavior are you developing?

Recall	Understanding	Critical Thinking	Problem Solving

Scenario (Stimulus):

Reading passage, pictorial stimulus, object, . . .

Questions usually are multiple choice, but they can be open-ended.

The item set is different. Table 4.4 provides a template for the item set much like the one in Table 4.3. Remember, however, that an item set has a stimulus and a set of items. The item set is especially useful for problem solving.

As shown in these templates, the process of writing a good multiple-choice item generally is the same:

1. Identify the content and mental behavior desired.
2. Write the stem in a question format.
3. Write the correct answer.
4. Write distractors that have the same grammatical and content structure as the correct answer but are clearly wrong.

Although these four steps may seem simple, you will be surprised at how many items that you write fail to perform when tried with students. Item writing to match your instruction is not easy. Having a clear purpose and making this purpose clear to students is a first step. Chapters 9 and 10 give advice on how to improve these items once they are drafted. A strong aspect of this advice involves student evaluation of items.

Do's and Don't's for Writing Multiple-Choice Items

In the next five sections, some rules are presented and items are used to illustrate the use of the rule or the violation of the rule. Although some of these rules are based on research, this research is not very extensive. Therefore, these rules are not laws that should never be broken. In fact, much of the validity of these rules comes from the opinions of experts in the field of educational measurement. And these testing specialists don't always agree (Haladyna & Downing, 1989a). As an item writer, you should use your best judgment regarding when to invoke or not to invoke these rules. As noted previously, the "rules" are merely advice to follow in most circumstances. Table 4.5 provides a summary of these item-writing rules. Review this table before reading and then select sections to read following your interest and expertise.

TABLE 4.5
A Handy Summary of Multiple-Choice Item-Writing Rules

Content Concerns

1. Base each item on something important for students to learn. Avoid trivial content.
2. Emphasize higher level thinking at the expense of recall.
3. Avoid both overly specific and overly general knowledge.
4. Focus each item on a single mental behavior instead of a complex chain of behaviors.
5. Avoid cueing students to a right answer to another item.
6. Avoid opinion-based items.
7. Avoid trick items.

Format Concerns

1. Identify a format presentation style and follow it consistently.
2. Use the question format instead of the completion format.
3. Use the best-answer format when you can.
4. Avoid the true–false and the complex multiple-choice formats.
5. Format the item vertically instead of horizontally.

Continued

TABLE 4.5 *Continued*

Style Concerns

1. Edit and proofread all items.
2. Keep vocabulary simple for the group being tested.
3. Use correct grammar, punctuation, capitalization, and spelling.
4. Minimize the amount of reading in each item.

Writing the Stem

1. Ensure that the directions to the student in the stem are very clear. The student should know exactly what is being asked.
2. Include the central idea in the stem instead of the choices.
3. Avoid window dressing (excessive verbiage).
4. Word the stem positively; avoid negatives like *not* or *except*.

Writing the Choices

1. Use as many good choices as possible. Generally, three seems to be about as many as we can write.
2. Make sure that only one of these choices is the right answer.
3. Vary the position of the right answer so that no one position usually has the right answer.
4. Place choices in logical or numerical order.
5. Keep choices independent; choices should not be overlapping.
6. Keep choices homogeneous in content.
7. Keep the length of choices about equal.
8. Avoid using the choice *none of the above* or *all of the above*.
9. Avoid the choice *I don't know*.
10. Phrase choices positively; avoid negatives like *not*.
11. Avoid giving clues to the right answer.
12. Make all distractors plausible.
13. Use typical errors of students to write your distractors.
14. Use a correct but irrelevant statement as a distractor.
15. Avoid humorous choices.

Content Concerns

1. Base each item on an important outcome for the student to learn. Avoid trivial content.

Grant Wiggins (1989) has introduced and promoted the idea of authentic assessment—that what students learn should be realistic, meaningful, and applicable to life. Philosophically, no test item is authentic, because every test is an intrusion into a student's life. But we can make learning activities and test items interesting, thought-provoking, and meaningful. Test content should reflect some connection to the world outside of school and should convey to students that this is worthwhile to learn.

To achieve this, we do not test trivial content. Much criticism has been leveled at item writers who ask questions that don't deserve answers because they are so trivial. As a content/item writer, you can decide what is important and what is trivial. Following are some examples of trivial testing:

---

1. When was the Webster-Ashburton treaty signed?
2. Who wrote *Crime and Punishment*?
3. What is the capital of Delaware?
4. Where was the first group intelligence test administered?

Students should believe that what is learned and tested is really worth learning and testing.

2. *Emphasize higher level thinking.*

In the past, we teachers have overemphasized testing recall at the expense of teaching and testing higher level thinking. Chapter 2 was devoted to a simple taxonomy of higher level thinking that featured understanding, critical thinking, problem solving, and creativity. Writing items that tap these types of mental behavior is a challenge. This chapter and the three chapters that follow provide help in writing such items.

3. *Avoid overly specific and overly general knowledge.*

The idea of overly specific and overly general knowledge is very difficult to communicate. It refers to a continuum of specificity ranging from abstract to concrete:

Abstract ——————————————————————— Concrete

Love is a many splendored thing.   My boyfriend was
                                                   15 minutes late for our date.

At one extreme we have an item such as this:

Which is the most serious problem in the world?

A. Hunger
B. Education
C. Disease
D. Political ideology

Whole books have been written on each of these topics. There is probably no correct answer to this simplistic question; the question defies an answer because it is so abstract.

At the other extreme we have:

Who composed "The Icon of Seville"?

A. Barber
B. Romero
C. Lorca
D. Segovia

Although this second item might reflect violations of other item-writing rules in future sections of this chapter, the important point here is that it asks students for information that is extremely specific and perhaps even trivial.

The judgment of specificity is subjective, and you need to decide how specific or how abstract a given item must be to reflect adequately the learner outcome statement on which it was based.

4. Focus each item on a single mental behavior instead of a complex chain of behaviors.

Every test item should be based on a single mental behavior. There are two reasons for this advice. First, we like to see a clear connection between what we teach and what we test. Having an item serve multiple purposes is confusing. Second, if a test item represents a complex, multistage process to reach the correct answer, when a student misses the item, the teacher does not know what step in the process was not learned. So no single item will test problem-solving behavior very well because it is so complex. For problem solving, the item set might work or we might have to resort to the variety of constructed-response formats presented in Chapter 3 and further discussed in Chapters 5A, 6, and 7.

5. Avoid cueing the student to a right answer to another item.

When writing sets of items for a goal or an objective, there is a tendency to permit one item to provide sufficient information to answer an adjacent item. For example, consider a line of questioning focusing on the desirability of lima beans:

---

1. What makes boiled lima beans yucky?

   A. *Taste
   B. Nutrition
   C. Reputation

2. Do children typically like lima beans?

   A. Yes
   B. No

Item 1 or item 2 may be good items separately, but item 1 gives away the answer to item 2.

6. *Avoid opinion-based items.*

This advice derives from the value that items should reflect well-known and publicly supported facts, concepts, principles, and procedures. To test a student on an opinion about any content is unfair unless the opinion is qualified by some logical analysis, evidence, or person cited in the instructional materials. An example is:

Who is best admired for outstanding dramatic performances in film in the past ten years?

   A. Jane Fonda
   B. Shirley McLaine
   C. Meryl Streep

The idea of admiration is a personal appraisal, and, unless qualified as part of instruction, is very much a personal opinion. Qualified opinions for items are all right if the opinion has been included as part of the instructions.

7. *Avoid trick items.*

Trick questions are ones that are hard to define or illustrate. These questions are designed by devious item writers to get students to make a wrong choice. Such a strategy in item design misdirects, because the purpose of any test item is to measure an important learner outcome in a fair way. The successful learner is supposed to pick the right answer; the unsuccessful learner is supposed to pick a distractor. Tricky items tempt knowing students to pick a wrong answer because of another cue, even though they learned what they were supposed to learn. Look at the following example.

What is the most effective treatment for arthritic pain in a knee?

   A. Exercise
   B. Physical therapy followed by medication
   C. *Medication

·   The question illustrates that a wrong answer (B) may be tempting because it is the longest answer (violating another item-writing rule). Here's another example:

Marriage is said to be a contract between/among what principals?

  A. church and state
  B. *husband and wife
  C. husband, wife, and in-laws-to-be
  D. husband, wife, and the state

The grouping of three choices with similar answers leads students to select the choice that is unique from all others. Here "church and state" is not the right answer.

Another criticism of trick questions is that such a questioning strategy, if frequent enough, builds an attitude by the test-taker of mistrust and lack of respect for the testing process. There are enough problems in testing without contributing more through trick questions.

Format Concerns

1. Identify a format presentation style and follow it consistently.

With today's personal computer and word-processing programs, coupled with superior printers, there is no excuse for bad-looking tests. Today's tests can have a professional look that earns respect from colleagues and students and effectively communicates what you teach and test. Use an informal or formal style guide that gives you a standard way of presenting all items. The items presented throughout this book follow such a style guide. Chapter 9 discusses the style guide at greater length.

2. Use the question format instead of the completion format.

Earlier, several alternative multiple-choice formats were presented. Research has indicated that the question format is preferable to the completion format (Haladyna & Downing, 1989b). Although the two formats offer very little difference, the question format is simpler and more direct. In keeping with the idea that multiple-choice questioning should emphasize attainment of knowledge instead of reading, every tactic designed to make the item read more clearly should be employed. The question format appears to be directed toward that end and is recommended over the completion format.

Question Format:

For multiple-choice items, which format is recommended?

  A. *Question
  B. Completion
  C. Complex multiple-choice
  D. Multidimensional choice

Completion Format: If you use a completion format, *never* leave the blank in the middle or at the beginning of the stem. Although the completion format is *not* recommended, it can be used effectively. One way to write a completion format is to develop the stem so that the correct answer and all possible choices complete the sentence begun in the stem as shown below:

For multiple-choice testing, one should use the

   A. *question format.
   B. completion format.
   C. complex multiple-choice format.
   D. multidimensional-choice format.

There are several ways in which this format should *not* be employed:

The _____ format is the best way to format a multiple-choice item.

   A. completion
   B. *question
   C. complex multiple-choice
   D. multidimensional-choice

Child abuse is an example of _____ violence, whereas racism is an example of _____ violence.

   A. structural, aggressive
   B. physical, structural
   C. *physical, psychological
   D. psychological, structural

The formats shown above are complex for students and difficult to answer. These formats, particularly the second example, require more time to administer and reduce the time spent productively answering other questions. They also may increase student anxiety, which is a chronic problem with at least 25 percent of students. For all these reasons, the use of internal or beginning blanks in completion items should be avoided.

3. Use the best-answer format when you can.

One can use a multiple-choice format that requires the student to distinguish a right answer from the wrong choices or to choose among the best of several right choices. Because this was shown earlier, no example will be provided here. Although the best-answer format can look like a trick item, remember that one aspect of critical thinking is the ability to evaluate. In many circumstances, we have many right answers, but one is clearly the best. Thus, this best-answer format is useful for one aspect of critical thinking.

4. Avoid the true–false and complex multiple-choice formats.
Both formats were illustrated in Chapter 3, and the warning was given to avoid this format. As a viable substitute for true–false, the alternate choice is recommended. As a viable substitute for complex multiple choice, the multiple true–false is recommended. Research generally supports these recommendations (Albanese, 1992; Downing, 1992; Frisbie, 1993; Haladyna, 1993, 1994).

5. Format the item vertically or horizontally.
Any multiple-choice item can be formatted either way. The most conventional format is vertical, as shown:

> Which is the most desirable test format for measuring evaluating behavior?
>
> A. True–false
> B. Testlet
> C. Multiple true–false
> D. *Best-answer

This item could be reformatted horizontally:

> Which is the most desirable test format for measuring evaluating behavior?
>
> A. True–false   B. Testlet   C. Multiple true–false   D. *Best-answer

The latter format occupies less space and therefore is more efficient in terms of production costs. On the other hand, the "look" of the test is affected by items that appear cramped. If face validity is important, horizontal formatting should be avoided. Also, some researchers suspect that younger students may have difficulty with the horizontal format.

Another suggestion here to counteract the argument for the brevity of horizontal formatting is to use a two-column format for test items on any test. This format is more compact, and reading research suggests that columns are easier to read than wider pages of text. Modern-day word processing can easily produce two-column printing for multiple-choice tests. The next section more directly addresses the appearance of items.

Style Concerns

This section is devoted to how test items are presented. As mentioned earlier in this chapter, Chapter 9 has a more comprehensive section on style.

1. Edit and proofread all items.

Depending on the purpose of the test and the time and other resources devoted to testing, one should always allow time for editing and proofreading. Although this topic is treated in more detail in Chapter 9, it is sufficient to say here that a test should look like a test and should follow high standards for testing if it is to do what was intended. Items that are written by a content expert may have editorial difficulties. Constant vigilance in editing and proofreading doesn't guarantee a good item but does provide some assurance that the item will perform as intended. Even with expert item development, as many as 40 percent of all items may fail to perform as intended in a formal testing program. Therefore, one should never overlook the opportunity to improve each item by subjecting it to editing and proofreading reviews.

2. Keep vocabulary consistent with the group of students being tested.

The purpose of any achievement test, as defined in this book, is to measure accomplishment—learning. Accomplishments are linked to learner outcome statements known as objectives or goals. The purpose of the test is *not* to test one's ability to read or translate the item. Therefore, vocabulary should be simple enough for the weakest readers in the group being tested. If reading is confounded with the achievement being measured, then the test score is likely to reflect reading ability more than what was taught and learned.

3. Use correct grammar, punctuation, capitalization, and spelling.

There are many reasons for such a rule. Every test is a reflection of the test maker. Errors of grammar, punctuation, capitalization, and spelling give the impression that the test was casually or improperly prepared. Such errors, though superficial to some, may signal a deeper and more significant neglect, such as poor choice of content. In other words, they may be the tip of the iceberg of a more serious problem. Also, errors reflect badly on the teacher by making students wonder if the teacher knows the correct form.

Some experts in testing have cautioned that students might be distracted from the test-taking process by such errors. If this is true, then these errors have another negative effect in that they cause some students to lose concentration and fail to perform as they should. Such a failure is bias in testing and a very serious threat to validity.

4. Minimize examinee reading time.

In testing as in business, time is money. Efficiency relates to the cost of testing in terms of both time and money. Items that require much reading take longer to administer. Consider an important test with alternative forms and a fixed period. The test with wordy items requiring much reading will provide for fewer items per fixed period than the test with more succinctly written items.

Thus, one benefit of minimizing examinee reading time is that you can ask more questions. The number of items given in a fixed period directly affects the reliability of test scores and the adequacy of sampling. Because these are two important characteristics of test design, you should make a strong effort to minimize reading time. Unless lengthy reading is demonstrably necessary, such items should *not* be used. Consider the following item:

Under the Supreme Court guidelines, which of the following is a test for obscenity?

   A. *The material lacks redeeming social value.
   B. The material is a threat to moral standards of the area.
   C. The material contributes to the commission of sex crimes.
   D. The material is the cause of sexual perversions.

The repetitious wording of the choices is a common error that makes the reading of the item a little tedious. The item should be edited. For example:

Which of the following is an appropriate test for obscenity under Supreme Court guidelines?

   A. *Lacks redeeming social value
   B. Threatens moral standards
   C. Contributes to sex crimes
   D. Causes sexual perversion

Some items can be very long and involved. As an item writer, you should decide if it is worth all the reading by the student to arrive at a right answer. Generally, items should be as brief as possible, because each item is a scorable unit, and reliability is governed by the number of scorable units. The more the better. By having shorter items, you can place more items on the test and get more reliable results. Also, with more items that are briefer, you can increase the sampling of content which affects validity.

Writing the Stem

1. Ensure that the directions in the stem are very clear. The student should know exactly what is being asked.

The item stem should always phrase the problem to be answered by each choice in a clear and unambiguous way. The test taker should always know what is being asked in the item.

This vocabulary item provides little or no information in the stem regarding the right answer.

Levitation is

   A. a principle of physics.
   B. defying gravity.
   C. light-hearted chit-chat.

When an item fails to perform with students as intended, there can be many reasons. One reason may be that the stem did not clearly present the problem to most students. This lack of clarity is difficult to detect when the item is originally drafted, but item review or tryout will often reveal that an item did not perform for this reason. We refer to this problem as an *unfocused stem.*

2. Include the central idea and most of the phrasing in the stem.

One fault in item writing is to have a brief stem and most of the content in the choices. Two examples follow.

River City

   A. has an air pollution problem.
   B. was under water during the flood.
   C. has insufficient police protection.
   D. *needs more firefighting equipment.

Ageism is

   A. *a negative attitude toward old people.
   B. physical abuse of the aged.
   C. prejudice against old people.
   D. the frequent use of discrimination against the aged.

These items require too much reading of choices and make the evaluation of items very complex and therefore difficult. If the objective of the first item is to identify a problem in River City, the question could be more effectively rephrased to include more material in the stem and less in the choices, as follows:

What is the most significant problem affecting River City?

   A. Budget
   B. *Insufficient firefighting equipment
   C. Inadequate police force

What best defines ageism?

   A. Prejudice against old people
   B. Discrimination against old people
   C. Physical abuse of the aged

A common error in writing an item is the use of repetitious phrases in each choice:

Occlusion of the right coronary artery by a thrombus would most likely result in

   A. infarction of the lateral wall of right ventricle and the right atrium.
   B. infarction of the lateral left ventricle.
   C. infarction of the anterior left ventricle.
   D. infarction of the anterior septum.

The item should read:

Occlusion of the right coronary artery by a thrombus would most likely result in infarction of the

   A. lateral wall of the right ventricle and the right atrium.
   B. lateral left ventricle.
   C. anterior left ventricle.
   D. anterior septum.

3. *Avoid window dressing (excessive verbiage).*

Some items contain words, phrases, or entire sentences that have nothing to do with the problem. They may have been added to make the problem sound more realistic, to give it substance. For example:

The night was clear, the moon was yellow, and the leaves came tumbling down. Who shot Stagger Lee?

  A. Billy
  B. Stagger Lee
  C. His girl friend
  D. The Gambler

This is window dressing. A better version is given in the example:

Who shot Stagger Lee?

  A. *Billy
  B. Stagger Lee
  C. His girl friend
  D. The gambler

In problem solving, where the student is supposed to sort through information and select what is relevant to solving a problem, extraneous information is actually necessary:

A compact disc at the music store was priced at $9.99, but it was marked at a 20% discount. Sales tax was 6%. Linda had $9.00 in her purse. Would she have enough money to buy this disc?

This item requires the student to sift through much information to figure out which is relevant and which is not. This is a perfectly legitimate questioning strategy that does *not* contain window dressing.

4. *Word the stem positively; avoid negative phrasing.*

This rule is based on a consensus of testing experts who feel that the use of negative words in the stem has negative effects on students and their responses to such items. This advice can be taken several ways, and each is illustrated.

First, stems should not contain a negative, as illustrated:

Which is *not* a benefit of multiple-choice testing?

A. Great potential for content validity
B. Great potential for high reliability
C. *Appropriate for measuring aspects of performance
D. Objectivity

A better way to phrase such an item is to remove the *not* and make the item a multiple true–false with more choices. Another variation of this rule is that when you use a negative word, it should be emphasized by being in boldface type, capitalized, or underlined so the student does not read through the *not* and forget to reverse the logic of the relationship being tested.

The marginal maxillary branch of the facial nerve enervates all of the following EXCEPT?

This type of item is probably better suited to a multiple true–false format.

Writing the Choices

Writing the correct answer and the distractors is the hardest part of multiple-choice item writing. We have fifteen specific rules, as Table 4.5 shows.

1. Use as many good choices as possible. Generally, three seems to be about as many as we can write.
The ideal number of choices for a test item is a matter of considerable debate and study in testing (Haladyna & Downing, 1989a, 1989b). A summary of this research indicates that there is a slight advantage to having more choices per test item, but is it worth the extra effort to write three or four distractors? Haladyna and Downing (1994) studied the number of useful distractors per item on the average for four well-developed standardized tests. They found that most items contained only one or two good distractors. If these results generalize to most multiple-choice situations, one would be inclined to write fewer distractors and concentrate on their quality instead of their quantity. This is my advice here. It matters not how

many distractors one produces for any given multiple-choice item, but it does matter if each distractor is working. Chapter 10 provides more information on the properties of working distractors.

One criticism of this approach is that guessing plays a role in determining a student's score. The use of fewer distractors will increase the chances of a student guessing the right answer. However, the probability that a student will increase his or her score significantly over a 20-, 50-, or 100-item test by pure guessing is infinitesimal. Any test user knows that if a test contains three choices, the lowest average score for a student who lacks knowledge and guesses randomly throughout the test is 33 percent. To control guessing, give the student enough test items to the extent that guessing will *not* influence a test score. This logic is sound for two-choice items as well, because the floor of the scale is 50% and the probability of a student making 20, 50, or 100 successful random guesses is very close to zero.

2. Make sure that only one of these choices is the correct answer.

Since much of test theory and test scoring equipment pertains to one correct answer per item, it seems reasonable to recommend that there be only one correct answer. Of course, if the best-answer format is used, it is possible to have more than one correct answer. In this instance, the best answer should *clearly* be the best answer, so that there still is only *one* correct answer.

Given that multiple-choice test items are often imperfect, there may be occasions where, unintentionally, more than one correct answer exists. In these instances, more than one right answer should be accepted.

A principal advantage of performance tests for measuring problem solving and creativity is that more than one answer is possible and tolerated. In these events, multiple choice is not a viable option.

3. Vary the position of the right answer so that no one position usually has the right answer.

Generally, the correct answer should be distributed about equally over the possible right-answer positions. If four-choice items are being used, the correct answer should be located about 25 percent of the time at each position. Any serious departure from this rule may cause higher performing students to see a pattern that may tip them off to guessing right answers and performing higher than they should perform. Or low performers may randomly select a choice position such as C, and accidentally get a higher score than deserved by pure luck. Random guessing is not a serious factor in tests of more than 10 items. Although research on the likelihood that a certain position will be randomly chosen over any other position is inconclusive, most test-makers and experts on testing recommend that the correct answer for any test be balanced. Therefore, the position of the right answer is a concern.

4. Place choices in logical or numerical order.

Numerical answers should be arranged in ascending or descending order.

Wrong	Right
What is the cost of an item that normally sells for $9.99 that is discounted 25%?	What is the cost of an item that normally sells for $9.99 that is discounted 25%?
A. $5.00 B. *$7.50 C. $2.50 D. $6.66	A. $2.50 B. $5.00 C. $6.66 D. *$7.50

Remember that the idea of the item is to test for knowledge in a direct fashion. If a student has to hunt unnecessarily for a right answer, time is wasted.

Logical ordering is more difficult to illustrate, but some examples offer hints at what is meant by this rule:

Which are considered the language arts?

A. Reading, writing, and arithmetic
B. Writing, reading, and grammar
C. *Reading, writing, speaking, and listening
D. Reading and writing

While such a questioning strategy may be criticized for other reasons, this popular format is additionally and unnecessarily confusing because the four possible terms (reading, writing, speaking, and listening) are presented in an inconsistent order. A more logical ordering and presentation is:

Which are considered the language arts?

A. Reading and writing
B. Writing, reading, and arithmetic
C. Reading, writing, and grammar
D. Reading, writing, speaking, and listening

5. Keep choices independent; choices should not be overlapping

This subtle item-writing fault is very much like the advice on interitem cueing. If choices are overlapping, they are unlikely to be correct. If an overlapping choice is correct, then the item is ambiguous and may have two correct answers. This is easiest to show with a mathematics problem like the following.

What age range represents the physical "peak" of life?

- A. 11–15
- B. 13–19
- C. 18–25
- D. *24–32
- E. Over 32

In such numerical problems, having ranges that are close makes the item more difficult. More important, choices A, B, C, and D in this example slightly overlap. If the answer is age 25, one can argue that both C and D are correct, although the author of the item meant C. This careless error can be corrected easily by developing ranges that are distinct. Avoiding overlapping options also will prevent embarrassing challenges to test items.

6. Keep choices homogeneous in content.

The use of choices that are heterogeneous in content is often a cue to the student. Such cues are not inherent in the intent of the item but an unfortunate accident. Therefore, the maintenance of homogeneity of options is good advice. For example:

Which is the least likely cause of a sudden wind storm in the Sonoran desert?

- A. Two weather fronts colliding
- B. Local heating
- C. *Coastal weather disturbances from the west
- D. Tropical storms from the Gulf of Mexico or the Gulf of California

---

7. Keep the lengths of choices about equal.

One common fault in item writing is to make the correct answer the longest. This may happen innocently. The item-writer writes the stem and the right answer and, in the rush to complete the item, adds two or three hastily written wrong choices that are shorter than the right answer. For example:

> Which dishwashing strategy is most likely to eliminate soap scum on glasses?
>
> A. Hand washing
> B. A liquid dishwasher detergent
> C. A power dishwasher detergent
> D. *Begin by rinsing all glasses in a lime solution. Then wash the dishes. Rinse in the lime solution again. Rinse in water. Air dry.

If the longest answer is a distractor, the item might be considered a trick question.

8. Avoid using the choices **none of the above** and **all of the above.**

Research has shown that "none of the above" has several negative characteristics that suggest that it *not* be used. Perhaps the most obvious reason for not using this format is that a correct answer obviously exists and should be used in the item. There is no advantage to omitting the right answer from the list of choices.

"All of the above" is a very popular choice. One reason may be that, in writing a test item, it is easy to identify two or even three right answers. The use of the option "all of the above" is a good device for capturing this information. However, the use of this option may be helping testwise students. For instance, if a student has partial information (knows that two of the three options offered are correct), that information can clue the student into correctly choosing *all of the above.*

One alternative to the "all of the above" choice is the use of the multiple true–false format. Another alternative is to ensure that there is one and only one right answer.

Because the purpose of a test item is to test knowledge, using "all of the above" seems to draw students into test-taking strategies more than directly testing for knowledge. For that reason, it is recommended that these options *not* be used.

9. Avoid "I don't know."

A popular choice for tests intended for young children is this option. The intention is to minimize the role of guessing in multiple-choice testing. Unfortunately, not all children or even all adults treat this option the same way. A study by Sherman (1976) showed systematic differences between groups of children by region, gender, personality variables, and ethnic background. Why would anyone want to use an option that benefits some groups of test takers at the expense of others? The "I don't know" option appears to have great potential for producing bias in test scores. Therefore, it should be avoided.

Besides, if students do not know the right answer, then by responding to the option "I don't know," they have, in fact, chosen the right answer, and you have to given them credit for not knowing.

10. Phrase options positively; avoid negatives like not.

It was recommended that stems be phrased positively. The same advice is offered for choices. The use of negatives such as *not* and *except* should be avoided:

Which is an example of bad taste?

    A. Not watching *Beavis and Butthead*
    B. Boiled lima beans
    C. Not going to the opera

Such questions tend to be unnecessarily difficult. Difficult questions do not necessarily pose a problem. Still, if the standards for evaluating student performance are high, artificially hard items make high test scores less likely. Therefore, the use of negative options should be avoided for that reason.

11. Avoid various clues to the right answer.

This general advice pertains to a collection of common clues to item writing: (1) clang associations, (2) ridiculous options, (3) formal prompts, (4) specific determiners, and (5) faulty grammar.

Clang associations include phrases in the stem that are repeated in options. Such connections often provide a clue to the right answer. For example:

Who are the "Magnificent Seven?"

    A. A pro basketball team
    B. *A group of seven fictional Western heroes
    C. A protest group made famous during the Vietnam War crisis
    D. A rock group

The use of the term *seven* in B. is a clue for those who don't really know the right answer.

Ridiculous options may be intended for humor or merely accidental. This second type of clue can be viewed as highly implausible, so much so that no test-taker would choose it:

> Who is responsible for the MTV network programming concept?
>
> A. Leonard Bernstein
> B. Dick Clark
> C. Andrew Rooney

You might be surprised to know that even on high-quality standardized tests containing four or five options per item, two or more choices may be so implausible that they are seldom chosen. We have a propensity to write implausible choices. The use of ridiculous choices makes guessing easier by reducing the number of useful distractors in a test item.

The third of these clues, *formal prompts,* is found in the way options are presented:

> Which is an example of a reptile?
>
> A. Bear
> B. Fox
> C. Coyote
> D. *Dinosaur

The first three are part of a set and are more plausible than the last option, which happens to be the right answer. If four options contain a set of three related options, a student may think that the odd option is the right one. The main idea here is that the item should contain a homogeneous set of options, with one option being right and the other options being distractors. A trick question leads one to choose the odd choice when another choice is correct.

The fourth type of clue, *specific determiners,* are so extreme that seldom is any choice containing a specific determiner correct. Some examples of specific determiners are *absolutely, always, never, completely, totally,* and *forever.* For instance:

> What is the most likely cause of debilitating text anxiety in young children?
>
> A. Total loss of self-concept
> B. Complete obsession with getting a high grade
> C. Moderate fear of failure

A fifth type of clue is *faulty grammar* in the choices. It is possible to give away an answer through a grammatical error. For instance:

> The best way to increase the reliability of a test is to
>
> A. increase test length.
> B. removing poor-quality items.
> C. making the test readable to all test-takers.

The careless construction of choices reveals that the right answer is the only grammatically correct choice.

12. Use plausible distractors.

Multiple-choice test items are designed to measure knowledge. Therefore, the right answer must be right, and the wrong answers must be clearly wrong. The key to developing wrong answers is plausibility. The idea behind plausibility is that the item should be answered correctly by those who possess this knowledge and answered incorrectly by those who do not possess this knowledge. A plausible distractor will look like a right answer to those who lack this knowledge. The plausibility of a distractor can be statistically analyzed, but the scientific development of plausible distractors has escaped discovery. Writing plausible distractors comes through hard work and is the most difficult part of multiple-choice item writing. Examine the following example:

> Why did Todd fail to hand in his homework?
>
> A. He was at baseball practice.
> B. Aliens stole it.
> C. His dog ate it.

While this first may be plausible in this make-believe story the student has read, options B and C are pretty far fetched. I know, you've heard those excuses before.

Some advice is offered toward the objective of developing plausible distractors in other rules. Chapter 10 is devoted to the statistical study of plausibility, but this is only an emerging science.

13. Use typical errors of students to write your distractors.

If completion items are given—open-ended items without choices—students will provide both the correct answer and some plausible wrong answers that are actually common student errors. The most frequent wrong answers should be the best distractors. In item writing, the good plausible distractor comes about through a thorough understanding of common errors. Experienced teachers expect students who have not learned to say or do certain things. These become plausible distractors.

14. *Use a correct but irrelevant statement as a distractor.*
In looking for plausible distractors, it is often useful to find phrases that are familiar and relevant to another item but absolutely incorrect in the context in which they are offered. For example:

Which fruit is the best source of potassium?

    A. Oranges
    B. *Bananas
    C. Apples
    D. Grapefruits

While bananas is the right answer, some of the other answers may be correct for other items, such as "What is the best source of protein?" or "What is the best source of Vitamin C?"

Avoid the use of humor.
While humor is a valuable tool in teaching and learning and can do much to lessen tension and improve the learning environment, it is *not* recommended for test items. Items containing humor can reduce the number of plausible distractors and in so doing may make the item artificially easier. Stems containing humor may encourage the student to take the test less seriously. Because the test is intended to measure knowledge, humor detracts from this purpose and does no good. Limited research on the use of humor shows that although in theory humor should reduce anxiety, for highly anxious test-takers the use of humor may actually increase anxiety. The safe practice is to avoid humor.

Rule 99

This rule is my favorite. It states that since most of these rules do not have the common ground of expert agreement and research, *break any rule you want.* But be responsible to your students for writing good items. If an item doesn't work, throw it out or revise it. You may find that when you do violate a rule, you generally have a good reason, and the item may work despite the advice contained in this chapter.

Summary

In this chapter, we have studied the anatomy of a multiple-choice item, reviewed the types of mental behavior best tested by multiple choice, reviewed the pros and cons of using multiple choice over the essay (open-ended) format, learned how to write multiple-choice items, and reviewed some guidelines on how to write these items. To add to this long chapter, we have the large number of formats we studied in Chapter 3. Table 4.1 showed how the multiple-choice format can be used to test different types of higher level thinking. Table 4.2 provided examples of item shells to get you started. Table 4.5 summarized the recommended rules (do's and don't's). Many examples were provided. Thus, you should have a good array of knowledge and skills to improve your multiple-choice item-writing ability.

References

Albanese, M. A. (1992). Type K items. *Educational Measurement: Issues and Practices, 12,* 28–33.

Downing, S. M. (1992). True–false and alternate-choice item formats: A review of research. *Educational Measurement: Issues and Practices, 11,* 27–30.

Frisbie, D. A. (1992). The status of multiple true–false testing. *Educational Measurement: Issues and Practices, 5,* 21–26.

Haladyna, T. M. (1991). Generic questioning strategies for linking teaching and testing. *Educational Technology: Research and Development, 39,* 73–81.

Haladyna, T. M. (1992a). Context-dependent item sets. *Educational Measurement: Issues and Practices, 11,* 21–25.

Haladyna, T. M. (1992b). The effectiveness of several multiple-choice formats. *Applied Measurement in Education, 5,* 73–88.

Haladyna, T. M., & Downing, S. M. (1989a). A taxonomy of multiple-choice item-writing rules. *Applied Measurement in Education, 1,* 37–50.

Haladyna, T. M., & Downing, S. M. (1989b). The validity of a taxonomy of multiple-choice item-writing rules. *Applied Measurement in Education, 1,* 51–78.

Haladyna, T. M., & Downing, S. M. (1994). How many options is enough for a multiple-choice test item? *Educational and Psychological Measurement, 53,* 999–1010.

Haladyna, T. M., & Shindoll, R. R. (1989). Item shells: A method for writing effective multiple-choice test items. *Evaluation and the Health Professions, 12,* 97–104.

Sherman, S. W. (1976, April). *Multiple-choice test bias uncovered by the use of an "I don't know" alternative.* Paper presented at the annual meeting of the American Educational Research Association, Chicago.

Wiggins, G. (1987). Teaching to the (authentic) test. *Educational Leadership, 76,* 41–47.

5 High-Inference Performance Formats

5A. Writing Items

IN CHAPTER 2, WE LEARNED ABOUT THE DIFFERENT TYPES OF COGNITIVE, affective, and psychomotor behaviors that can be taught and tested. We use the low-inference item for student behavior that is easily observable. Some student outcomes are indirectly demonstrable and less tangible. For these, the term *high-inference* was used, because although we know what we are supposed to be observing, it can be inferred only by a content expert (you, the teacher). The term *performance test* refers to a constructed-response format where either a high-inference rating scale or a low-inference observation method is used to score the response. This chapter concentrates on writing high-inference performance items, and Chapter 6 concentrates on low-inference performance item formats. This chapter has two parts, 5A and 5B. Part 5A discusses writing high-inference items. Part 5B discusses scoring responses to high-inference items. Each topic is significant, complex, and unique enough to receive separate treatment.

This chapter discusses:

- Types of learner outcomes that are compatible with this format
- Reasons for high-inference performance testing and some cautions
- How to design high-inference items.

As in previous chapters, many examples are provided and discussed.

What Types of Learner Outcomes Require High-Inference Test Items?

As we learned in Chapter 2, several kinds of cognitive and psychomotor outcomes may require high-inference test items. These outcomes include knowledge and both mental and physical skills and abilities. As noted in Chapter 2, the line of demarcation between high-inference and low-inference is clear. Although this distinction was discussed in Chapters 1 and 2 and applied to item formats in Chapter 3, we need to review briefly the high-inference/low-inference distinction here and to provide more examples.

High-Inference and Low-Inference Behaviors

Table 5A.1 provides a list of high-inference and low-inference behaviors related to car repair and driving. The examples on the left from the Teen-Age Obedience Academy unit on car maintenance and safety all require expert teacher judgment because the things being taught and learned are abstract. We will want to use rating scales. The examples on the right are activities that a group of observers would agree were either done or not done. This is a major distinction in performance testing, one that we use consistently throughout this book.

TABLE 5A.1

Examples of High- and Low-Inference Student Behaviors at Teenage Obedience Academy Unit on Car Maintenance and Safety

HIGH-INFERENCE BEHAVIOR	LOW-INFERENCE BEHAVIOR
THE STUDENT WILL:	THE STUDENT WILL:
Drive safely.	Shift gears without "making music."
Clean the car thoroughly.	Take the car in for regular maintenance.
Operate a car competently.	Change a tire correctly.
Parallel park precisely.	Parallel park without hitting the curb.
Vacuum the car completely.	Correctly keeps gas mileage records for a year.
Wash the car thoroughly.	Wash the car correctly.
Wash the car windows effectively.	Use less then one bottle of window cleaner a month on her car.
Plan a trip by car responsibly.	Plan a trip to "Lost Wages," Nevada, for under $200.
Drive through rush hour capably.	Make a left turn at a busy intersection and, at the same time, tune in a favorite radio station.
Evaluate comparably priced cars in terms of appearance and reliability.	Figure out and pay monthly cost of car ownership, including car payments, insurance, gas, and maintenance.

Reasons for Using a High-Inference Item Format

Several factors have contributed to the emergence of high-inference performance testing in our schools.

School Reform

School reform describes ongoing efforts to make schools more accountable to the public, more effective, and more efficient. The report *A Nation at Risk* (1983) contributed greatly to public concern about schooling. Another factor that contributed to this concern was the perception that mental test scores have declined over the past two decades. Although the theory about declining test scores has been challenged (Berliner & Biddle, 1995), most educators believe that schools must reform to meet the new challenges we face in this rapidly changing and shrinking world. With increased diversity within our nation, social problems, increased crime, extreme poverty, homelessness, the AIDS epidemic, and dissatisfaction with big government, educators face a greater challenge than ever before.

School reform includes testing. Should tests always require students to choose answers, or should students construct answers? Many thoughtful essays on this topic have contributed to significant reform in testing (e.g., Wiggins, 1989). Hardy (1995) reported that performance testing is here to stay and dominates over half of the 50 states' testing programs already.

Political Factors

Ernest House (1991) identified two prevailing political philosophies in the United States. One extreme position is that the so-called underclass is unproductive and contributes greatly to social problems. In this view, it is the fault of the poor that they fail in school because it is their lack of cognitive ability that contributes to many of their problems (Herrnstein & Murray, 1994). A second extreme view is that school problems can be solved if we dedicate significant fiscal resources. Elected officials are policymakers who allocate resources at the national, state, and local levels, such as school districts. Because elected officials have political philosophies that may fall anywhere on this continuum, these policymakers affect perceptions of the value of performance testing. Politics plays an important role in the future of high-inference performance testing. Currently, performance testing has received strong support from these elected policymakers, but not without questions about feasibility and cost.

Higher Level Thinking

Educators have long been concerned about the fact that most educational achievement tests measure trivial, isolated fragments of knowledge involving mostly memorization of facts. Such material is easy to teach and test, and some teachers believe that the mind is a muscle and that memorization makes us better learners. This seventeenth-century notion, referred to as *faculty psychology*, persists today. Fortunately, an increasing number of educators believes that we can and should teach and test higher level thinking (Nickerson, 1989; Stiggins, Griswold, & Wikelund, 1989). The famous Bloom taxonomy was introduced in the mid-1950s to help educators define educational objectives that reflect higher forms of thinking (Bloom, Engelhart, Furst, Hill, & Krathwohl, 1956). But the heart of this problem is our failure to define such terms as *critical thinking, problem solving, metacognition, reasoning,* and *abstract thinking.* Without adequate definitions and training, teachers lack the knowledge and skills to teach and test for these desirable but elusive human qualities.

Cognitive Psychology

Behaviorism, rooted in stimulus–response learning theory, has existed for most of this century. Behavioral (instructional) objectives, mastery learning, criterion-referenced testing, essential elements of instruction, and many other educational innovations are behaviorally based.

Cognitive psychology offers an alternative view of student learning. Cognitive psychologists have been working on methods for developing mental abilities. For instance, an educational psychologist and researcher, Richard Lohman (1993) believes that certain kinds of mental abilities, called *fluid abilities*, can be taught, but that these abilities are developed slowly over years. Cognitive psychology provides a useful basis for thinking about various abilities and the simpler mental skills that make up these abilities. Because higher level thinking is a high priority in our increasingly complex society, we will turn more to cognitive psychology for answers about how to teach and test for higher level thinking. High-inference testing provides one approach to this kind of testing. But cognitive psychology has not yet answered many puzzling questions about higher level thinking. We still have a long way to go.

Accountability and Test Abuses

Accountability involves the exchange of information from an information supplier to a policymaker for the purposes of informing a policy or a resource allocation.

The public's need for accountability in the schools requires that we provide clear-cut indicators of what students have and have not learned. For decades, published standardized tests have provided this information using multiple-choice formats. Reports of declining test scores, while misleading and false according to Berliner and Biddle (1995), have motivated the public and legislators to reduce learning to statistical summaries of test scores for schools, districts, and states. In the city of Phoenix, for example, maps are produced that display neighborhoods color-coded by test scores, so newcomers can pick the "best schools." Test scores have been consistently used by the press, legislators, school boards, and others to evaluate our schools, districts, states, and the nation without considering the social capital of the community. This social capital consists of the material and spiritual resources available to children in the home and in the community. Schools have no control over the supply of social capital, yet can be held accountable for these powerful forces that affect student learning. The pressure for accountability has resulted in a ruthless test-score-improving industry (Cannell, 1989; Haladyna, Nolen, & Haas, 1991; Mehrens & Kaminski, 1989). Studies like one by Nolen, Haladyna, and Haas (1992) reveal various techniques for improving test scores, none of which deal with real learning. Others, like Mary Lee Smith and her colleagues, report that teachers teach to the test and as a result reduce their role from teachers to technicians (Smith, 1991). Scott Paris and his colleagues report on the negative effects of testing on students (Paris, Lawton, Turner, & Roth, 1991). These studies and others have revealed that the reduction of student learning to test scores is misguided because student learning is too complex to reduce to a single test score. Although accountability is necessary, to achieve it we will need to define more intelligently what we teach and test accordingly. Performance testing is an important element in overcoming this problem with accountability. But it too can be corrupted by reductionism in thinking. Performance test scores are only indicators of complex human behavior, not a summary.

Multiple-Choice Teaching

Much debate has surrounded the "evils" of multiple-choice testing (Shepard, 1991, 1993; Wiggins, 1989). Shepard argued that multiple-choice testing leads to multiple-choice teaching. In other words, teaching to multiple-choice tests involves low-level, undesirable learning. Others point out that most multiple-choice test items measure trivial material or simply ask students to recall something they have memorized. At the heart of this problem is the idea that multiple-choice test items measure one kind of cognitive behavior (trivial) and performance tests measure another, more important kind of cognitive behavior. Snow (1993) noted that research has not yet been done to prove this point. If you want to measure understanding and some types of mental skills and abilities, multiple-choice formats can be written to measure these behaviors effectively. If you want to test performance-oriented skill or mental or physical ability, high-inference performance items may work well. And there is room for both multiple-choice and performance testing.

Reasons for Caution in Using High-Inference Performance Test Items

Although my position in this book is that high-inference testing is often necessary, several reasons exist for exercising caution in its use. Although none of these reasons is overwhelmingly negative, these factors may diminish the effective use of high-inference tests.

Performance Testing Is the Only Answer

As pointed out throughout this book, the lack of definition of various types of higher level thinking has limited our ability to teach and measure them. Some advocates of performance testing insist that the performance item format is the *only* format one should use. Various types of higher level thinking can be measured with high-inference items, but sometimes multiple choice can be used effectively. When you have a choice between multiple-choice and performance item formats for mental skills and abilities, the multiple-choice item format provides more reliable results than a comparable performance format. So, if a type of higher level thinking can be measured with multiple choice, then this is preferable. But if the behavior calls for high-inference items, so that the opportunity to use multiple choice is inappropriate, then, of course, the performance item format should be used.

Cost

The cost of developing, field-testing, administering, and scoring high-inference items is significant. Hardy (1995) estimates that performance tests are from three to ten times as expensive as multiple choice. The low cost of multiple-choice testing is one reason why it has dominated achievement testing. Multiple-choice testing typically measures knowledge and some types of mental abilities. Performance tests measure many types of mental and physical skills and abilities that are difficult or impossible to measure with multiple choice. Therefore, comparisons between multiple-choice and performance item formats are generally invalid, because the two formats have different purposes. Nonetheless, you always have to ask: Can I afford to use a performance test item? Or can I afford *not* to use a performance test item?

Another important point regarding cost is that performance tests should be scored by teachers. If teachers are not compensated for district- or state-level testing, then the process of performance testing could be demoralizing. Because teachers must score these test results, this scoring provides a kind of inservice training that improves the teacher's ability to design better items and to score future student performance test results more consistently. The higher cost of performance testing is partially offset by this professional development factor.

Bias and Scoring Inconsistency

Because high-inference testing requires human judgment of student responses, tendencies exist for *scorer bias* and *inconsistency*. These two factors may detract significantly from the validity of test score interpretations and uses. This issue is discussed further in Chapter 5B. Bias and inconsistency are serious threats to effective high-inference performance testing.

Summary

In this section, we have examined the arguments favoring high-inference testing. Though tending to be costly, high-inference testing is necessary in most educational and training programs. To measure knowledge (recall or understanding), multiple-choice testing seems very suitable. In the area of mental skills and abilities, multiple-choice items may work very well, while other abilities are well suited to high-inference or low-inference performance items. With physical abilities, performance testing seems appropriate. As the educational reform movement continues, teachers will use high-inference performance items increasingly and more effectively to measure higher level student learning outcomes.

We can alleviate some problems in using performance test items by better defining what we want to measure. We also need to be selective about what we choose to test using a high-inference item format because of its cost. Problems of scorer bias and inconsistency can be handled but are serious threats to validity. These topics are more adequately discussed in Chapter 5B.

Writing the High-Inference Item

As noted in Chapter 3, a high-inference test item contains several basic parts: (1) question or instruction, (2) response conditions, (3) student response, (4) rating scale or set of rating scales used to judge students' responses with respect to some abstract trait. The four main steps involved in writing the high-inference item are:

1. Consider the ability or skill being developed.
2. Write the instruction or question.
3. Specify the conditions for performance.
4. Provide the evaluation criteria (rating scales and point values).

Sources for Items

Chapter 2 emphasized avoiding memory-type questions and using several types of higher level thinking, such as problem solving, critical thinking, and creative thinking or production. Grant Wiggins and other test reformers have steadfastly maintained that student learning should occur in a meaningful context where students perform for their own good and see the intrinsic merit in what they do. The alternative is performing tasks that seem mindless, meaningless, or irrelevant.

Where can we find good material for this meaningful, contextualized, relevant learning? A variety of good answers follow.

1. Real life. Draw from real life, using problems and situations encountered daily by children and their parents. A fertile source of this kind of material is the daily newspaper. Social issues, news features, charts and graphs, editorials, entertainment, classified advertisements, and even sports pages provide a basis for problem solving, critical thinking, and creative thinking or production. News magazines are also a good source of such information and ideas. A basic need in life, eating, can be explored by using the food shopping section of the newspaper, usually published on Wednesdays. Food shopping is a daily, weekly, or biweekly problem that must be solved. It is complex because of shopping comparisons, coupons, and health factors (fat content, cholesterol, calories, and other evils).

Social issues, new laws, societal problems, news events, television, and neighborhood events or problems can be used to generate interesting and relevant complex test items. Unfortunately, item writing is a creative act, so shortcuts are seldom available. On the other hand, the collection of good ideas for testing provides a basis for future teaching and testing. Good teachers typically collect good ideas, jokes, materials, techniques, and test items, and then use them repeatedly.

2. Curriculum. Perhaps this is the most obvious source, but with any school-based testing program, the existing curriculum framework is the official currency for any test. Planning for classes that include testing should revolve around the curricula that exist for the intended group of students. National associations like the National Council of Teachers of Mathematics (NCTM) release curriculum frameworks representing their official curriculum and evaluation standards. Future teaching and testing might strongly consider the recommendations from a professional peer association like the NCTM.

3. Professional development textbooks. A variety of authors have developed textbooks for teachers-in-training and teachers that specialize in subject-specific professional development reflecting current trends toward seamless instruction. One example is a book by Anthony, Johnson, Mickelson, and Preece (1991) that emphasizes the testing of literacy. Hein and Price (1994) have a similar focus on active science assessment, which identifies the current problem with tests and addresses how to measure performance in science. Books like these serve a valuable purpose to teachers in that they provide the context in a subject matter for significant reform in current testing practices.

4. Research. Researchers are constantly exploring new ways to teach and test. A foundation in current thinking provides a basis for designing your own items. For instance, reading comprehension is a major focus in elementary schools and a necessary ability in education at every level. Traditional reading comprehension tests have come under attack. A more modern view of reading comprehension is that it is a constructive process that is shaped not only by the encounter between the student and the printed page but by that student's life experiences and perspectives. Reading comprehension is a constructive process calling for innovative alternative ways to gain insights into students' reading ability. Examples at the end of this chapter provide some insight into how reading items might be written in the future.

Conditions

A critical part of a high-quality, high-inference performance test item is the list of conditions. This list should provide a clear picture of what students can do to complete the task. The standard for performance also should be explicit. Clarity of purpose and expectation are critical to writing a good high-inference performance test item.

This section begins with a discussion of factors that item-writers should consider. Examples are provided, and there is a discussion of these examples, referring to the template in Table 5A.2. This template follows the discussion in this section and provides an overview of the specific issues you must address when designing your items.

Type of Outcomes Desired

Based on the types of mental behavior discussed in Chapter 2, we can choose the single behavior or set of behaviors that we think the item represents. For instance, if we want the student to generate original ideas or inventions, we would choose either creative thinking or creative production. Or we might want to present a problem for which we have an answer. Some problems require creative solutions,

TABLE 5A.2
Template for a High-Inference Test Item

TYPE OF OUTCOMES DESIRED:

Recall	☐	Understanding	☐	Problem Solving	☐
Critical Thinking/Predicting	☐			Creativity/Thinking	☐
Critical Thinking/Evaluating	☐			Creativity/Production	☐

Integrated or not?	☐	Are subject matters being integrated?
Process or product?	☐	Are we concerned with how something is done or only with the result?
Meaningful context?	☐	Have we chosen a task that is meaningful, authentic, realistic, significant, or important to the student?
Clear instruction to student?	☐	Student needs to have a clear understanding of what he/she is to do to complete the assignment.
Materials provided?	☐	What materials or supplies are needed to do this? Does the school supply these or does the student get her/his materials?
Time limit given?	☐	How long does the student have to complete this? Be specific.
Scope of response described?	☐	Indicate what kind of response is appropriate. Remember that some students will do the minimum and some will overwhelm you.
Consultation allowed?	☐	Can parents, students, teachers give feedback and provide other assistance? How much and when?
Collaboration encouraged?	☐	Can students work together? What are the conditions, rules, guidelines?
Corrective allowed?	☐	Do we allow the student to redo the work, to improve it, to polish it until it is wonderful?
Computers allowed?	☐	Do we allow or insist that a computer be used to develop the result or write our report of results? If so, what conditions do we have regarding spell checker and grammar checker?
Criteria?	☐	Are we going to share the scoring rubric(s) with the student?
Point values for grading?	☐	Did we tell the student the value of this item toward her or his grade?
Student checklist?	☐	Did you provide a brief checklist for the student to remind her or him what is expected?

so we would cover two categories: problem solving and creative thinking. Critical thinking may be featured in an item or may be part of problem solving or creative thinking. As we think about abilities, as opposed to the simpler skills that make up an ability, our item might be so complex that it includes several types of cognitive behaviors.

Integrated versus Exclusive Subject Matters

In designing any high-inference performance test item, you will need to think about an integrated test versus a single-subject test. An increasing practice in schools is to create integrated thematic units of instruction that involve language arts, mathematics, and other subject matters. For instance, the Arizona Student Assessment Program's annual performance test is integrated, with reading, writing, and mathematics tested in a single context. In choosing an integrated test, you will need to decide if scores will be developed for each subject or if subject matter scores are combined. Generally, scores are developed for each subject, especially because grades are assigned by subject and not in an integrated way.

Process or Product

Let's take an example of a young chef making macaroni and cheese from a packaged mix. There are three steps in the process of making this wonderful dish—four, if you count turning on the burner on the stove. We can view the teaching of chef ability as a process:

"Did our young chef follow the three (or four) observable steps?"

or as a product:

"How did the macaroni and cheese taste?"

The three steps are observable (low-inference), and the taste evaluation is done subjectively using a rating scale (yummy . . . yucky) which is more subjective, abstract, and therefore high-inference.

A difference exists between how a skill or ability is performed and the result of that performance. In writing a high-inference item, if you are concerned with technique or steps in a procedure, then the *process* is your objective. For instance, in mathematics, teachers often require students to follow a problem-solving algorithm that contains certain steps. Your problem is to decide whether the process is something that can be objectively observed or something more holistic. If it is objectively observed, then it is a low-inference activity (Chapter 6). If it is holistically rated, then we will use a rating scale (Chapter 5B). Generally, if you are interested in a process, you probably will turn to a behavioral checklist like those shown in Chapter 6, because processes usually have observable steps that can be nicely handled with a checklist.

In designing your item, make clear to your students what you are trying to accomplish: process or product. Your scoring criteria will reflect this concern. In the early stages of learning a complex skill or ability, process may be your emphasis; but later you probably will be more concerned with the product that results because of the process you have taught. Writing is a perfect example. Persuasive writing is an ability that is developed over a long time. Certain steps are recommended in writing a creative persuasive essay. Once the student has mastered the process of writing, later persuasive essays might focus more on results than on how well the process was followed.

Meaningful Context

Grant Wiggins (1993), a leading proponent of reform in testing, argues that all teaching and learning and testing should be done in meaningful contexts that are relevant to the learner. Wiggins is given credit for coining the phrase *authentic assessment* to reflect student performance that models realistic encounters in life. Constructivism, an emerging approach to thinking about teaching and learning, also encourages learning that is meaningful to the learner. The teaching of lower level skills, while always necessary, should *never* be an end in itself. All knowledge needs to be applied in some way to solve more complex problems, to think critically, or to create. The challenge to us is to create situations, tasks, encounters, or problems that are recognizable to the student, realistic, meaningful, interesting, relevant, and useful. Can you construct a testlike atmosphere in which the student can learn and show successful learning at the same time?

Clear Instruction to the Student

The question or instruction to the student should be clear. Lack of clarity will result in a student response that is far from expected or the variability of student responses might be such that the exercise is not worthwhile. Often the test item becomes the instruction, and the student learns while the task is performed. The statement of what the student should do is crucial, as is the list of other concerns in the template in Table 5A.2. Examples are given at the end of this chapter.

Materials Provided

Many performance test items require more than just writing. They may require a model, exhibit, product, invention, work of art, or the like. It is important to explain to students whether you or the school will provide materials or whether the student must find her or his own materials. If the latter is true, the cost of materials becomes a factor. If students are economically disadvantaged, as a growing number unfortunately are, your assignment may be unfair. Be certain to specify what each student will need and what you will supply.

Time Limit

Some performance test items may take only a few minutes as part of a formal sit-down test, but other items might require a major effort over a few days, weeks, or even months. You need to specify the time limit and the consequences for late work. For example, if work is late, as it invariably is for some students, do you offer extended time limits, do you accept legitimate excuses, or is the time limit strict? Time limits should be clearly specified, and all students should know beforehand the consequences for late work.

Scope of Response Described

Students come in all types. Some will give you long, complicated responses, while others will give only the minimum. Can you specify clearly what you expect in a response? If it is writing ability you want to measure and you get a sample of writing, you might assess a word limit or page limit. With computerized spell checkers and word counters, this can be easy. For an art or science project, share your expectations with your students. The criteria and point values discussed later in this section bear on this scope of response. Directions to students should state explicitly what kind of response you expect.

Consultation

Consultation involves students asking others for advice or help. You will need to decide if consultation is desirable or to be encouraged. With performance testing, consultation is often natural, and teachers do not have the means to prevent students from consulting. In general, consultation is desirable because it resembles what we do in real life when we solve complex problems. Make clear to students that self-responsibility is a key issue and that each student is accountable for her or his final performance or product.

A major issue here is the idea of a take-home test. A study by Weber, McBee, and Krebs (1983) with college-age students shows higher motivation, more effort, and better performance with a take-home test, where consultation is possible. These researchers state that cheating did not seem to be a problem. In general, however, cheating was reported to be a widespread problem. A national survey showed that 89 percent of American high school students reported that cheating is common at their school (Karlsen & Newmark, 1995). Most of this cheating involves copying someone else's homework. If student consultation is encouraged, then the take-home test avoids the kind of cheating where improper consultation may occur. Of course, detecting copying (plagiarism) is another matter.

I have found the take-home test to be very desirable with mature graduate students. Students reported that they worked harder, learned more, and felt more satisfied with the results, despite the perception that they did "extra" work. Therefore, the take-home test may be a viable option when strict time limits in school are not possible or desirable. For less mature learners and with a grade at stake, these students may be inclined to take shortcuts or to make less effort. You might want to experiment with this option. If it works, students may be more motivated, work harder, and learn more.

Collaboration

With many real-life performance tasks and the increasing use of cooperative learning, students are often encouraged to work with others on a project. You will need to decide if a student can collaborate with others. If so, the issue of credit toward the grade will force you to establish policies about the extent of collaboration and how credit is assigned. A common complaint among cooperative learners is that not everyone is pulling an equal load. One or two students usually work harder and are more productive than the others, but the compensation is the same for all members of the cooperative team.

Correctives

Mastery learning is a behavioral teaching method that calls for stating clear outcomes, allowing sufficient time for learning, assigning relevant learning activities, giving frequent formative quizzes to help students diagnose learning difficulties, and designing and giving comprehensive summative tests, with opportunities for relearning and retesting when learning is not sufficient. Mastery learning is a powerful method of instruction, with a long history of research supporting its use. An important feature of mastery learning is allowing additional time for each student to learn at a desirable achievement level. This means that each student is given time to fix what needs to be fixed. Correctives provide a helpful step in the learning process, where students are allowed to correct or otherwise improve their work as they complete their performance task. This idea of polishing is an authentic activity that many adults have an opportunity to use in their work and life outside of work. In fact, we might argue that polishing is a critical aspect of most activities we do in life.

Will you allow individual students to engage in a review of their work, to seek constructive criticism, and to improve their product? Correctives can occur in any stage of development and be a continuous process, because as we said before the performance task is a learning activity as well as a test activity. The final product is a result of student–teacher collaboration. This partnership can ensure a steady, motivated effort.

The Role of Computers in Performance Tests

Computers play an increasing role in our lives. It is now hard to imagine writing without a computer. Computer laboratories and computers in the classroom are becoming increasingly commonplace. Many students have computers and extensive experience and ability in computerized design and graphics. Because a large portion of performance tests are written, should computers play a role? Will you disadvantage students who do not have computers at home? A good policy is to encourage computer use and to make computers available for doing assignments. In most universities today, computer commons are the rule rather than the exception, and it is hard to imagine a college student without good computer skills.

Interestingly, a recent research study by Powers, Fowles, Farnum, and Ramsey (1994) compared handwritten and word-processed versions of identical student writing. Handwritten responses received higher scores than identical word-processed responses, suggesting a bias for handwriting. Another team of researchers (Wolfe, Bolton, Feltovich, & Bangert, 1995) reported that a bias exists when students are expected to use word processing but are not comfortable with it. These researchers also found no differences in performance between handwritten and computer-written writing when the students were comfortable with word processing. Thus, the belief that word processing produces better writing would not be supported by either team of researchers. On the other hand, word processing offers a wealth of opportunities to improve one's writing and present it in its best light.

Adult life invariably involves computers. Written work can often be computerized. Excellent, user-friendly word-processing programs are available. Even first graders may write their stories on computers and illustrate their work from graphic arts files. Every student should have the opportunity to learn to use the computer to write, to use the spell checker, the grammar checker, the Thesaurus, and other writing aids, because these are natural helpmates in life, and they teach us to use available tools to do excellent work. Students become better motivated to perform when they have computer access. The computer skills they acquire have lifelong and career implications. Making computer use a necessary condition in writing seems to have dual benefits: (1) to help students complete performance tests and (2) to increase their abilities with computers.

Criteria

The rating scales you will use to evaluate student performance should be shared with students before their projects are submitted to you. The design of this rating scale or set of rating scales is shown in Chapter 5B. It is very important to be honest with students and inform them that you are a judge and that your judgment is fallible, but that you are doing your best. They have to accept your judgment, but, as the critical thinkers you have developed, they will want to argue with you about the merits of their work. This is a delicate problem. On one hand, you want to maintain good will and a positive class environment by letting students have their say. On the other hand, you have to make the final decision. Each teacher has to decide where to draw the line between these two opposing concerns. This puts pressure on you to have good, clear items and effectively and consistently used rating scales.

Self-Reflection

Self-reflection (self-regulation) is a newer idea that has to do with students' self-analysis and strategizing to plan future learning to be more successful. Sometimes it is a good idea to get students to write in a journal or diary reflections about learning so that they can plan strategies for improving themselves and use their journals to chart their progress. Self-reflection provides a rich opportunity to get students to think about their responsibility to themselves and how they might succeed in future work. Self-reflection is never graded but should be viewed as a motivational device to be used in concert with performance tasks. It is also important to ensure that self-reflective writing, like test results, is strictly confidential and not shared publicly.

Point Values for Grading

Most test items and assignments have value toward student grades. Grading systems may vary, but the most sensible way to tie a good performance into the course grade is to assign points for completion of the task. Points can be used to establish a student grade, in this example:

Grade:	A	B	C	D	F
Points:	1,000–900	899–800	799–700	699–600	Under 600

Student Checklist

This final entry in the template is a friendly reminder to students about what specific items, actions, or results should be done in the performance. The checklist is something that the student can use to review work before it is submitted. It is usually very simple and contains three to five behaviors that the student checks "yes" or "no." Each item is usually a question. The checklist is a way to ensure that the student is attending to the task and does not digress or drift away or do the task superficially. In summary, this checklist says: "Did you remember to do all the things you were supposed to do?"

Summary

This section provided a template for developing a high-inference item. Although the list of concerns in the template in Table 5A.2 may seem overwhelming at first, it gives you an idea of the enormity and complexity of performance testing as well as the intrinsic merit of such testing in developing a complex mental or physical skill or ability.

Examples of Items

This section contains examples of performance test items and a discussion of each example. The main purpose of this section is to give you some ideas about the variety and complexity of well-written performance test items. These examples do not exhaust the long list of performance formats given in Chapter 3. For each item, we refer to the template in Table 5A.2 to make some comment about the item. Not all items are perfect. Most do not follow the template strictly and need further refinement and polishing. In fact, the high-inference performance items I have reviewed that were either teacher-made or professionally produced seldom have all the ideal elements of a well-written test item. When you use the template to evaluate these items, you will discover missing elements. But there is a good reason for this. Early drafts of performance test items need constant attention and polish before they work as expected. This is usually a long, slow developmental process.

Notice that every item does *not* represent a single category of higher level thinking. To answer a good performance item successfully, several types of mental behaviors are usually needed. It is difficult to capture such a complex mixture of behaviors from multiple-choice formats. This is why performance type items are so highly prized.

1. Reading Comprehension

In this section, we will first define reading comprehension and then present a set of items from a single reading passage to show the variety of testing strategies possible. As with the other examples, we will use the template to reflect on the qualities of the item and to determine if the item can be improved (which invariably it can).

Reading Comprehension
This is a process of constructing meaning from text that involves one's prior knowledge and experiences as well as general ability. In other words, readers connect the author's information and clues with their own prior knowledge to create meaning from text. Readers' prior knowledge and ability weigh heavily in the quality of reading comprehension. Our cultural perspective also affects how we understand what we read. In this framework, reading is an ability that consists of many complex cognitive aspects: (1) using what the reader knows from the past, (2) asking questions of oneself to determine what needs to be known, (3) having a purpose in reading, (4) monitoring one's reading to determine if the purpose is being achieved, and (5) using what one has read to think critically. According to Barr, Blachowicz, and Wogman-Sadow (1995), this definition of reading comprehension has emerged over the last two decades and is based on considerable reading research. Cognitive psychology plays a strong role in this emerging definition.

Some Reading Comprehension Testing Strategies Involving Different Formats
Table 5A.3 presents a short passage on goldfish. The set of items is open-ended and provides a basis for measuring students' understanding of what has been read. The first question asks students for a title, which involves creativity and some critical thinking. The second item reflects students' understanding, the second type of mental behavior discussed in Chapter 2. The third and fourth items are examples of critical thinking, consistent with the previously offered definition of reading comprehension. The fifth item calls for understanding the concept of breathing in fish and humans and for more critical thinking. We also obtain a brief writing sample. The checklist at the end of the item is not intended for grading but as a reminder to students about how to prepare the answers.

Some other item formats can be used in a situation like this one. One is written or oral retelling, which is a free recall process that requires students to write or tell in their own words what they just read. The use of questions, as seen in Table 5A.3, gives the readers clues about what they have read. Written or oral retelling does not provide these clues. On the other hand, teachers must use an explicit or implicit rating scale to determine the extent to which reading comprehension was demonstrated in the written or oral retelling. Both written and oral retelling have built-in biases. For instance, with written retelling, students' writing ability will affect the teacher's judgment. Students' oral speaking ability will also affect the teacher's

TABLE 5A.3
Outcomes: Understanding (Reading Comprehension)

Student: Read the story and answer the questions in the spaces provided on your paper.

GOLDFISH

Goldfish are wonderful pets. Goldfish open and close their mouth as they swim. This is how they get air from the water into their body. The water comes out of their gills which are at the back of their heads. You should put an air pump in the bowl so the fish will have more air in the water. You will have to keep the bowl clean and give the fish a little fish food each day.

You don't have to have much room to have a goldfish. All you need is a bowl and fresh water. Some fish like salt water, like we find in the ocean. Goldfish like fresh water. Don't forget to put in a few stones and plants in your bowl. Be careful and don't give your goldfish too much food or it will die. Goldfish eventually grow very large.

1. What is a good title for this story?
2. What is the main idea of this story?
3. What would happen if you feed your goldfish too much food?
4. What would happen if you did not clean the goldfish bowl?
5. Think about how you breathe. Tell how fish breathe differently from you. Write at least two sentences.

You have 30 minutes to answer all five questions.

CHECK YOUR WORK.

_____ Did you use end marks for your sentences?

_____ Did you use capital letters at the beginning of your sentence?

_____ Did you check your spelling?

Commentary Using the Template

Integrated or not:	No. Language Arts.
Process or product:	Product.
Meaningful context:	Not necessarily. May be more interesting to some than others.
Clear instructions:	Very detailed.
Materials provided:	None.
Time limit given:	Yes.
Scope of response given:	No for the first four questions, yes for the fifth question.
Consultation encouraged:	No.
Collaboration encouraged:	No.
Correctives allowed:	No.
Computer allowed:	No.
Criteria:	No.
Point value for grading:	Not given.
Student checklist:	Given. Done.

judgment. Other forms of bias may come from student appearance, attractiveness, gender, ethnic or racial background, personal hygiene, height, and weight.

Despite some of these handicaps, one benefit of the act of retelling is improved written or oral expression. Also, a written retelling might be added to the student portfolio (discussed in Chapter 7).

2. State Law

Table 5A.4 presents a test item intended for junior high or high school social studies that deals with a state law or potential state law about seatbelt use for infants. Legislatures struggle with issues like these, so this is good material that affects parents and future parents.

Students first have to read and understand the article, and then identify the issue. Then students take a position and develop supporting arguments for and against legislation. Students might do additional research or interview some legislators or parents. Students draft essays, have a friend or teacher seek more evaluative feedback, and complete the work, using criteria offered by the teacher for grading. In this case, students are invited to perfect their work for maximum point value.

3. Food Shopping

Table 5A.5 provides a simple problem with correct answers. The meaningful context is buying food for a family. The student figures out how to save money when shopping. The materials provided for this exercise are Sunday's and Wednesday's newspapers containing food advertisements. Some students may not have access to these materials. The teacher should clarify who supplies what. Although the item is promising for teaching mathematics problem solving in a meaningful context, as the discussion in Table 5A.4 shows, the item needs much polish before it will be ready for student use. The danger in using an unpolished item like this one is that good students are likely to do well, but poor students are likely to become confused and quit. I have observed young students who were unprepared for problems like these and had not received adequate instruction crying from frustration. Using unclear items without enough instructional background can be very harmful.

4. Environmental Issues

Table 5A.6 gives the item for a high school test. This item was developed by Dr. Marc Becker of the Glendale (Arizona) Union High School District, where such innovative assessments have been ongoing for many years. The item addresses

TABLE 5A.4
Outcomes: Creative Thinking and Persuasive Writing

Read the article "Study Finds Children Unbuckled" in the Wednesday, October 20, 1993, issue of the *Phoenix Gazette*.

Write a two-page persuasive essay on either issue:

a. Should parents be held accountable for the death of an unbuckled child (under the age of 18) when they are driving a car and have an accident?
b. What should our state law be regarding the safety restraint of children in cars?

You can have your initial draft reviewed by me or a parent or a classmate or friend. You are responsible for the final essay.

This activity is worth a total of 160 points: 40 points for effective writing, 40 points for writing mechanics; 40 points for persuasive writing; 40 points for good solution.

If you are not satisfied with your point total, you can rewrite your essay until it is perfect.

Commentary Using Template

Integrated:	Yes. Social Studies and Writing points given.
Process or product:	Product.
Materials provided:	None.
Time limit:	Not specified in item.
Scope of response:	Two pages, about 500 words.
Consultation:	Yes, anyone can be consulted.
Collaboration:	No.
Correctives:	Yes, very clear.
Computers:	Yes, but on a limited basis.
Criteria:	Yes, very clear. But the actual rating scales should be given to students.

TABLE 5A.5
Outcome: Problem Solving

You are responsible for food shopping this week. You have a list of things to buy. For every dollar you save with coupons, you can buy *any* food item you like, as a treat.

Clip coupons from the previous Wednesday paper and the Sunday supplement on food. Using Wednesday's paper, create a table showing what you should have paid, how much you saved, on items on your shopping list. Tell us what percent of the total food bill you save using coupons and how much money you saved. What did you buy with your savings? (50 points).

Due: January 9.

Commentary Using the Template

Integrated or not:	Problem-solving. Yes, involves Language Arts, Mathematics, higher level thinking.
Process or product:	Product.
Meaningful context:	Yes, student should be able to identify with problem in a personal way.
Clear instruction:	Very detailed.
Materials provided:	It is implied newspapers will be available.
Time limit given:	There is a due date.
Scope of response given:	None given, but assume short answer and one data table.
Consultation encouraged:	No, but it is possible.
Collaboration encouraged:	No.
Correctives allowed:	No.
Computer allowed:	Not mentioned.
Criteria:	Not given in the example, but the item needs to show specifically on what criteria students are being graded. It would appear that students' thought processes would be evaluated.
Point value for grading:	Not given, but a final draft of this item should contain a specific point value that is used in the grading policy.
Student checklist:	Not given. But a good performance item would have a brief checklist reminding the student of what needed to be done.

TABLE 5A.6
Outcomes: Informative Writing and Speaking Ability

The Student Will:

a. Select a local environmental problem from a list.
b. Gather information about the problem.
c. Write a proposal outlining a solution to the problem.
d. Write the proposal using word processing.
e. Construct a graph or table to summarize a main point, using graphics and spreadsheet software.
f. Submit the proposal in draft and final form to illustrate editing.
g. Orally defend the solution advanced in the proposal to the class in a five-minute presentation.

Partial Directions to the Student

You have been chosen by the County Commissioner's Office to serve on a citizen task force. As a member of this task force, you will be asked to propose a solution to an environmental problem affecting our county. Choose an environmental problem listed below:

water conservation	nonhazardous use of pesticides
recycling of garbage	soil conversation
waste management	air pollution

Write your proposal recommending a solution to the problem that you have selected. Your proposal solution should be based on scientific data. It is important that you summarize these data in one or more tables or graphs.

When you have completed your written proposal, you will be called upon by the County Commissioner to present your solution to the County Supervisors and defend it orally.

Maximum length of proposal:	10 pages single-spaced
Time for completion of proposal:	8 weeks
Time for oral presentation:	5 minutes
Point value:	1,000 points

Commentary Using the Template

Integrated or not:	Problem-solving. Yes, involves Language Arts, Mathematics, higher level thinking.
Process or product:	Product.
Meaningful context:	Yes, personal account.
Clear instruction:	Very detailed.
Materials provided:	None. But it is implied that computers and software are available.
Time limit given:	Yes.
Scope of response given:	Yes, 10 pages single-spaced for the written work. One oral response of five minutes.
Consultation encouraged:	Yes.
Collaboration encouraged:	No.

Continued

TABLE 5A.6   *Continued*

Correctives allowed:	Not mentioned here. But a drafting process ensures some quality control.
Computer allowed:	Definitely.
Criteria:	Not given in the example, but the item needs to show specifically on what criteria the student is being graded. It would appear that this is a Language Arts' assignment.
Point value for grading:	Given. Major part of grade.
Student checklist:	Not given. But a good performance item would have a brief checklist reminding the student of what needed to be done.

Source: Used with permission of Dr. Marc Becker, Glendale Union High School District, Glendale, AZ.

---

many aspects of higher level thinking in a meaningful context. Technically, the item addresses most points of the template.

5. Planning a Dinner

The item shown in Table 5A.7 involves planning a dinner party for five people. This planning is a daunting task; several possibilities for testing student behaviors are possible. We might be interested in the creativity of the menu, or we might be interested in the budgeting process and costs related to shopping. We also might want to test for planning ability, which involves critical thinking and problem solving. The basic activity has many facets and offers teacher and students many options.

When the template is used to check the item, we find that some elements are missing. Most of these would be easy to fix. The one major problem is adequacy of criteria. We showed that five criteria are to be used, but the student has no clue about what creativity, thoroughness, logic, or presentation mean. It is hoped that the teacher can make this clear before students begin their projects.

6. Telling a Story

Table 5A.8 is a narrative writing project of a personal nature. Presenting the story to the class may be a problem for shy children, and there are many in school. The item is extremely detailed in procedure, leaving little for students to guess about what to do.

TABLE 5A.7
Outcomes: Creative Thinking, Critical Thinking, Problem Solving

You are responsible for planning a dinner for four friends or family members. You are completely in charge of planning the menu, budgeting, purchasing the food, preparing the food, setting the table, picking up dishes, and, of course dishwashing.

Prepare a written plan that addresses the following criteria:

1. Creative menu
2. Budget under $50.
3. How you purchased the food.
4. Timing—use a time-and-task schedule.
5. Problems that you might encounter.

The plan should be no more than two or three pages and should contain one time-task chart.

You will be graded on (1) creativity of your menu, (2) thoroughness of your plan, (3) staying within your budget, (4) logic of your plan, and (5) presentation.

Total Points: 500

	Commentary Using Template
Integrated or not:	Problem-solving. Yes, involves Language Arts, Mathematics, higher level thinking.
Process or product:	Product.
Meaningful context:	Yes, personal account.
Clear instruction:	Very detailed.
Materials provided:	None. But it is implied that computers and software are available.
Time limit given:	Yes.
Scope of response given:	No.
Consultation encouraged:	Not mentioned.
Collaboration encouraged:	No.
Correctives allowed:	Not mentioned.
Computer allowed:	Not mentioned.
Criteria:	Not given in the example, but the item needs to show specifically on what criteria the student is being graded.
Point value for grading:	Given.
Student checklist:	Not given. But a good performance item would have a brief checklist reminding the student of what needed to be done.

TABLE 5A.8
Outcomes: Narrative Writing and Speaking Abilities

In less than 2,500 words, tell a short story that involves you. Tell about the best thing you ever did, the most exciting thing you ever did, the happiest moment of your life, or something interesting you did recently. Here are some things to do to help you finish this project:

1. Choose a topic. You are free to choose among the above or pick something else that is interesting that others might enjoy reading and hearing about.
2. Prepare a brief outline of what you are going to say. Remember that 2,500 words is about ten pages of double-spaced type on the computer.
3. On your first draft get your main ideas down. Don't worry about spelling, punctuation, grammar, and sentence structure yet.
4. Edit your work. Now worry about spelling, punctuation, grammar, and sentence structure. Remember, use the active voice when possible.
5. Choose a classmate or friend, parent, or teacher to review your work. Ask if the topic is interesting? Ask if the writing is good (that is, no spelling errors, correct punctuation, no grammar errors).
6. Revise your writing. Use the spell checker and grammar checker. Make changes that you think will improve your work.
7. Get another review from a classmate, friend, parent, or teacher. Polish your work.
8. Present your story to the class using expressive speaking techniques we have learned. Remember pitch, volume, gestures, etc.
9. Turn in your first, second, and final drafts.

You will have two weeks to complete this work.

Commentary Using the Template	
Integrated or not:	No. Language Arts.
Process or product:	Product.
Meaningful context:	Yes, personal account.
Clear instruction:	Very detailed.
Materials provided:	None. But it is implied that computers and software are available.
Time limit given:	Yes.
Scope of response given:	Yes, two weeks for the written work. One oral response.
Consultation encouraged:	Yes.
Collaboration encouraged:	No.
Correctives allowed:	Definitely. This is an important aspect of writing.
Computer allowed:	Yes.
Criteria:	Not given in the example, but the item needs to specifically show on what criteria the student is being graded.
Point value for grading:	Not given, but a final draft of this item should contain a specific point value that is used in the grading policy.
Student checklist:	Not given. But a good performance item would have a brief checklist reminding the student of what needed to be done.

This project is a significant one. The item is high quality. It needs point values and criteria for grading. More information about the availability and desirability of computers is needed.

Summary

This chapter and its companion chapter, 5B, provide a complete treatment on writing and scoring responses to high-inference test items. There are many valid reasons for using these types of items, and also some cautions. You will want to select carefully the times you use these types of items because of their high cost of scoring. For a classroom teacher this is a personal, not compensated, expense. At the school, district, and state levels, performance testing has a bright future and will continue to be used to help policymakers make decisions and allocate resources. Writing performance items can be aided by understanding the complexity of these items and attending to the various aspects, as shown in the template in Table 5A.2. Table 5A.9 summarizes these six items and speculates about what kinds of higher

TABLE 5A.9
Summary of Items Presented Showing Behavior Types Tested and Topics

	TYPES OF BEHAVIOR TESTED	TOPIC	TABLE
1	Reading comprehension	Goldfish	5A.3
2	Critical thinking Creative thinking Persuasive writing	New state law	5A.4
3	Problem solving Critical thinking (evaluating) Recall and understanding	Food shopping	5A.5
4	Problem solving Critical thinking Creative thinking Recall and understanding	Environmental issues	5A.6
5	Creative production Problem solving Critical thinking	Planning a dinner	5A.7
6	Narrative writing Writing skills	Telling a story	5A.8

level thinking may be tested. The six examples provided do not capture the full array of possible performance type items. Chapter 3 lists the variety of formats that might be used to give you a better idea of the potential here.

References

Anthony, R. J., Johnson, T. D., Mickelson, N. I., & Preece, A. (1991). *Evaluating literacy: A perspective for change.* Portsmouth, NH: Heinemann.

Barr, R., Blachowicz, C. L. Z., & Wogman-Sadow, M. (1995). *Reading diagnosis for teachers,* 3rd ed. White Plains, NY: Longman.

Berliner, D. C., & Biddle, B. J. (1995). *The manufactured crisis.* Reading, MA: Addison-Wesley.

Bloom B. S., Engelhart, M. D., Furst, E. J., Hill, W. H., & Krathwohl, D. R. (1956). *Taxonomy of educational objectives.* New York: Longmans Green.

Cannell, J. J. (1989). *How public educators cheat on standardized achievement tests.* Albuquerque, NM: Friends for Education.

Haladyna, T. M. (1994). *Developing and validating multiple-choice test items.* Hillsdale, NJ: Lawrence Erlbaum Associates.

Haladyna, T. M., Nolen, S. B., & Haas, N. S. (1991). Raising standardized achievement test scores and the origins of test score pollution. *Educational Researcher, 20,* 2–7.

Hardy, R. A. (1995). Examining the costs of performance assessment. *Applied Measurement in Education, 8,* 121–134.

Hein, G. E., & Price, S. (1994). *Active assessment for active science.* Portsmouth, NH: Heinemann.

Herrnstein, R. J., & Murray, C. (1994). *The bell curve: Intelligence and class structures in American life.* New York: Free Press.

House, E. R. (1991). Big policy, little policy. *Educational Researcher, 20,* 21–26.

Karlsen, L., & Newmark, J. (1995). Crib sheet: Cheating is widespread though students know it's wrong. *The Phoenix Gazette,* March 29, p. 12.

Lohman, D. F. (1993). Teaching and testing to develop fluid abilities. *Educational Researcher, 22,* 12–23.

Mehrens, W. A., & Kaminski, J. (1989). Methods for improving standardized test scores: Fruitful, fruitless, or fraudulent? *Educational Measurement: Issues and Practices, 8,* 14–22.

National Commission on Excellence in Education. (1983). *A nation at risk: The imperatives for educational reform.* Washington, DC: U.S. Department of Education.

Nickerson, R. S. (1989). New directions in educational assessment. *Educational Researcher, 18,* 3–7.

Nolen, S. B., Haladyna, T. M., & Haas, N. S. (1992). Uses and abuses of achievement test scores. *Educational Measurement: Issues and Practices, 11,* 9–15.

Paris, S. G., Lawton, T. A., Turner, J. C., & Roth, J. L. (1991). A developmental perspective on standardized achievement testing. *Educational Researcher, 20,* 2–7.

Powers, D. E., Fowles, M. E., Farnum, M., & Ramsey, P. (1994). Will they think less of my handwritten essay if others word process theirs? Effects on essay scores of intermingling handwritten and word-processed essays. *Journal of Educational Measurement, 31,* 220–233.

Shepard, L. A. (1991). Psychometrician's beliefs about learning. *Educational Researcher, 20,* 2–9.

Shepard, L. A. (1993). The place of testing reform in educational reform—A reply to Cizek. *Educational Researcher, 22,* 10–13.

Smith, M. L. (1991). Put to the test: The effects of external testing on teachers. *Educational Researcher, 20,* 8–11.

Snow, R. E. (1993). Construct validity and constructed-response tests. In R. E. Bennett & W. C. Ward (Eds.), *Construction versus choice in cognitive measurement: Issues in constructed response, performance testing, and portfolio assessment* (pp. 45–60). Hillsdale, NJ: Lawrence Erlbaum Associates.

Stiggins, R. J., Griswold, M. M., & Wikelund, K. R. (1989). Measuring thinking skills through classroom assessment. *Journal of Educational Measurement, 26,* 233–246.

Weber, L. J., McBee, J. K., & Krebs, J. E. (1983). Take home tests: An experimental study. *Research in Higher Education, 18,* 478–483

Wiggins, G. (1989). Teaching to the (authentic) test. *Educational Leadership, 76,* 41–47.

Wiggins, G. (1993). *Assessing student performance: Exploring the purpose and limits of testing.* San Francisco: Jossey-Bass.

Wolfe, E. W., Bolton, S., Feltovich, B., & Bangert, A. W. (1995). *The influence of computers on student performance on a direct writing assessment.* Paper presented at the annual meeting of the American Educational Research Association, San Francisco, April.

5B. Scoring

IN CHAPTER 3, WE LOOKED AT DIFFERENT PERFORMANCE ITEM FORMATS. The first part of this chapter, 5A, addressed issues surrounding high-inference performance testing and advice on how to design high-inference items. We also examined six examples of performance items using the template given in that chapter. In this section of Chapter 5, we examine the scoring of a student's response to a high-inference performance item. Because high-inference performance testing in the schools is a young science, some controversy exists in how to design a rating scale and score results. Researchers are busy studying problems and coming up with solutions. This section of Chapter 5 will provide background on some of these issues and also suggest best practices. Because the measurement of writing ability is the most advanced, examples come from high-quality writing testing programs exclusively. My hope is that you can use these guidelines and examples to apply to other high-inference performance fields.

Abstract High-Inference	Tangible Low-Inference
Quality of writing	Weight
Sentence fluency	Size
Creativity in a short story	Time
Completeness of the assigned effort	Width
Originality of the story	Length
Thoroughness in completing project	Distance
Organization of thoughts	Height
Adequacy of a written response	Length
Clarity of writing	Density
Persuasiveness of a persuasive essay	Yes/no
Management of resources	Right/wrong
Rigor of treatment of a topic	Go/no go
Command of language	Pass/fail
Detail in preparing a report	Present/absent
Effectiveness of a solution	Number of times observed

The Rating Scale (Scoring Rubric)

A rating scale is a device used to record observations in graded categories. It is used for rating characteristics that are *abstract* (high-inference) as opposed to *tangible* (low-inference). As you can see in the many examples that follow, abstractions on the left must be judged by experts. Concretions (the opposite of abstractions) on the right can generally be objectively observed by anyone. Although low-inference behaviors on the right might be the easiest to observe, many important outcomes of schooling involve the kinds of abstract things found on the left.

Types of Rating Scales

Three common types of rating scales are (1) numerical, (2) graded-category, and (3) descriptive.

Numerical Rating Scale

The numerical rating scale is the layperson's scale. It is easy to construct and use, and it always provides a numerical result. For example, someone might ask you to rate a recent movie you saw on a ten-point rating scale. Although you don't see this scale, you might visualize it in the following way:

Movie:

Texas Chain-Saw Dentist Meets Freddy on Elm Street on Friday the 13th

1..10

Unfortunately the numerical rating scale suffers from several deficiencies that suggest that it *not* be used. The scale often has more scale points than the typical human being can discriminate. Each user has to make up her or his interpretation of what each numerical rating means. We can do better than this.

Graded-Category Rating Scale

The graded-category rating scale is the most popular. Like the numerical rating scale, it contains numerical rating scale points. We often refer to this as the *Likert scale* after its inventor, Rensis Likert. However, it is more explicit about the interval between points and the meaning of each point. For example, a rating scale used to respond to student performance might be a five-point Likert rating scale, as the following example shows. In this example, a soccer goalie is being evaluated on his or her performance.

How Would You Rate the Goalie's Performance?

Excellent	Good	Fair	Poor	Very Poor
1	2	3	4	5

The graded-category rating scale also can be used to measure a particular quality of a performance or a product. For instance, suppose a student turned in a project representing a plan for a rapid transit system as part of a college course on urban development. The rating scale used to evaluate one part of the plan, say the usefulness of the plan, is as follows:

How Useful Was This Plan?

Very Useful	Useful	Neither Useful Nor Useless	Useless	Very Useless
5	4	3	2	1

Notice that we associate points with each phrase, showing the relative value of the rating. The number of points for a Likert scale is five, but as few as three or as many as seven could be used. Generally speaking, more rating scale points are better, up to a limit of seven. The point scale may run from low to high or from high to low, but the point values should be consistent with the kind of interpretation you want. Positively worded rating scale points might have higher point values than negatively worded options.

The greatest strength of the graded-category scale is its ease of construction. Table 5B.1 contains a brief catalogue of graded-category rating scales for various occasions. Another strength is that each scale point has some basic meaning on a continuum from high to low. Each scale point also has a number value that we can assign and interpret accordingly. In Chapter 8, rating scales form the basis for measuring affective traits of students via a survey.

Among the weaknesses of the graded-category rating scale is that the meaning of each rating scale point is open to interpretation. What does "useless" in the previous example really mean? While graded-category scales are good for student surveys as used in Chapter 8, they are *not* recommended for high-quality, high-

TABLE 5B.1
A Brief Catalogue of Graded-Category Rating Scales

TRAIT	POSSIBLE RATING SCALE POINTS
Degrees	Extremely, Rather, Somewhat, Hardly, Not at All
Difficulty	Extremely Difficult, Difficult, Moderately Difficult, Easy, Very Easy
Comparison with the normal distribution	Far Above Average, Above Average, Average, Below Average, Far Below Average
Comparison with a general standard	High, Average, Low
Likability	Like, Indifferent, Dislike
Likability	Like, Not Care, Dislike
Desirability	Very Desirable, Desirable, Neutral, Undesirable, Very Undesirable
Frequency	Very Often, Often, Sometimes, Seldom, Hardly Ever
Comparison	Very Much, Much, Some, Little, Very Little
Degrees	Extremely, Much, Somewhat, Hardly, Not at All
Agreement	Strongly Agree, Agree, Neutral, Disagree, Strongly Disagree
Wellness	Very Well, Well, About as Well as Most, Poorly, Very Poorly
Favor	Strongly in Favor, Favor, Moderately Opposed, Strongly Opposed
Answer to a question	Yes, Maybe, No
Enthusiasm	Very Enthusiastic, Enthusiastic, Unenthusiastic, Very Unenthusiastic
Time	Daily, Weekly, Monthly, Annually
Goodness	Good, Fair, Poor
Approval	Strongly Approve, Approve, Disapprove, Strongly Disapprove
Dependability	Very Dependable, Dependable, Undependable, Very Undependable
Like myself	Very Much Like Myself, Like Myself, Unlike Myself, Very Much Unlike Myself
Dependability	Very Dependable, Dependable, Undependable, Very Undependable
Favorableness	Very Favorable, Favorable, Uncertain, Very Uncertain
Originality	Very Rare, Rare, Common, Very Common
Neatness	Very Neat, Neat, Average, Sloppy, Very Sloppy
Realistic	Very Realistic, Realistic, Unrealistic, Very Unrealistic

inference performance tests. Despite this recommendation, there are times when you might want to use this type of rating scale for a performance test, especially when the time available to develop the rating scale is short and scoring is holistic, as in our two previous examples. The use of the graded-category rating scale is a compromise between the numerical rating scale and the next one we will discuss, the *descriptive* rating scale.

Several comments may be appropriate about Table 5B.1. First, more rating scale points are desirable whenever you have a choice. Second, the use of the neutral middle score is controversial. Some experts favor it and some oppose it because it allows you to be uncommitted on a rating. You must decide whether the middle term is worth the effort.

Descriptive Rating Scale

A descriptive rating scale differs from a graded-category rating scale in one major way: Each rating scale point has a phrase, sentence, or even paragraph describing what is being rated. The person doing the rating has a better chance to know exactly what is to be rated. For example, taking an item from Chapter 5A, we will rate student performance on writing a narrative essay about a personal experience. The descriptive rating scale appears in Table 5B.2. This scale is useful in performance testing because it identifies five clear-cut, ordered categories of performance that range from unscorable (0 points) to a very high level (4 points).

Generally, testing experts recommend the descriptive rating scale for performance tests because it is the richest in description and the easiest to use. It overcomes the inherent problem with the graded-category scale concerning the meaning of each rating scale point. On the negative side, descriptive rating scales are harder to create, and considerable training is needed to get raters to use these scales with consistency.

The descriptive rating scale is always recommended if resources are sufficient. For classroom teaching, the development of descriptive rating scales is a good idea, but the cost in terms of time needed to develop and perfect it may be prohibitive. Once the descriptive rating scale is perfected, it can be reused time after time. Also, we have some excellent sources of descriptive rating scales. For example, Marzano, Pickering, and McTighe (1993) have developed a large assortment of descriptive rating scales that might be adopted or adapted for classroom purposes.

TABLE 5B.2
Descriptive Rating Scale
A Narrative Writing Rating Scale to Measure an Aspect of Writing Ability

	SCORING CATEGORY
U	**Unscorable:** The ideas/content scale is somewhat more dependent on the mode of discourse than are the other traits; therefore, a response that does not attempt to produce a narrative(story) must be designated unscorable (U) on the ideas/content scale. However, a narrative that tells a story seemingly unrelated to the topic of the prompt may be scored. (See score point 1.) Papers also may be rated unscorable if they (1) are blank, illegible, or not written in English or (2) cannot even broadly be constructed as an attempt to respond to the topic of the narrative prompt. (The chief evaluator should confirm responses that seem to fall into the latter category.) If a story is incomplete, rate it based on the content that exists.
1	**No real story or an extremely brief or unclear story.** Narratives rating a score of 1 in the I/C scale suffer from some very major weaknesses in development. They may be very brief, doing little more than describing what's happening in the prompt drawings. Some 1s offer a flat listing of events with no development of plot or character. Some present a plot outline with very few or very vague supporting details, while some responses may go off on a tangent, losing the original plot entirely.
2	**A dull, trite story or an extremely brief or unclear story.** Narratives rating a score of 2 in the I/C scale suffer from some very major weaknesses in development. They may be brief, doing little more than describing what's happening in the prompt drawings. Some 2s offer a flat listing of events with no development of plot or character. Some present a plot outline with very few or very vague supporting details, while some responses may go off on a tangent, losing the original plot entirely.
3	**A reasonably good, well-developed story.** The 3 writer succeeds in telling a fairly good story. The story has a main point with some fairly good development of characters and/or action. Support is sufficient; enough details are provided to make the plot clear and the story interesting; some originality in the ideas adds to the plot or character development. There may be some rambling, but overall the details are relevant to the plot.
4	**An engaging or exceptional story.** The 4 writer succeeds in telling an interesting story. The narrative has a clear plot with a main point. Character and plot are well developed. Details support the action, provide a setting or background, and add interest. Stories may have a lot of action or conversation. Some papers may contain very original, imaginative, or entertaining ideas—perhaps a twist of plot or an unexpected event or particularly satisfying conclusion. Overall, 4 papers stand out from all the rest.

Source: E. A. Witt, "Issues in Constructing an Analytic Scoring Scale for a Writing Assessment." Used with permission of The University of Iowa.

Types of Descriptive Scales

Unfortunately, the issue of descriptive rating scales is not simple as it first seemed. Two major distinctions need to be made here. First, there are *holistic* and *analytic* rating scales. The second distinction is between *generic* and *task-specific* rating scales. To select, adapt, or design your rating scales for classroom use, you will need to sort through the arguments and make a wise decision. The information in this section is based on recent research and practice and is not completely authoritative. Choose an approach to designing a rating scale that you think will work for your students and yourself.

Because the issues presented here are complex, this next section will use the assessment of writing ability as a basis for thinking about the issues. In this section, we will engage in some analysis of writing and link this analysis to rating scales used to measure writing skills and abilities. Table 5B.3 shows the construct of writing ability, five specific types of writing abilities that make up the general construct "writing ability," and six specific clusters of writing skills that are used to demonstrate specific and general writing abilities.

In theory, as teachers of writing, we teach writing knowledge and skills in the hope that writing ability is being developed. We presume that overall writing ability is a general construct that reflects a combination of this knowledge and these skills. We do not have a specific formula for exactly what knowledge and skills to teach. Most well-developed standardized achievement tests, like the Iowa Test of Basic Skills, provide good measures of knowledge and specific writing skills in a multiple-choice format. But a total score on such a test is *never* a substitute for actual writing. With this overview of writing, we can examine the issues of types of descriptive rating scales more critically and in a context we already understand. And we can figure out which practices will be best for measuring what you teach.

Holistic versus Analytic Rating Scales

To measure the main objective of writing instruction, which is general writing ability, you should use the holistic scale. Table 5B.4 contains a holistic rating scale for writing ability that was used in the Arizona Student Assessment Program. Writing ability may not be well defined enough for this to be useful. Nevertheless, although each teacher may have a slightly different definition of writing ability, the holistic rating addresses the general construct of writing ability. A holistic rating scale is easy to adopt, adapt, or design. In fact, the rating scale in Table 5B.4 is general, nonspecific, and applicable to a variety of situations. We could assign any writing to the class and apply this rating scale to evaluate overall writing ability.

TABLE 5B.3
Definition of the Construct of Writing Ability

Construct: Writing Ability	Communication by means of the written word.

SPECIFIC WRITING ABILITIES	
ABILITIES	**DESCRIPTION**
Descriptive	Describes an object, place, or person, enabling the reader to visualize what is being described and to feel that he or she is very much part of the writer's experience. Writer's purpose is to create a strong and vivid image or impression in the reader's mind.
Persuasive	Attempts to convince the reader that a point of view is valid or persuade the reader to take a specific action. Writer's purpose is to persuade the reader.
Expository	Gives information, explains something, clarifies a process, or defines a concept. Writer's purpose is to inform, clarify, explain, define, or instruct.
Narrative	Recounts a personal experience or tells a story based on a real event. Writer's purpose is to recount an experience or tell a story in a concise and focused way to create some central theme or impression in the reader's mind.
Imaginative	Tells a story based on the writer's imagination. The story is basically fictional, but the writer may use his or her experience and knowledge of people or situations to bring a special flair or flavor to the writing. Writer's purpose is to entertain the reader or write for the author's own pleasure.

ANALYTIC TRAITS	
TRAIT	**DESCRIPTION**
Ideas	The heart of the message, the content of the piece, the main theme, together with all the details that enrich and develop that theme. Ideas are strong when the message is clear and enlivened with interesting and important ideas.
Organization	The internal structure of a piece of writing, the thread of central meaning, the pattern that holds everything together. Organization is strong when the piece begins meaningfully, proceeds logically, and creates a sense of anticipation that is ultimately systematically fulfilled.
Voice	The writer coming through the words, his or her wit and feeling, the sense that a real person is speaking to us and cares about the message. Good writers impart a personal tone and flavor to the piece that is unmistakably his or hers alone.
Word choice	The use of rich, colorful, precise language that communicates not just in a functional way but in a way that moves and enlightens the reader. Strong word choice may depend more on the skill of using words precisely than on his or hers alone.

Continued

TABLE 5B.3 *(Continued)*

TRAIT	DESCRIPTION
Sentence fluency	The rhythm and flow of language, the sound of word patterns, the way in which the writing plays to the ear—not just to the eye. With good fluency, sentences vary in length and style, and they are so well crafted that reading aloud is a pleasure.
Conventions	The mechanical correctness of the piece—spelling, grammar, usage, paragraphing, capitalization, and punctuation (handwriting neatness excluded). Writing that is strong in conventions has been well proofread and edited.

Source: Adapted from G. H. Roid (1994), "Patterns of Writing Skills Derived from Cluster Analysis of Direct-Writing Assessment," *Applied Measurement in Education, 7*, pp. 159–170, with permission of the publisher, Lawrence Erlbaum Associates, Inc.

TABLE 5B.4
Holistic Rating Scale for Writing Ability

POINTS	DESCRIPTION
4	A 4 paper will be written in a style appropriate to the genre being assessed. It will be well organized, will be clearly written, and will meet the needs of the author and the reader. It will contain sufficient details, examples, descriptions, and insights to engage the reader. The author will bring closure through a resolution of a problem or a summary of the topic (poetry excepted).
3	A 3 paper will be written in an appropriate style and format. It may appear to be well organized and clearly written but may demonstrate minor lapses in the communication to the reader. It may be missing some details and/or examples, or may offer incomplete descriptions and fewer insights into the characters and/or topics. The author may not sufficiently close the piece of writing and may leave the reader "hanging" or may offer the reader an inappropriate closing or ending.
2	A 2 paper may show an incomplete or inadequate knowledge of the skills assessed. Significant flaws may be evident as the author fails to address the prompt in an appropriate manner; ideas may be conveyed in a random method; and very little is given in proof, details, facts, examples, or descriptions. Closure is often missing.
1	A 1 paper will barely attempt the task. The general idea may be conveyed, but there will be a definite lack of understanding by the author of format or procedure.
0	Assign a 0 if the student fails to attempt the paper.
N/S	Assign a N/S (Not Scorable) if the response is illegible or unreadable.

The negative aspect of using a holistic rating scale is that a single holistic scale is seldom adequate in terms of reliability. Because we have such a narrow range of ratings, 0 to 4, a student receiving a rating of 3 might just as easily receive a rating of 2 or 4 from another rater. Also, the holistic scale is subject to many biases in scoring and interrater inconsistency, which we will address later in this chapter. Also, unless the holistic rating scale is extremely detailed and well defined, teachers and other content experts are likely to use their personal definition. Fortunately, the example provided in Table 5B.4 is very detailed.

Analytic rating scales are richer in description and detail. They have good diagnostic value for teachers because they more directly address what teachers easily teach: skills. Referring back to Table 5B.3, we can see that the state of Oregon's writing assessment uses six analytic traits representing six specific writing skills. Rating scales would be developed for each trait that can be used by trained teachers or curriculum experts for rating student writing.

Analytic trait scoring has an obvious major advantage: From the standpoint of teaching, testing, and using test results to help students learn, the analytic traits provide each student with a diagnosis of her or his writing skills. For instance, if a student has trouble with sentence fluency, then a series of exercises can be designed to work on this deficiency. Teachers like analytic scoring for this reason. Another positive point is that a combination of analytic scores provides a more reliable measure of holistic writing ability than a single holistic rating. How can this be? The answer is that a series of interrelated measurements is usually more reliable than a single measurement. In other words, more ratings are better than fewer ratings.

However, there is a down side to the use of analytic rating scale. The first is the high cost of scoring. If you assign writing to your 32 students, then you have 6 x 32 = 192 separate scores to report, six analytic scores for each student. Not only is this a major effort, but it is fraught with potential for rater inconsistency and bias, which we will address in the next section. Also, you are expected to make personal comments to all students regarding their writing. Another point is that a set of analytic skills does not actually constitute writing ability; practicing and perfecting six writing skills may not necessarily lead to becoming a more effective writer. Writing is very complex and involves more than six skills; it involves creativity and other forms of higher level thinking such as those introduced in Chapter 2.

This discussion was *not* intended to discourage you from using analytic rating scales and scoring. But first, make a realistic assessment of the effort and cost of analytic scoring. Experts in writing and some state testing programs seem committed to analytic scoring over holistic scoring because of the richness of information obtained (Roid, 1994).

Analytic scoring is more desirable from many standpoints, especially if you are interested in improving student writing. But if the only reason for testing is to measure writing ability for the class, school, or district, then holistic scoring is cost-effective and feasible. If you are really interested in improving student writing ability or the specific skills identified in Table 5B.3, then analytic rating scales should be used.

Generic versus Task-Specific Rating Scales

The second issue is generic versus task-specific rating scales. For any subject matter, including writing ability, a variety of items (tasks) is possible. Given the variety of possible test items a student might answer and given that many teachers and testing agencies allow students to choose items from a list to maximize their motivation for writing, scoring can be a problem because the variability in the difficulty of the writing task may influence the rating.

We can use a generic rating scale that addresses a general aspect of a writing skill we are testing or we can use task-specific rating scales, where each rating scale has been uniquely designed for each item. Witt (1995) discusses the problem we face here: Do we use the generic rating scale to increase generalizability of results, or do we design a unique rating scale for each item to maximize interrater consistency and reliability? Because items differ in difficulty, the use of task-specific rating scales muddies the water of providing a uniform scale to interpret results. Students may inadvertently choose a hard item or an easy one, and then results will not be comparable. Table 5B.5 contains a brief example of a task-specific rating scale developed for a student response to the analysis of a story.

TABLE 5B.5
Task-Specific Rating Scale

Clip coupons from the previous Wednesday's paper and the Sunday supplement on food. Using Wednesday's paper, create a table showing what you should have paid, and how much you saved on items on your shopping list. Tell us what percentage of the total food bill you save using coupons and how much money you saved. What did you buy with your savings? (50 points).

POINTS	DESCRIPTION
50	Answered all questions correctly. Was clear and accurate in presentation.
30	Answered all questions but made one or more errors. Minimally acceptable.
10	Made many errors or presented data poorly. Not satisfactory.
0	No response or inappropriate response.

Generic rating scales seem like a good deal. You develop several good ones and use them universally. Unfortunately, there are some problems. First, a single rating scale seldom leads to a reliable test result. Second, no ability is so simple that a single rating scale can cover it. For measuring a single skill, a generic rating scale might be useful, but is the rating transferable to other skills? That is a tough question.

Task-specific rating scales are more expensive to create, one or more for each item. But task-specific rating scales seem true to what we are measuring and should provide students with more dependable results that can help students learn. Also, if the tasks are good ones, then we can use each with its set of rating scales year after year, just as a good comedian uses favorite jokes over and over.

Recommendations

The issue you face is holistic versus analytic and generic versus task-specific. We can summarize these recommendations with a handy 2 x 2 table:

	Holistic	*Analytic*
Generic	Cost-effective but lacking in diagnostic value	Desirable
Task-specific	Not recommended	Very desirable but expensive

Generic/holistic scales make sense from the standpoints of cost and consistency across tasks. But you get only one score per task, which can be unreliable. The generic/holistic rating scale yields your overall appraisal of writing ability with no diagnostic details to help the students learn. This provides a good overall, summative measure.

Generic/analytical scales are desirable because they apply to a variety of items but provide the diagnostic detail that the generic/holistic scales lack. For classroom testing, these make the most sense.

Task-specific/holistic scales should not be used, and no examples are provided in this chapter. Because a curriculum is specific about the abilities and the types of higher level thinking being developed, it is hard to imagine a use for such a scale.

Task-specific/analytical scales make sense from the standpoint of precision of what is taught and tested. They provide the most accurate attempt to respond to students' need for good information to improve learning. They also provide a more reliable index of student achievement because you can combine the multiple ratings obtained to form a more dependable total score. This attractive task-specific/analytical combination comes at a high cost: For every performance item, a set of descriptive rating scales has to be developed. For high-stakes testing programs at the school district or state level, these kinds of scales have been used successfully. But in a classroom situation, you are unlikely to invest so much time and effort constructing a rating scale for each item.

How to Develop a Rating Scale

Ideally, one develops a rating scale in response to a single trait. A single rating scale may be used for that trait. Or you may want to add together responses to several traits to get a total score. In the examples provided in this chapter on writing, we conceptualized that six specific analytical writing skills might be summed to get a score representing overall writing ability. In a previous section, we said that the holistic scale was appropriate for an overall appraisal of a specific ability, such as writing, or for a specific type of writing ability, such as persuasive writing. The analytic scales are appropriate for a more detailed analysis of skills that make up the ability.

The steps suggested in this section are intended for a high-inference performance test item and apply to a variety of rating scale types and situations. These steps are summarized in a template in Table 5B.6. Many of these steps represent an ideal situation, with a testing staff and many resources. For the purpose of classroom testing, you will omit some of these steps simply because they are not feasible.

1. *Identify a purpose or reason for using the scale.* That purpose is likely to be as part of the evaluation of students so that grades can be assigned. Another purpose is to help students understand what they have learned and need to learn in the future. This is diagnostic testing. Sometimes, these items are administered to evaluate the school district's student goals or a specific program.
2. *Define clearly what is to be rated.* This is important for two reasons. Students need to know the criteria by which they are being evaluated. Also, clear definition reflects your state of mind, showing what you intend to teach. If you can't come up with a clear definition of what you are teaching, then, indeed, you have a fundamental problem. This definition will likely address a specific or general ability such as writing or persuasive writing. We might also want to test using the types of higher level thinking introduced and described in Chapter 2, such as understanding, critical thinking/predicting and critical thinking/evaluating, problem solving, and creative thinking and production.
3. *Decide which scale you will use: holistic or analytic, generic or task-specific.* These decisions will come from your analysis and from the previous discussion of these issues. Generally, strive for the more desirable types, but be realistic about time and other resources.

TABLE 5B.6
Template for Developing a High-Inference Rating Scale to Rate Student Performance

Type of Outcomes Desired:

Recall ☐	Understanding ☐	Problem solving ☐
Critical thinking/predicting ☐		Critical thinking/evaluating ☐
Creativity/thinking ☐		Creativity/production ☐

Skill ☐	or	Ability ☐	If skill, then analytic scale is typically more suitable. If ability, then holistic scale is more suitable.

Holistic ☐	or	Analytic ☐	Analytic is recommended.
Generic ☐	or	Task-specific ☐	

How many rating scale points will be used? You should use 4 to 7 rating scale points. More is better.

       3 ☐   4 ☐   5 ☐   6 ☐   7 ☐

Developmental field testing? Should try out scale with a few examples of student work, and make appropriate revisions.
yes ☐   no ☐

Training for raters?
yes ☐   no ☐

Was bias studied?
yes ☐   no ☐

Was interrater consistency studied?
yes ☐   no ☐

Was reliability estimated?
yes ☐   no ☐

4. *Develop a draft of the rating scale.* This draft should be one that can be shared with the students as they consider how they will prepare for the performance. This rating scale contains the criteria you are using to judge their performance.

5. *Edit and proofread.* Be careful to edit and proofread your work. Your students will also be happy to point out the teacher's errors. (Students *love* to correct their teacher.)

6. *Administer your item on a trial basis, to look for problems and difficulties, such as lack of clarity, too difficult or too easy, insufficient information.* This field testing is done for high-stakes testing programs at the national, regional, and state levels, but is seldom practicable for classroom testing. Chapter 9 provides more information about this important step.

7. *Use your rating scale to evaluate the results of student performance.* See if what you just invented works satisfactorily. This is a difficult appraisal because you probably want all students to learn, but your scale should reflect the full range of behavior, from beginner to the most advanced.

8. *Determine the consistency of judges and the reliability of ratings.* Examine patterns for bias. These steps are necessary in high-stakes testing programs at the national or state level but are impractical for teachers in the classroom. Chapter 10 contains some advice about the statistical aspects of this.

9. *Evaluate results and make changes in items and rating scales for future uses of the items and rating scales.* The items and companion rating scales form a complementary set. If the set is well polished, you will be able to use the set year after year with modifications as needed.

Reliability and Interrater Consistency

Two related important issues are reliability and interrater consistency. As a classroom teacher, you will seldom study or be concerned about calculating actual coefficients of reliability and interrater consistency. But each is an important concept to consider when using your own performance test items. If an application of performance testing is at a school or school district level, or at a state level, and the stakes are high, then interrater consistency and reliability are crucial concerns. This section discusses the issues only generally and conceptually.

Table 5B.7 provides several hypothetical settings with three students, three judges, and four items. The upper half of the table shows consistent and inconsistent ratings for a single item for these three students. The lower half shows reliable and unreliable ratings when judges' scores are averaged for three items.

Reliability refers to the consistency of ratings. Ideally, a set of ratings should be identical from rater to rater and across repeated performances. Every score has a true component and an error component. The reliability coefficient is an estimate of the percentage of variation of test scores that is true relative to total variation. Practically speaking, the reliability of performance ratings is often lower than we would like. The ways to maximize reliability are to (1) have good descriptive rating scales, (2) train raters effectively and thoroughly, (3) have as many different ratings as feasible, (4) use rating scales with the maximum number of rating scale points—seven, and (5) maximize interrater consistency.

Interrater consistency is easier to understand. Do different raters give the same ratings for each performance? Generally, performance ratings are not as consistent

TABLE 5B.7
Examples of Consistent and Inconsistent Ratings

	CONSISTENT RATING			INCONSISTENT RATING		
	Judges Using a Seven-Point Scale			Judges Using a Seven-Point Scale		
Students	Judge A	Judge B	Judge C	Judge A	Judge B	Judge C
Larry	7	6	7	7	3	1
Moe	4	4	3	4	6	2
Curley	1	2	2	2	4	7

Examples of Reliable and Unreliable Ratings

	RELIABLE RATINGS			UNRELIABLE RATINGS		
	Judges Using a Seven-Point Scale			Judges Using a Seven-Point Scale		
Students	Item 1	Item 2	Item 3	Item 1	Item 2	Item 3
Larry	7	6	7	7	3	1
Moe	4	4	3	4	6	2
Curley	1	2	2	2	4	7

from rater to rater as we would like. To maximize interrater consistency, give good training to raters and eliminate inconsistent raters from the rating process.

As a teacher, what can you get from this? Rating scales like those in this chapter tend to produce undependable results; therefore, you should take steps to provide for fair treatment of students' performances. If students feel that ratings were not done properly, their performance should be rescored or, ideally, scored by another teacher. An average of two ratings should be taken. Because learning is the paramount concern, if results are based on just a few items and a single judge, we should be careful not to overweight these results or give them more credence than they deserve. Because these ratings are not as precise as we would like, we need to use them with caution.

Biases in Rating Performance

Inconsistency in ratings affects reliability. *Reliability* is a random error that can be positive or negative, large or small. We never know how much error we really have or whether this error is positive or negative, because it is random. Bias, by contrast, is directional error, whereby a subset of performers may be consistently overrated or underrated. Bias exists in different forms. Each is discussed in some detail here to give you insight into the problems of using rating scales effectively for high-inference performance testing. Table 5B.8 summarizes these biases for quick reference.

TABLE 5B.8
List of Rating Scale Biases and Brief Explanations

TYPE OF BIAS	EXAMPLE
Response set	Marks a rating of 4 for everyone on a five-point scale.
Leniency	Consistently overrates performance compared to other judges.
Severity	Consistently underrates performance compared to other judges.
Central tendency	Consistently rates at the center of the rating scale. Rates 3 on a five-point scale.
Proximity	Tends to rate about the same number as the adjacent rating scale used.
Halo	Tends to be influenced by the first of the items and rates other items similarly.
Logical	Tends to invent one's own definition of what is rating due to the inadequacy of the rating scale (applicable to graded-category and numerical scales)
Lack of interest	Is not involved in the process and rates inconsistently because of lack of interest.
Idiosyncrasy	Makes peculiar judgments that show little pattern with other more consistent raters. Usually someone who is quirky or wants to undermine the process.
Other biases	The most serious and most complex problem in rating. Particularly troublesome when the performer is viewed by the rater.

1. Response set is the tendency of the rater to mark in the same place when rating someone or something. This response-set tendency also applies to multiple-choice testing. One easy way to counteract or detect response set is to reverse the rating scales from high to low or low to high when using a set of analytical scales. Raters in a response set may contradict themselves, thus letting you know of the problem.

2. Leniency error is the tendency to give high positive ratings despite differences among the persons or things being rated. In other words, everyone or everything gets a high rating, with no discrimination apparent. This tendency should not be confused with a situation in which all persons or things being rated are actually outstanding.

3. Severity error is the tendency to give low, negative ratings regardless of how different the persons or things being rated are. This is the opposite of the leniency bias. Severity can be serious in that it may result in undeserved negative conclusions based on such ratings. Consider the situation in a high school graduation test where performance is being rated by two severe teachers. A borderline student might fail because of this. That is why the study of bias is so important.

4. Central tendency error is the tendency to give middle ratings regardless of how different the persons or things being rated are. This tendency is often the result of a rater not wanting to look too lenient or too severe. It is the "wimp" tendency, to avoid taking a stand on what is being rated. Central tendency errors tend to lower reliability because most scores concentrate toward the center of the scale.

5. Proximity error is the tendency to give ratings very similar to the one just given for a different trait. This would occur in the case of rating a set of analytical traits. It is probably the result of careless thinking or laziness in doing the ratings. If, for example, item 5, representing the analytical trait of voice, were given a high rating, then item 6, representing the analytical trait of conventions, also would be given the high rating, even though 5 and 6 are very different and the student being rated differs on 5 and 6.

6. Halo error is the tendency for the rating of performance to be influenced by the first impression. For example, if the first analytical trait is ideas and the student has an excellent rating on ideas, this high rating might carry over to all other analytical traits. The halo tendency is a natural human behavior when rating on a series of traits. Though we may be unconscious of it, we are still influenced by it. This serves as a warning to those being rated—the first impression is really important.

7. Logical error is the tendency to believe that a vaguely worded performance trait is what you think it is as opposed to what it really is. For example, if the analytical writing trait is ideas and is not especially well defined in rater training, you may interpret it in a personal way that is unlike all other judges. This error of interpretation can be counteracted by better training and monitoring of raters and by using high-quality descriptive rating scales. Also, this error is likely to occur with a holistic, generic scale.

8. Lack of interest error is the tendency of a rater to give ratings in a manner that is inconsistent because the rater sees no value to performing the rating. This lack of interest can be very harmful to the rating process. For a rating of someone else or something, lack of interest is difficult to note.

9. Idiosyncratic error is the tendency to give unexpected and unpredictable ratings due to a variety of reasons. This tendency is counteracted by throwing out highest and lowest ratings for a set (as is done in Olympic Games judging in diving, boxing, and figure skating). These unusual ratings are called *outliers*, as they occur beyond the normal pattern of responses. If you see outliers, you may want to question or challenge the ratings. Or you may want to eliminate them because of the potential threat to students where important decisions may be made based on these results.

10. Other biases are insidious, so we need to be vigilant for them. Table 5B.9 lists some of these specific forms of bias. Many of these occur when students perform in front of the rater, as in the visual and performing arts. *Gender bias* separates boys from girls or men from women based on gender instead of what is being rated. *Ethnic bias* separates persons based on ethnic background instead of what is rated. *Racial bias* would be similar to ethnic and gender bias. *Personal appearance* may influence a rating, such as type of clothing worn, hair style, jewelry worn, and the like. *Physical attractiveness* may also bias a rater. *Height* may be a source of bias; tall people tend to get higher ratings than short people. This tendency carries over to *weight*, or more specifically to being overweight.

Writing skill/penmanship in any handwritten test (which is a measure of a person's knowledge) or a performance test where the result is written may result in a biased rating. Word processing evidently produces a bias. Powers, Fowles, Farnum, and Ramsey (1994) showed that identical computer-generated writing received systematically lower scores than the original handwritten result. One speculation they offered was that raters give the benefit of the doubt on handwritten test results. Another speculation is that word-processed writing is so easy to read that errors are more easily found, resulting in a lower rating.

There are statistical methods for studying these kinds of biases. In formal testing programs, the study of bias is essential to maintaining a testing program's integrity. Chapter 10 briefly describes these methods and provides references to more extensive treatments of this topic.

How can you avoid bias in performance ratings? Insofar as possible, try to avoid knowing who the performer is when rating the performance. If a student com-

---

TABLE 5B.9
Examples of Bias in Rating Performance

TYPE OF BIAS	EXAMPLE
Gender	Performance differences between boys and girls may be due to rating bias instead of true performance.
Ethnic	Ratings among ethnic groups may differ when it can be shown on another measure that such differences don't exist.
Racial	Ratings among racial groups may differ when it can be shown on another measure that such differences don't exist.
Attractiveness	Physically attractive persons may get higher ratings on a performance than less attractive persons.
Height	Taller people may get higher ratings than shorter people.
Writing ability	Writing ability may influence the rating of written performance when the construct being measured is *not* writing ability.
Penmanship	Penmanship ability may influence the rating of written performance when the construct being measured is *not* penmanship.
Word processing	One study has shown that the use of word processing leads to lower performance than handwritten performance (Powers et al., 1994), suggesting that the two modes of presentation are not comparable.
Reading ability	Reading ability influences the rating of performance when the construct being measured is *not* reading ability.

---

plains about a rating, everything should be done to investigate the potential that some hidden bias is affecting that rating instead of actual performance. It is easy to underrate or overrate a student's rating because of some existing factor, such as any of those mentioned in the previous section and listed in Table 5B.9.

One solution concerning these biases is to counsel raters not to be influenced by the factors in Table 5B.9. Another solution is to advise those being rated to take safeguards against undesirable ratings due to these biases.

Another solution involves the student. If a student is performing in front of judges, that student should ensure that factors that may influence the rater in a negative way should not be present—for example, wearing a sweatshirt and ragged jeans at a piano recital. If a student is presenting a written report, that student should know that unattractive presentation or irrelevant factors may count against her or him. Although some of these biases are beyond the control of individuals being rated, some conditions are under their control. If, indeed, personal appearance and grooming inadvertently enter into ratings, those being rated ought to understand that this unfair hidden agenda in ratings can be potentially helpful or harmful.

Finally, if these solutions do not work, there are statistical methods of detection that can be used to identify biased raters and remove them from the rating process. We don't want to get into that here, but as mentioned earlier in this chapter, Chapter 10 discusses this topic in greater detail.

Training Raters

For classroom testing, the following is *not* realistic or feasible. For testing programs at the school, district, or state levels, the following steps are highly recommended. If test scores have a high-stakes use, then such practices should be mandatory. In fact, failure to train raters for high-stakes test use may put testing program personnel into legal battles where their defensibility will be in question.

1. Identify raters carefully. Raters must be willing and motivated to do their best. Uninterested raters will weaken the rating process. It is strongly recommended that teachers be compensated for scoring performance tests, because of the complexity and added burden of this work.

2. Conduct a highly effective training program for raters. If the stakes for rating are very high, the training program can be extensive. For example, in the oral examination of physicians in medical specialties, it is common for training programs to include extensive lessons on the rating process, even including videotaped performances where the examiners interact. Part of this training involves examination of student performances of high, average, and low quality. Eventually, each rater develops skills in reading or observing a student behavior and then consistently classifying the response or behavior into one of the available rating categories provided.

3. Validate raters. Study rating patterns to find if their ratings are valid. This is the only opportunity to weed out those raters not useful to the process or to correct rater problems that always crop up.

Ideal Number of Raters and Number of Items

This section is intended for readers who are more involved in performance testing at a district, region, or state level, more than for classroom teachers. It deals with the process of training raters of performance and the steps we take to ensure that their ratings are consistent with themselves and others. This discussion will be general but will focus on a training session in which twelve teachers are being trained to score 1,000 writing samples in the elementary grades.

Number of Raters

For any classroom, the number of available raters will be one: you. It is hard to imagine any other alternative. Partnerships with other teachers or within the school organization may provide mutual benefits if teachers work together to score performance tasks. With effective training, scoring ability can reach a very high level.

The issue of how many raters are needed for a performance task has been the subject of some study (Saner, Klein, Bell, & Comfort, 1994). More raters per student response create a more desirable condition than only one rater. As the number of scorable tasks increases, there is less need for multiple raters. If you use six analytic scales per student, then having only two raters is acceptable. With good training, the need for additional raters can be lessened, according to Saner et al.

Number of Items (Scorable Tasks)

As stated previously, the more scorable tasks you can develop, the better reliability is likely to be. But scoring more tasks takes more time and is less realistic. You need to decide how much is enough in terms of time, resources, and motivation. If students' grades rely on your judgments, you will want to have enough tasks to grade during the grading period. Try to maximize this number.

Examples of Rating Scales to Score Performance Items

Given the comprehensive treatment on rating scales as a background for the development efforts you are likely to undertake to write and scale your items, this last section of this chapter is devoted to showing different examples of rating scales and discussing the advantages and disadvantages of using each kind. These examples were taken from various sources, mostly school districts, state testing programs, or national or federal testing programs.

1. Developmental/analytic/generic

The rating scales in Table 5B.10 were developed in the Bethel (Washington) School District to reflect the analytic traits from Table 5B.3, which are taken from the Oregon Writing Assessment. There are some very attractive features of this presentation of a rating scale for scoring a writing performance. First, we have a three-phase developmental sequence that reflects our common understanding of the development of student ability: emerging, competent, and exemplary. Purves (1993, p. 189) presents a rating scale with a similar structure, except that the three stages are basic, proficient, and advanced. Although these three stages may not be refined enough to reflect the actual development of writing, these are workable.

TABLE 5B.10
Developmental Analytic/Generic Rating Scales for Writing Ability

ATTRIBUTES	EMERGING	COMPETENT	EXEMPLARY
Ideas and content are clearly developed.	Lacks a central idea and purpose; sketchy details, random thoughts.	Clear and focused; support is attempted but details are limited, predictable.	Clear, focused, and interesting; holds reader's attention; details enrich the piece.
Writing is well organized.	Lacks direction, ideas, details; events are helter skelter; no clear introduction or conclusion; transitions are weak or bewildering.	Introduction and conclusion recognizable, placement of details sometimes confusing, transitions sometimes work well, reader can usually follow what's being said.	Order, structure, presentation are compelling; smooth transitions; strong introduction and conclusion; details fit.
Writing has strong voice when appropriate.	Writer seems uninvolved, indifferent; writing is flat, lifeless, mechanical; reader is not involved; piece is monotonous.	Writer seems sincere but not fully involved; piece is pleasant, acceptable, sometimes personable, but not compelling; readers sometimes interact with writer.	Writing is individualistic, expressive, engaging; writer is involved; language is natural yet provocative; paper is honest and from the heart; reader interacts with writer.

Continued

Table 5B.10 *(Continued)*

ATTRIBUTES	EMERGING	COMPETENT	EXEMPLARY
Writing demonstrates fluency in sentence structure.	Paper difficult to follow or read aloud; sentences choppy, incomplete, rambling; irregular, awkward, monotonous word patterns.	Sentences tend to be mechanical rather than smooth, occasional awkward constructions, dialogue sometimes sounds stiff, little variety in sentence length or structure.	Writing has easy flow and rhythm; strong and varied sentence structure; dialogues sounds natural; easy to read out loud.
Writer uses effective word choice.	Lacks direction; ideas, details, events are helter skelter; no clear introduction or conclusion; transitions are weak or bewildering.	Ordinary language but conveys message; images are there but lack detail or precision; functional words but lacks punch.	Writing is interesting, precise, and natural; imagery is strong; powerful verbs; fresh, appealing expression.
Conventions are accurately followed.	Numerous errors in usage, sentence structure, spelling, or punctuation distract or make text difficult to read; paragraphing irregular or absent; extensive editing required.	Errors in usage; sentence structure, spelling, or punctuation tend to distract but are not overwhelming; paragraphs sometimes run together or start in the wrong places; moderate editing required.	Demonstrates correct usage, sentence structure, spelling, and punctuation; paragraphing is sound; writer may manipulate conventions for style; only light editing required.

Second, we have placed the categories representing the rating scale points so the rater can see the three possible ratings on a page.

Table 5B.11 provides a different type of developmental scale, a holistic/generic scale that can be applied to any writing. This rating scale was developed by teachers from a local school district in Oregon. Although the holistic/generic scale suffers from several deficiencies, its use to assess general writing ability for any writing sample makes it attractive from the standpoint of ease of use.

Serial List

This rating scale, shown in Table 5B.12, is normally task-specific and contains a number value and a serial list of points to consider when rating the student. The one shown in the table comes from the Arizona Student Assessment Program at a time when task-specific rating scales were used. The program has since changed to generic rating scales. Serial lists can be long, which places the teacher/rater in the tenuous and stressful situation of having to apply complex criteria to a student product.

The main idea with the serial list is to classify any student response into one available category, given the rich detail provided for each category. It is expected that teachers are trained in the various levels using actual student examples from

---

TABLE 5B.11
Holistic/Generic Developmental Scale

SCORE	KEY WORD	DESCRIPTION
5	Strong	Writer in control—skillfully shaping and directing the writing—evidence of fine tuning
4	Maturing	More control, writer has confidence to experiment—about a draft away
3	Developing	Writer begins to take control, begins to shape ideas—writing gaining definite direction, coherence, momentum, sense of purpose
2	Emerging	Moments that trigger reader's/writer's questions—stories/ideas buried within the text
1	Beginning	Searching, exploring, struggling, looking for a sense of purpose or way to begin

TABLE 5B.12
Serial List

A 4 response	• Contains both a picture and an explanation that indicate a clear understanding of the pattern
	• Contains a picture showing a whole divided into four equal parts
	• Contains an explanation that enhances the picture by comparing the size of each piece using either sentences or computation, or a combination of both
A 3 response	• Contains a picture that indicates a clear understanding of the pattern but only an attempt at an explanation
	• Contains an explanation that indicates a clear understanding of the pattern but only an attempt at a picture
	• Has limited detail in the picture or the explanation
A 2 response	• Offers an adequate picture only
	• Offers an adequate explanation only
	• Contains an explanation that does not enhance the picture
	• May be difficult to understand because of errors in language and grammar
A 1 response	• Makes some attempt at a picture or an explanation
	• Is unclear
A 0 response	• Fails to attempt the question or provides an incoherent response
A N/S (nonscorable) response	• Is illegible or unreadable

the test. While the serial list might be useful for high-stakes testing programs, it is unlikely that you would use one for classroom testing.

Hybrid

Table 5B.13 presents the hybrid scale, which combines a graded-category rating scale with a descriptive rating scale. Thus, the teacher can learn the more complex descriptive rating scale and use the graded-category summarizing term for a handy reference point. The rating scale in the table is generic/analytic.

TABLE 5B.13
Hybrid

POINTS	SUMMARIZING TERM	DESCRIPTION FOR COHERENCE
5	Exceptional	Writing exhibits outstanding supporting details for the topic sentence. The writer unifies thoughts in organizing the extra detail into a logical and effective essay.
4	Commendable	Writing exhibits sufficient supporting details to support the topic sentence and is coherent in the organization of those details.
3	Adequate	Writing exhibits some supporting reasons for the student's topic sentence, but is unified with sporadic coherence.
2	Poor	Writing exhibits little to no supporting reasons for the student's topic sentence and is scattered in thought and coherence.
1	Very poor	Writing shows a lack of clear sense of direction. Topic is undefined and organization is unclear.
0	No response	No response was given.
0	Off topic	Writing is not salient to the item (prompt).

Superficial Rating Scale

The previous examples have offered you choices, each with its particular strengths and weaknesses. No rating scale or system of rating scales will be ideal if you consider cost, time to score, reliability, bias, and interrater consistency. However, there is one type of scale that should *never* be used. This scale is referred to as *superficial* because it is "quick and dirty." It represents a superficial attempt to score student writing. The scale is holistic and generic:

0—blank
1—attempt, not to the point, off base
2—partial response
3—almost complete response
4—complete response, well developed

Summary

A companion to the previous chapter, this chapter focused on scoring student responses to high-inference performance test items. The development and use of rating scales to score high-inference items is expensive and time-consuming. Such testing is often necessary to measure complex mental abilities and types of higher level thinking that are often overlooked in everyday teaching and conventional multiple-choice tests. There are few shortcuts in scoring high-inference tests and plenty of hazards to avoid along the way. However, the overall benefit to students outweighs this added burden. I hope this chapter has afforded you enough guidance and examples to adopt, adapt, or create rating scales and methods for scoring student responses that will allow you to help students develop mental abilities and other forms of higher level thinking.

References

Marzano, R. J., Pickering, D., & McTighe, J. (1993). *Assessing student outcomes.* Alexandria, VA: Association for Supervision and Curriculum Development.

Powers, D. E., Fowles, M. E., Farnum, M., & Ramsey, P. (1994). Will they think less of my handwritten essay if others word process theirs? Effects on essay scores of intermingling handwritten and word-processed essays. *Journal of Educational Measurement, 31,* 220–233.

Purves, A. (1993). Setting standards in the language arts and literature classroom and the implications for portfolio assessment. *Educational Assessment, 1,* 175–200.

Roid, G. H. (1994). Patterns of writing skills derived from cluster analysis of direct-writing assessments. *Applied Measurement in Education, 7,* 159–170.

Saner, H., Klein, S., Bell, R., & Comfort, K. (1994). The utility of multiple raters and tasks in science performance assessments. *Educational Assessment, 2,* 257–272.

Witt, E. A. (1995). *Issues in constructing an analytic scoring scale for a writing assessment.* Paper presented at the annual meeting of the American Educational Research Association, San Francisco, April.

6 Low-Inference Performance Formats

IN CHAPTER 2, WE LEARNED ABOUT THE DIFFERENT KINDS OF COGNITIVE, affective, and psychomotor outcomes that can be tested in the class. In Chapter 3, we examined many different types of formats for writing test items. The major distinction discussed in Chapter 3 was between selecting an answer from a list of choices and constructing an answer. When students construct the answer, we have two possible inferences: high and low. Chapters 5A and 5B dealt with high-inference testing. This chapter is about low-inference testing.

This chapter contains a discussion of the following:

- Different types of student outcomes that are measured with the low-inference item format
- The anatomical difference between high- and low-inference item formats
- Strengths of low-inference item formats
- Limitations of low-inference item formats
- Four different low-inference item formats
- How to design four different types of low-inference item formats
- Score results for each type
- Examples of each of these formats with reference to an item-writing template

What Types of Learner Outcomes Require Low-Inference Test Items?

To review, the development of any student's abilities requires complex combinations of five types of student behavior: (1) recall, (2) understanding, (3) critical thinking, (4) problem solving, and (5) creative behavior (thinking and production).

With a student outcome that requires performance instead of selection of choices, you can interpret the performance in a high-inference or low-inference way.

With high-inference behavior, you are assessing an abstract quality of a process or a product, so you use a rating scale. With low-inference behavior, you are assessing a tangible, concrete quality of a process or product, so you use observation and simply note whether a desired behavior or characteristic is present or absent. The following chart below shows high- and low-inference student learning outcomes:

Measures of High-Inference Skills/Abilities	Measures of Low-Inference Skills/Abilities
Effectiveness of a new procedure	Baseball batting average
Quality of house construction	Time for 100-meter freestyle swim
Beauty of newly refurnished room	Number of trophies for ballroom dancing
Eloquence of a speech	Number of paintings sold
Effectiveness of a new state law	Number of marathons won
Convincingness of an essay	Number of pieces of furniture made
Tastiness of a new dish	Number of prize-winning recipes

As you can see from this chart and similar ones in previous chapters, the distinction between high- and low-inference testing is fundamental. If you want to know about the tastiness of a new dish you have created in your kitchen, then tastiness is an abstract quality. If we want to know how much four servings of this dish cost, that involves a very tangible, concrete observation.

Anatomical Differences between High- and Low-Inference Items

Table 6.1 shows the main difference between high- and low-inference items. The item stem, conditions, and student response are identical. The only difference is in the method of scoring. However, this difference in scoring derives from an earlier consideration when designing the item: What exactly do we want to measure? If the trait being measured is abstract and requires an inference, then we are in the realm of high-inference testing where we use rating scales. High-inference testing is more judgmental and fallible with respect to errors of measurement, judge consistency, and bias. If the trait being tested is plainly visible, with a right answer or a simple observable behavior, then we use low-inference scoring. With low-inference

TABLE 6.1
Anatomical Differences between High- and Low-Inference
Constructed-Response Items

HIGH-INFERENCE ITEM	LOW-INFERENCE ITEM
Question or instruction	Question or instruction
Conditions	Conditions
Student response	Student response
Inference using a rating scale or set of rating scales	Direct observation using a key, checklist, simple yes–no observation, or instrument-aided observation

testing, we avoid most of these problems associated with the rating scale, such as low reliability, judge inconsistency, and bias. With low-inference items, we trade in our rating scale for simple observation or a set of correlated observations, which we call a checklist.

Strengths of Low-Inference Items

We have many good reasons for using low-inference items.

Easily Adaptable to Processes

Low-inference items are best suited to visible, observable, sequential processes, such as the steps you might follow in making a pot of coffee. If you can identify the actual steps that can be observed in a process, then a low-inference test item is desirable and appropriate.

Easily Adaptable to Qualities of Products

With some products, low-inference items can be used to identify aspects of the product that are readily observable. For instance, if a brake mechanic is inspecting your car, the mechanic may focus on how the car stops, when you last had your brakes tested or inspected, whether your brake light works, whether the brakes make noise when applied or grab when applied, and whether your brakes "chatter." (Is there anything more boring than chatter from a set of brakes?) This inspection involves a systematic checklist.

Direct Observation

High-inference items require an expert judge to observe a student response and then rate the student performance or product using three to seven judged rating scale categories for some abstract idea such as clarity, persuasiveness, completeness, or originality. We are prepared to admit that we cannot see these abstract qualities, but we can make a guess about each based on our expertise. High-inference testing is sometimes referred to as *indirect observation*. This leap of faith from a student process or product to this abstract concept is a problem in high-inference testing because of the possibility of poor interrater consistency and judge bias.

With low-inference items, we typically do not have that problem. With the brake inspection problem, we can see what is happening. We can watch the performance step by step and note if certain events occurred or not. Two observers can see the same set of events and report the same result with the low-inference item. We have no leap of faith. *Direct observation* is desirable because "seeing is believing."

Interrater Consistency

When two judges agree in their judgments, the degree of this agreement can be represented by an index of interrater (interjudge) consistency. With rating scales, this degree of consistency is too often lower than we would like. With direct observation via a low-inference item, this consistency should be nearly perfect. For instance, if you and I observed the brake inspection, we probably would agree on the results of the specific tests being run. We typically have high interrater consistency with a low-inference item.

Some educators call interrater consistency *reliability*, but this is not really correct. Reliability is a different type of consistency. However, low interrater consistency will contribute to low test score reliability.

Objectivity

When two raters or observers get the same result when viewing the same process or product, we consider the scoring process to be *objective*. Objectivity is good because it minimizes the threat of low interrater consistency. Low-inference items tend to be objectively scored.

Reliability

Reliability refers to the consistency of test results for the same product or performance from time to time or at one time (internal consistency among item performances). Low-inference scoring tends to produce more reliable test results because measurement error is very low. We seldom compute a reliability coefficient for a set of low-inference items. If we did, it would be very high.

Bias

With high-inference items, we have a persistent threat of bias because the rater has to make this translation between the abstract characteristic being rated and the rating scale categories provided. We learned in Chapter 5B about different types of bias and its effects on students being rated. Because we are directly observing something via a low-inference item, bias is less likely. With the low-inference item, all observers are seeing the same thing, so the chance of bias is very slim. But it is possible that two observers having the same bias can produce identical (consistent) results that are biased. The credibility of the judges comes into question here, because the performer and other spectators also can judge performance and find out whether a standard was met. For instance, during a recent basketball game, all 19,362 fans saw our favorite player get punched by an opposing player, but the three referees (judges) didn't see what the rest of us saw, so no foul was called on the opposing player. Were they biased? Or were we biased? The point is that observation is *somewhat* free of the threat of bias, but bias is always a threat.

Summary

In this section, we have examined strengths of low-inference testing. Low-inference testing works especially well with physical and mental skills and abilities, where each step can be seen. Also, with processes that involve simple events, whether requiring timing, weighing, or measuring, low-inference testing seems very appropriate. Such factors as direct observation, high interrater consistency, objectivity, high reliability, and minimizing of bias contribute to the desirability of using a low-inference item.

Limitations of Low-Inference Performance Test Items

You probably are wondering why anyone would ever bother with any other type of scoring if low-inference scoring is so good. Here are some of its limitations to report.

Worthwhile Student Learning Outcomes

Most worthwhile student outcomes reflecting higher level thinking lend themselves to high-inference scoring. Most of the examples we see in national and state testing programs involve rating scales to assess abilities, such as writing. It is difficult to find high-quality student learning that can be assessed using low-inference items. The only dependable type of higher level thinking that can be observed directly with a low-inference item is a problem that has a known answer, such as a mathematical problem or an essay question.

Another important point is that many responses to a higher level thinking item may have multiple correct responses, that require a high-inference judgment. It would be good if we could transform that situation into an observable set of steps that are common to all problems and their solutions.

Efficiency

Both high- and low-inference items require expensive and time-consuming administration and scoring. There are no shortcuts. Each student must be individually tested instead of group tested. Therefore, you need to examine why you are doing performance testing and choose your performance tasks cautiously. Although you may want to test a variety of low-inference tasks, the amount of time needed will quickly and greatly surpass the time available.

Summary

The low-inference format has many worthwhile qualities. For various types of simple student learning, the low-inference formats presented in this chapter work well and are appropriate. For the most desirable types of student learning involving the many abstract complex mental abilities of problem solving and critical thinking, the low-inference format seldom applies usefully and we turn to the high-inference format.

Four Different Low-Inference Formats

This section introduces and discusses four unique low-inference formats.

1. The Open-Ended Question or Instruction (Also Known as the Essay Item)

This brings us to a controversial issue regarding the essay format. For any open-ended item with a correct answer, we also could construct a comparable multiple-choice item. Testing specialists often compare the multiple-choice and the essay format for measuring recall of facts, understanding, and some types of critical thinking and problem solving. Studies have shown over and over that when measuring simpler types of behaviors, such as recall, understanding, and even limited forms of higher level thinking such as problem solving and critical thinking, multiple-choice and essay versions of the same question seem to reflect the same type of mental behavior (Bennett, Rock, & Wang, 1990; Haladyna, 1994, 1995). Given that multiple-choice format provides more reliable results at a lower cost, you might be inclined to use the multiple-choice format instead of the essay format. Nonetheless, the essay format is presented in this chapter as a viable low-inference format because it continues to be popular and often used. Further, the essay gives a sample of student writing that can be independently analyzed as a high-inference test.

Variations in the essay format. There are three types of essay formats: completion, short-answer, and extended-answer.

Generally, the *completion* format is the most objectively scored, the most reliable, and the easiest to write and score results. However, it fails to measure much in the way of higher level thinking. We use this format for the simplest behaviors, recall and understanding. Generally we use right/wrong scoring for the completion.

Who played the hand in the fine film *Addams Family Values*?

The *short-answer* format is the most highly recommended (Coffman, 1971). It offers a set of questions that focus on a topic or related set of topics in a chapter, unit, or course of study. In a fixed period for testing, the short-answer essay is a useful format for covering material. Scoring for the short-answer may be right/wrong, or we might use a checklist to detail specific elements of a correct answer.

> Why is it a bad idea to leave a tuna fish sandwich out overnight before enjoying it for lunch the next day?

The *extended-answer* essay format is often criticized because of ridiculous examples such as: *Define truth* or *Discuss the history of the world*. But this format is applicable to critical thinking (predicting or evaluating) and problem solving, where we have a right answer in mind and scoring can pretty much pinpoint the qualities of the right answer using a checklist or simple right/wrong scoring.

> Discuss the role of peanut butter and jelly in the creation of the classical luncheon menu for the school child, tracing the history of this sandwich with the agricultural development of our nation.

Table 6.2 shows examples of essay items written for a variety of student behaviors. None of these items conform to the ideal items presented later in this section. None of these items follow our template for writing items. These items merely suggest approaches to completion, short-answer, and extended-answer items that involve both right/wrong and checklist scoring reflecting types or combinations of higher level thinking.

There also are two special cases of essay formats. The first is the take-home essay briefly discussed in Chapter 3. Among the principal advantages of this format is the ability to work on a problem or activity for an extended period. Among its disadvantages is the possibility that the student will compromise the security of the test and get help. Another format discussed and evaluated in Chapter 3 was the oral examination. Although this method is very desirable in that it gets students to speak and perform orally, it is very time-consuming. Also, you could use either a checklist for evaluating performance or a rating scale, so this format might appear in either high- or low-inference settings.

Scoring essay items is a daunting task for any teacher. Ideally, this is what testing specialists recommend for scoring an essay test, whether we have a right answer or a checklist.

1. Score each item for all students, then move to the next item.

In this way, you keep a consistent mind set when scoring all item 1 responses, then all item 2 responses, and so on. Don't score a student's entire paper and then move on to the next student's paper. The following schematic shows the right and wrong ways to score. Imagine a test with four students and three items.

TABLE 6.2
Examples of Essay Items

MENTAL BEHAVIOR	ITEM
Recall	What is the most critical age in cognitive development for a child?
Recall	What is the best predictor of future school achievement?
Understanding	Produce five examples of onomatopoeia referring to family members.
Understanding	List four food groups and give one example of each.
Problem solving	Which is the fastest route from the east side of San Jose to the west side?
Critical thinking–predicting Problem solving	Estimate the effects of a high fat diet for an fifty-year old overweight male smoker with respect to health care costs and life insurance liability.
Critical thinking–evaluation	Compare the caloric values of hamburgers, pizza, and tacos.
Problem solving Critical thinking–evaluation	You are considering refinancing your home. You have four financing options. Evaluate each and determine which will benefit you most over a five-year period.
Critical thinking–evaluation	Discuss at least three pros and three cons for using an essay test for twelve students in high school Honors Physics.
Problem solving	Determine the cost of shipping three-pound packages with dimensions 12" x 18" x 14" to Japan so that you can better price the product you are selling there.
Critical thinking–predicting	Given current economic realities and current government economic policies, discuss the future of inflation in the United States over the next four years.
Critical thinking–evaluation	Contrast and compare the roles of R2D2 in the movie *Star Wars* with the role of the Robby the Robot in the movie *The Day The Earth Stood Still.*

Items	RIGHT WAY			WRONG WAY		
	1	*2*	*3*	*1*	*2*	*3*
Anna	A	E	I	A	B	C
Savanna	B	F	J	D	E	F
Lana	C	G	K	G	H	I
Rosannadanna	D	H	L	J	K	I

Doing it the right way, you score all four answers to item 1 first, then all four answers to item 2, and then all four answers to item 3. Doing it the wrong way, you score all three of Anna's answers first, then all three of Savanna's answers, and so on. The reason for this advice is that you should use criteria consistently in scoring each item. If you score across items, you may forget your criteria and not score consistently.

2. Do not give students options, such as "Choose 3 of the 5 items listed below."

One student may choose three easy items; another may choose three hard items. One student may choose three items from one part of the domain of knowledge; another student may choose from another part of the domain. The resulting test scores will not be comparable.

3. Provide students with your key and your model answers.

Students tend to imitate teachers. Model answers help students learn and prepare them for future essay tests with you. You will notice improvement in their second and third sets of essays as they learn more about your preferences and style.

4. Make comments on each student paper.

Compliment students when justified, point out their errors in thinking, give them hints about future study strategies, or offer other bits of constructive criticism. *Never* be negative or sarcastic; such behavior is unproductive.

5. Mix the papers periodically.

Students' papers should occasionally be shuffled, like a deck of cards. This practice counteracts a form of bias that comes with fatigue, boredom, or increasing frustration as a teacher grades papers. If all the good papers are on top, the grader may grade by the order of the papers instead of actual responses.

6. Don't confuse writing ability or writing skills with whatever you are measuring.

It is easy to lose sight of what the essay test is supposed to measure. This is an honest error. The most obvious bias is that a student's handwriting may influence your scoring. As noted in a previous chapter, the use of word processing apparently biases scoring. With essay scoring, penmanship may be a deciding factor. Another bias is the student's writing ability. A good writer may get a higher score than deserved. One form of bias that has been observed in the past is the length of sentences; longer sentences result in higher scores (Coffman, 1971).

The essay format has a long history of use and probably will continue to be used to test student recall, understanding, critical thinking (predicting and evaluating), and problem solving. Using a checklist or right/wrong scoring eliminates many forms of bias that have troubled the essay format traditionally. If multiple-choice is a viable alternative, I strongly recommend its use instead of the essay format, because of the hazards of essay testing described here and in Chapter 5B.

2. Simple Observation Format without a Measuring Instrument

All item formats in this chapter require teacher observation of a single student behavior or student-initiated processes or products. This section deals with a single event. Two types of simple observation are (1) without and (2) with a measuring instrument. Here I address the first of these two types. This kind of observation means simply making a record of the presence of a behavior, event, action, process, or product. Observation is not very complex. In other cases, observation simply means recording some characteristic of a person or process.

Although observation may be inherently simple, do not turn away from it. It has many uses in teaching, particularly in such areas as early learner education, special education (particularly for students with severe physical or mental handicaps), physical education, industrial arts, science, mathematics, home economics, foreign languages, medical education, health education, and job training, among many others.

Here are some examples of simple observation, drawn from a variety of instructional settings and situations. The fact that each is presented as a list should *not* imply a checklist. Unlike a checklist, these lists contain discrete simple behaviors that require a teacher or other observer to note whether something happened or was done. These observations do not require judgment.

This format is so simple that often you don't even have to write an item. Simply note if you see the behavior or product or not. You might record the result as

---

Examples of Simple Observation

_____ Walks without support.

_____ Correctly spells all 100 words.

_____ Puts equipment away before bell rings.

_____ Swims 50 yards.

_____ Uses graduated cylinder to measure liquids.

_____ Turns in all homework on time.

_____ Solves Type I problems.

_____ Makes correct change for any purchase up to $10.00.

_____ Drinks from a cup.

---

evidence for assigning a grade or simply record behavior as part of the everyday development of each student.

Sometimes, test-makers will assemble a set of simple observations into an inventory. For example, _An Inventory of Primary Skills_ (Valett, 1970) is an example of 300 simple observations arranged into sets to form test scores. This inventory has the elements of a checklist but is really a set of independent observations.

While simple observation has many good qualities such as objectivity, freedom from bias, accuracy, high interjudge agreement or consistency, and high reliability, its main limitation is that the most important outcomes of schooling in this era of educational reform, including most types of higher level thinking and mental abilities, are not well suited to simple observation. Another significant limitation is that these observations are done individually, which is very time-consuming.

Despite these limitations, simple observation continues to be a viable low-inference method of testing because some student outcomes require the teacher's observation.

3. Simple Observation with a Measuring Instrument

Like the previous type of item format, instrument-aided observation is direct and very accurate. That is because the measuring instruments we typically use are precise: a watch or clock, timer, scale, or ruler. In some settings, such as military training, job training, or science laboratories, complex measuring instruments are used. Instrument-aided observation is quick, easy, precise, and objective. We can hardly question the accuracy or validity of such measurements. Here are some examples of instrument-aided observation:

Examples of Instrument-Aided Observation

_____ Writes numbers through 50 within 5 minutes.

_____ Constructs a pulley system with which a person who weighs less than 100 pounds can lift a 100-pound object.

_____ Swims 100 yards in less than 3 minutes.

_____ Installs a water pump in any General Motors car (vintage 1987–1994) in less than 25 minutes. (Pump must operate correctly.)

_____ Constructs a new egg carton in which 12 eggs survive a 20-foot fall.

These items vary considerably in type and complexity. All require simple observation, observable events, and the use of a measuring instrument.

4. Items Requiring a Checklist

Suppose that your goal is to teach students to perform a sequence of steps—for instance, to carry out a laboratory routine, conduct an interview, give a speech, or

---

Performance Checklist:
Brewing a Pot of Coffee

Yes No

____ ____ 1. Empties leftovers from previous use.

____ ____ 2. Rinses out the pot.

____ ____ 3. Fills the pot with water.

____ ____ 4. Pours the water into the top container.

____ ____ 5. Empties the coffee grounds container.

____ ____ 6. Wipes it clean.

____ ____ 7. Puts filter in container.

____ ____ 8. Fills it with four scoops of coffee.

____ ____ 9. Puts the container in the appropriate slot.

____ ____ 10. Turns the switch to "on."

play a musical instrument. These behaviors are observable parts of the performance. Sometimes, you may want to analyze the results of performance, such as a painting, an essay, a skit or play, a poem, a short story, a solution to a major problem we face in our society, interpretation of complex data, or a business letter. These are products.

A checklist is a device for marking a sequential set of observations. The behaviors or characteristics being checked must be observable, and each observation must be dichotomous (e.g., pass/fail, seen/unseen, yes/no, done/undone). These observations must make up a set that is preferably, though not necessarily, sequential. For example, suppose you want to find out if a new teacher has mastered brewing a pot of coffee in the faculty lounge, an important aspect of becoming a teacher. If a performance problem exists, observation coupled with this checklist can spot an incompetent performance in this important professional skill, so professional help can be given. The coffee-making example on page 163 is a performance checklist. This is a standard procedure for visible performance. The list of activities can be viewed by any judge with great accuracy.

A product checklist is a little different. It involves inspection of a student product to find out if certain characteristics are present or absent:

Product Checklist

TSW will create a new tasty salad for the faculty potluck next week.

Yes No

_____ _____ 1. Procedures for making salad provided to other faculty.
_____ _____ 2. Items analyzed for cholesterol, fat, and calories.
_____ _____ 3. Amounts needed clearly specified.
_____ _____ 4. Cost of materials estimated.
_____ _____ 5. Time needed to prepare item given.
_____ _____ 6. Recipe shared with everyone.

The product checklist is ordinarily not sequenced. The preceding example comes from an assignment to new teachers who must bring a potluck item to a faculty dinner. In this particular school, where extremely high standards are used, the teacher must state the procedures (in other words, provide a recipe), ensure that the salad contains good stuff (no wicked fat or high calories), give the amount of salad fixings needed, estimate the cost, and estimate the time it takes to prepare the salad.

TABLE 6.3
Template for a Low-Inference Test Item

TYPE OF OUTCOMES DESIRED:

Recall	☐	Understanding	☐	Problem Solving	☐
Critical Thinking/Predicting	☐			Creativity/Thinking	☐
Critical Thinking/Evaluating	☐			Creativity/Production	☐

Integrated or not?	☐	Are subject matters being integrated?
Process or product?	☐	Are we concerned with how something is done or the end result?
Meaningful context?	☐	Have we chosen a task that is meaningful, authentic, realistic, significant, or important to the student?
Clear instruction to student?	☐	The student needs to have a clear understanding of what he or she is to do to complete the assignment.
Materials provided?	☐	What materials or supplies are needed to do this? Does the school supply these, or does the student get her or his own materials?
Time limit given?	☐	How long does the student have to complete this? Be specific.
Scope of response described?	☐	Indicate what kind of response is appropriate. Remember that some students will do the minimum and some will overwhelm you.
Consultation allowed?	☐	Can parents, students, and teachers give feedback and provide other assistance? How much and when?
Collaboration encouraged?	☐	Can students work together? What are the conditions, rules, and guidelines?
Corrective allowed?	☐	Do we allow the student to redo the work, to improve it, to polish it until it is wonderful?
Computers allowed?	☐	Do we allow or insist that a computer be used to develop the result or write our report of results? If so, what conditions do we have regarding spell checkers and grammar checkers?
Criteria?	☐	Did we inform the student about how the responses are scored?
Point values for grading?	☐	Did we tell the student the value of this item toward her or his grade?
Student checklist?	☐	Did you provide a brief checklist for the student to remind her or him of what is expected?

Summary

In this section, you have looked at four low-inference item formats. They differ mainly in the nature of what is measured and in the scoring. The most significant of these four formats is the essay, which can be scored right/wrong or with a checklist. The essay is usually considered an unattractive alternative to multiple choice by testing specialists. All four formats share a tendency toward simple observation, objective scoring, and high interrater consistency. All formats avoid the problems of rater inconsistency and bias encountered with rating scales. However, it is difficult to find applications of these four formats for the most important outcomes of good schooling, namely the mental abilities and types of higher level thinking featured in Chapter 2.

Writing the Low-Inference Test Item

This section contains some generic steps for writing low-inference performance test items. As noted previously, these steps are identical with those for high-inference performance test items, with one exception. Instead of a rating scale to score results, you will use observation or a checklist. The template in Table 6.3 is virtually identical to the template in Table 5A.2 in Chapter 5A. The recommended steps are as follows:

1. Consider the student outcome being developed.
2. Write the instruction or question.
3. Specify the conditions for performance.
4. Provide the evaluation criteria (checklist or observation system and point values).

As with high-inference items, stating the conditions in the item is crucial for many reasons. The main advantage to students is that once the desired behavior is known, its measurement is objective. Students know the results at the time of the test or even before, because they know the criteria ahead of time.

The Search for Content

This was discussed in a previous chapter but is worth mentioning briefly here. Use your curriculum guide or framework. If it is not specific enough or is uninspiring, use your creativity to explore the outside world, otherwise known as *real life*. Many real-life problems could be adopted or adapted for a low-inference performance. Another good source are specialty books published for selected subject matters. One excellent source for elementary science is Meng and Doran (1993), which contains many ideas and examples of science items. In reading, we referred to books by Anthony, Johnson, Mickelson, and Preece (1991) and by Barr, Blachowicz, and Wogman-Sadow (1995). The NCTM standards provide some source material in mathematics. Regardless of your content inspiration, much work lies ahead designing and adapting activities for various types of higher level thinking. But it is good to tap a variety of resources, share your ideas with others, and have them share their ideas with you.

Examples of Items

This final section of the chapter contains several examples of low-inference performance test items from a variety of sources. There is a brief discussion of each item. As with Chapter 5A, we will use the template in Table 6.3 as a means of evaluating each item.

Informal Reading Inventory

Chapter 5A contained a definition of reading comprehension that was research-based and in line with innovations in the teaching of reading. In this section, we will examine a popular new technique for assessing reading ability that involves low-inference observation.

The informal reading inventory (IRI) is widely used today to determine each child's independent, instructional, and frustration reading levels. The purpose of this assessment is to find the child's strengths and weaknesses. Commercial IRIs are available (see Barr, Blachowicz, & Wogman-Sadow, 1995, for a list). Or you may want to develop your own. This section is for the home-grown version.

An IRI has five basic components:

1. A reading passage that is of good literary quality and is appropriate and interesting for the student
2. A set of open-ended questions that are dependent on reading the passage
3. A set of words in order from easiest to hardest, derived from this passage
4. A set of clear directions
5. Clear-cut scoring

In the IRI, the student first reads from the word list, then proceeds to an oral reading task, then to a silent reading task, and then to a listening task. According to Barr et al. (1995), all scoring is objective and quantitative but requires a certain amount of clinical judgment of these results to make a final determination of student reading ability.

The IRI is a diagnostic test, not appropriate for grading or high-stakes purposes. Nonetheless, it is an important type of format for measuring reading. Although an entire item cannot be reproduced here because of its length and complexity, interested readers should consult Barr et al. (1995) for a comprehensive treatment of this topic.

Hiebert and Calfee (1992), in their review of IRIs, found reports of much irregularity in their use and importance for classroom grading or student placement. Nonetheless, the usefulness of IRIs seems to be increasing as we formalize the process of using low-inference measures with the IRI.

Essay Item with a Checklist

Table 6.4 contains a single essay item with an easy-to-use grading checklist. Because the student has clear instructions and the grading checklist, that student is likely to give a high-quality response. This example is typical of essay testing. Instead of testing for recall or understanding, however, the item goes further to make a choice for a specific setting and defend that choice. Understanding is shown by providing three examples, which the teacher must judge as correct/incorrect.

Problem Solving with Right/Wrong Scoring

Table 6.5 provides a problem-solving item dealing with car maintenance. There is one and only one right answer. This kind of problem is typical of problem solving in mathematics, and we have many lifelike applications like this one. If the item is not very specific, a student might make a correct assumption that you haven't considered. For instance, a student might figure the cost of his or her labor at $50/hour into the problem, something you hadn't considered. Would you give credit to that student for a correct assumption that led to an answer different from yours? I hope your answer is yes.

Problem Solving with a Product Checklist

Table 6.6 gives a real-life example of the problem encountered in planning a Thanksgiving Day dinner for twelve people. The specific item only asks for three specific things that can be evaluated using a product checklist. In this instance, the product is a written one containing information.

Despite the limited focus of the checklist in Table 6.6, this activity could be evaluated along a number of other dimensions. For example, you could evaluate the dinner in terms of creativity, using a high-inference approach, a rating scale. You

TABLE 6.4
Outcome: Essay Item with a Checklist

As a first-year teacher in a second-grade class, briefly state whether you will use general or specific rules, and why. Give three appropriate examples of the particular type of rules you will use. (16 points).

Grading Checklist

ACTIVITY	POINTS	COMPLETED?
Chose specific rules.	5	Yes ☐ No ☐
Gave at least one reason.	5	Yes ☐ No ☐
Gave three appropriate examples (2 points for each).	6	Yes ☐ No ☐

{Note: This is part of a formal sit-down test.}

Commentary Using the Template

Integrated or not:	No
Process or product:	Product
Meaningful context:	Yes, student should be able to identify with problem in a personal way.
Clear instruction:	Very detailed.
Materials provided:	No materials are necessary.
Time limit given:	Implied.
Scope of response given:	Clearly indicated.
Consultation encouraged:	No.
Collaboration encouraged:	No.
Correctives allowed:	No.
Computer allowed:	Not mentioned.
Criteria:	Given.
Point value for grading:	Given.
Student checklist:	Given.

Source: Author is Jennifer (Murphy) Schuman, Education student at ASU West.

TABLE 6.5
Outcome: Problem Solving with Right/Wrong Scoring

Compare the cost of having the oil changed on your car by a car dealer versus a discount store versus doing it yourself. Show the percentage of saving for the least expensive option compared with the second least expensive option. Show all calculations. (20 points)

Commentary Using the Template

Integrated or not:	Problem-solving. Yes, involves mathematics, higher level thinking.
Process or product:	Product.
Meaningful context:	Yes, student should be able to identify with problem in a personal way.
Clear instruction:	Yes.
Materials provided:	No materials are necessary.
Time limit given:	None given. Assume a sit-down test.
Scope of response given:	Clearly indicated.
Consultation encouraged:	No.
Collaboration encouraged:	No.
Correctives allowed:	No.
Computer allowed:	Not mentioned.
Criteria:	Assume that answer must be correct for credit.
Point value for grading:	Given.
Student checklist:	Not relevant.

might want to analyze dietary content addressing issues of fat content, calories, and the like. Other dimensions can be added to make the problem more complex and challenging.

Writing Ability with a Product Checklist

Table 6.7 is a product checklist for a writing sample involving a business letter written by the student. The checklist is so explicit that a motivated student could use the checklist to produce a perfect letter. With this activity, you might employ correctives, letting the student know that she or he can work at this until it is per-

TABLE 6.6
Outcome: Problem Solving with a Product Checklist

You have been assigned to plan and serve Thanksgiving Dinner for twelve people. The dinner can be traditional or nontraditional. You are the boss. Your first step is to prepare a plan containing a budget. Figure out the cost of a Thanksgiving Day dinner for twelve people. Show how you arrived at your answer. The following checklist will be used to evaluate your answer.

ACTIVITY	POINTS	COMPLETED?
Lists the menu.	10	Yes ☐ No ☐
Shows detail for costing.	15	Yes ☐ No ☐
Arrives at figure correctly.	15	Yes ☐ No ☐

Your response is due on March 17. You may consult with family members or a friend, but your work is your responsibility.

Commentary Using the Template

Integrated or not:	Problem-solving. Yes, involves mathematics, problem solving.
Process or product:	Process.
Meaningful context:	Yes, a very common problem.
Clear instruction:	Yes.
Materials provided:	No materials are necessary.
Time limit given:	Yes.
Scope of response given:	Clearly indicated.
Consultation encouraged:	Yes.
Collaboration encouraged:	No.
Correctives allowed:	No.
Computer allowed:	Not mentioned.
Criteria:	Assume that answer must be correct for credit.
Point value for grading:	Given in checklist.
Student checklist:	Not relevant.

TABLE 6.7
Outcome: Writing Ability with a Product Checklist

Using the computer, write a business letter to the High-Energy Health Club announcing your resignation. Make sure that they understand that (1) you have met your obligations in your contract and (2) the monthly deduction from your paycheck to pay for membership should end immediately. Their address is: High-Energy Health Club, 700 East 22nd Street, Chickahominy, VA, 70707. (24 points)

Check All That Apply (3 points per check)

_____ 1. Business letter was written using a word-processing program.
_____ 2. Spell checker was used correctly.
_____ 3. Student sought feedback from fellow student or teacher or parent.
_____ 4. No spelling errors.
_____ 5. No grammatical errors.
_____ 6. Proper greeting was used.
_____ 7. Proper ending was used.
_____ 8. *Friendly* font (Times Roman or Helvetica) was used.

Commentary Using the Template

Integrated or not:	Problem-solving. Yes, involves writing and computer skills.
Process or product:	Product.
Meaningful context:	Yes, a very common life activity.
Clear instruction:	Yes.
Materials provided:	Yes, need a computer and printer.
Time limit given:	No.
Scope of response given:	Clearly indicated.
Consultation encouraged:	Not mentioned.
Collaboration encouraged:	No.
Correctives allowed:	No.
Computer allowed:	Yes.
Criteria:	Very clearly spelled out in checklist.
Point value for grading:	Given in checklist.
Student checklist:	Not relevant.

fect. The student might be assigned to add this work to her or his portfolio. {See Chapter 7 for information on portfolios.}

Physical Ability with a Performance Checklist

The example in Table 6.8 comes from the Housekeeper Licensing Examination. The example shows 12 specific activities to be performed and their point values. This checklist does not ask how well each task was performed. If you wanted to know the quality of the each performance, that is a high-inference matter requiring a rating scale.

Simple Observation with an Instrument

Instead of providing a single item, the following examples each require the use of an instrument. These are simple in nature and reflect diverse subject matters including mathematics and science.

Simple Observation with an Instrument for a Science Class

____ ____ 1. Distance traveled by solar-powered vehicle
____ ____ 2. Time needed for plant seed to germinate in different solutions
____ ____ 3. Relative weights of rocks and minerals of different densities
____ ____ 4. Amount of electricity and cost to recharge a rechargeable battery

---

These items have observable results that can be scored right/wrong. All probably represent mental skills/abilities. All represent complex thinking. The range and types of items possible are extensive, because they are all lifelike problem solving. We probably would not want to use a template with these items because of their simplicity.

TABLE 6.8
Outcome: Physical Ability with a Performance Checklist—Housekeeper Licensing Examination

Clean the kitchen. Cleaning supplies are provided. You have one hour to complete the tasks. You will be evaluated on the following:

ACTIVITY	POINTS	COMPLETED?
Top of refrigerator cleaned.	2	Yes ☐ No ☐
Range hood cleaned.	10	Yes ☐ No ☐
Cobwebs removed.	5	Yes ☐ No ☐
Cabinet doors cleaned and polished.	15	Yes ☐ No ☐
Stove top cleaned.	10	Yes ☐ No ☐
Window sills and window frame dusted.	5	Yes ☐ No ☐
Pictures dusted.	2	Yes ☐ No ☐
Top of door frames dusted.	2	Yes ☐ No ☐
Backsplash and countertop cleaned.	10	Yes ☐ No ☐
Sink cleaned.	10	Yes ☐ No ☐
Wastebaskets and recycling can emptied.	12	Yes ☐ No ☐
Floor washed/vacuumed.	17	Yes ☐ No ☐

Commentary Using the Template

Integrated or not:	No. Physical ability.
Process or product:	Process.
Meaningful context:	Yes, a very common life activity.
Clear instruction:	Yes.
Materials provided:	Yes, cleaning supplies.
Time limit given:	Yes.

Continued

TABLE 6.8 *Continued*	
Scope of response given:	Clearly indicated.
Consultation encouraged:	Not mentioned.
Collaboration encouraged:	No.
Correctives allowed:	No.
Computer allowed:	Not relevant.
Criteria:	Very clearly spelled out in checklist.
Point value for grading:	Given in checklist.
Student checklist:	Not relevant.

Summary

This chapter has analyzed low-inference performance testing where either right/wrong, simple observation, or checklist scoring is used. This type of testing is somewhat free of the problems associated with rating scales, such as low inter-rater consistency, low reliability, and bias. But this format does not apply to all types of higher level thinking as well.

Table 6.1 provides an analysis of the differences between high-inference and low-inference items. Table 6.3 provides a template much like the one in Chapter 5A for high-inference item writing. This template, when used, should guide you to the sound construction of low-inference items to meet your needs. The latter part of this chapter gave examples of low-inference items and their associated scoring systems. For the most part, these methods are simple. Items are easy to write, and responses are easy to score. Testing would serve us better if we could think of complex tasks that require low-inference items and scoring systems.

References

Anthony, R. J., Johnson, T. D., Mickelson, N. I., & Preece, A. (1991). *Evaluating literacy: A perspective for change*. Portsmouth, NH: Heinemann.

Barr, R., Blachowicz, C. L. Z., & Wogman-Sadow, M. (1995). *Reading diagnosis for teachers*, 3rd ed. White Plains, NY: Longman.

Bennett, R. E., Rock, D. A., & Wang, M. (1990). Equivalence of free-response and multiple-choice items. *Journal of Educational Measurement, 28,* 77–92.

Coffman, W. E. (1971). Essay examinations. In R. L. Thorndike (Ed.), *Educational Measurement,* 2nd ed., (pp. 271–302). Washington, DC: American Council on Education.

Haladyna, T. M. (1994). *Developing and validating multiple-choice test items.* Hillsdale, NJ: Lawrence Erlbaum Associates.

Haladyna, T. M., & Ryan, J. (1996). *The instrumentality of test item formats.* Submitted for publication.

Hiebert, E. H., & Calfee, R. C. (1992). Assessing literacy: From standardized tests to portfolio and performers. In S. J. Samuels & A. E. Farstrup (Eds.), *What research has to say about reading instruction.* Newark, DE: International Reading Association.

Meng, E., & Doran, R. L. (1993). *Improving instruction and learning through evaluation: Elementary school science.* Columbus, OH: ERIC Clearing House for Science, Mathematics, and Environmental Education.

Valett, R. E. (1970). *An inventory of primary skills.* Belmont, CA: Fearon.

7 The Portfolio: Collections of Student Work

THE PORTFOLIO IS A UNIQUE FORMAT FOR COLLECTING STUDENT DATA. Because of its growing prominence as both a teaching and a testing device, this entire chapter treats this topic. This chapter:

- Starts with a definition of the portfolio
- Provides an analysis of the portfolio's strengths and weaknesses
- Tells how to design one type of portfolio
- Describes how to score the results

The methods and technology for portfolio development and use as a testing tool are relatively new and unresearched. Portfolio development poses many logistical problems, not the least of which is developing teacher skills in designing and using portfolios in the classroom. Technical problems with scoring affect the validity of interpretation of portfolio results and the reliability of scores derived from portfolios. But for many reasons provided in this chapter, portfolio use should increase. As we gain more experience with its use, many logistical and technical problems will be solved.

What Is a Portfolio?

A portfolio is a collection of student work, usually contained in a folder. It contains a series of high-quality, meaningful tasks, assembled in order of completion to reflect the student's best work. The portfolio might contain assignments, project results, reports, and other writing; it also might reflect attitudes, self-reflection, and other indicators of affective characteristics associated with learning. The portfolio also should contain the grading criteria, so that students know the value of their work as related to their grade for a subject, such as language arts.

Is the portfolio an item or is it a type of test? In the context of a book on item writing, the portfolio is viewed as a type of superitem, much like the item set described in Chapter 3. The portfolio constitutes a unified and coordinated approach to measuring the types of higher level thinking seen in the development of an ability, such as reading or writing.

Although most of the contents of the portfolio may resemble performance items shown in Chapters 5A and 6, some major differences exist between performance items and the portfolio.

1. The portfolio is a series of performances that vary considerably in time taken to complete each assignment.
2. Tasks vary considerably in scope.
3. The results of assignments have been polished to the extent that they seldom resemble the original first effort.
4. The portfolio contents reflect the passage of time and the developmental nature of the ability being learned.
5. The portfolio represents a sort of partnership between the teacher/mentor and the student/learner, reflecting their collaboration and cooperation.

Gearhart and Herman (1995) state that the use of the portfolio supports long-term projects that would not be possible with a typical performance test. A portfolio also supports student revision of the work, showing how polishing leads to higher quality work. The portfolio provides a context both for presenting work and for receiving constructive criticism to improve future work. The portfolio seems ideal for developing student abilities in reading, writing, mathematical problem solving, and critical thinking. In creative fields such as architecture, photography, musical composition, dance, and interior design, the portfolio has had a long and honorable history for exhibiting a creative person's best work. So a portfolio can also document the development of creative ability.

According to Wolf (1989), the portfolio has three major components:

1. *Biography:* This part shows the developmental history of a significant project or product. The biography's purpose is to give the reader an impression of what the student was at the beginning and how far the student has traveled at the end.
2. *Range of works:* The range of works includes the variety of assignments contained in the portfolio. Table 7.1 contains a table of contents of examples of eighth- and ninth-grade students' writing for a middle school.
3. *Reflections.* Students may be asked to critique their own work or to reflect on how they have changed in their performance, what they have learned, and what they need to do to improve.

For What Content and Mental Behavior Should a Portfolio Be Used?

An outstanding feature of a portfolio is its adaptability to a variety of educational settings. In this section, the most obvious uses of a portfolio are listed. As a teacher,

TABLE 7.1
Examples of Portfolios of Writing Samples

ENGLISH 8	ENGLISH 9
Dialectical journal containing poems, passages, imitation of another author's style	Essay supporting a generalization
	Journal entry
Autobiographical incident	Translation of passage into students' own voice and style
Problem solution	
Analysis: Speculation about causes	List of inferences regarding an author's intent
Evidence of the writing process	Evidence of all phases of the writing process
List of outside works read	Best writing sample (students' choice)
Best writing sample	List of outside works read

you might see additional or different ways that a portfolio can be used to collect a set of works from the student for a specific purpose.

Table 7.2 provides a partial listing of content areas or types of abilities that might justify the development of a student portfolio. This table provides only a brief glimpse and sampling of content and types of mental behaviors. Note that the mental behaviors sampled are almost universally abilities. We have agreed that developing abilities is the long-term objective of any instructional program.

The most interesting entry on the list in Table 7.2 involves encountering a lifelike problem. Grant Wiggins (1989) has been a leading proponent of *authentic assessment*, a term coined to reflect assessment focused on lifelike, meaningful, relevant types of student learning. This last category in Table 7.2 offers opportunities to study problems intensively; research issues; and produce solutions, recommendations, proposals, new laws, inventions, policies, and procedures. It is the richest and most fruitful category in terms of genuine learning, but it is also the most difficult to complete. As teachers, we have the least experience and know-how in designing challenging activities that address this category. Nonetheless, the portfolio seems an ideal vehicle toward this end.

If you are interested in more comprehensive information about portfolios, including a fuller range of options and possibilities, some excellent books have been devoted to this topic alone. Glazer and Brown (1993) and Tierney, Carter, and Desai (1991) have written books on portfolio assessment dealing with literacy (reading and writing). A book edited by Belanoff and Dickson (1991) provides a broad perspective on portfolio design and assessment. This book includes contributors from various fields.

TABLE 7.2
Types of Content and Mental Behaviors Suitable for a Portfolio

CONTENT	SPECIFIC CONTENT	MENTAL BEHAVIORS EXHIBITED
Language arts	Reading, writing, speaking, and listening	Critical thinking and creative abilities
Mathematics	Numerals, geometry, statistics and probability, measurement, problem solving	Critical thinking and problem solving abilities
Science	Biological, physical, and earth sciences	Understanding and critical thinking, problem solving and creative abilities
Social studies	History, psychology	Understanding and critical thinking, problem solving and creative abilities
Visual and performing arts	Acting, authoring, musical composition or performance, painting, photography, sculpting, theatrical performance	Creative abilities
Unstructured life encounters requiring integrated use of subject matters above	Economic, diet and nutrition, family and home, government, health, social problems, transportation, world of work	Understanding and critical thinking, problem solving and creative behavior (thinking and production)

Types of Portfolios

Table 7.3 summarizes five types of portfolios. Wolf (1989) suggested the ideal portfolio, while Valencia and Calfee (1991) suggested the other four types.

It should be noted here that tradeoffs exist in the choice of a type of portfolio. The *ideal* portfolio is "ideal" from the standpoint of modeling or displaying good instruction, but it contains no desirable properties that we can measure consistently and report validly. This kind of portfolio is probably good instructionally but does not serve well to document student growth and achievement. The *showcase* portfolio is a mainstay in the visual and performing arts and in some sciences. It will continue to be used in these contexts. In the mainstream of a core curriculum, the showcase portfolio is probably less useful. It is very unstandardized and not likely to lead to good measurement of student learning. The *evaluation* portfolio is

TABLE 7.3
Types of Portfolios

Ideal

The *ideal portfolio* is a low-stakes effort that is probably not used for grading or for school or teacher accountability. Its purpose is to show student growth and self-reflection in learning. This ideal portfolio is intended to help students become effective learners and evaluators of their work. This type of portfolio is probably the friendliest and least threatening. In a class, the completion of this portfolio might be accepted as a precondition for a grade, but not graded. If it is graded, the nonthreatening aspect disappears and the threats to validity discussed in the next section might creep in.

Showcase

The *showcase portfolio* is a more familiar type. It contains a collection of students' best work. Self-selection and self-reflection are essential. This type of portfolio is unlikely to be a good choice for accountability or grading because it is unstandardized and self-reflection is not a typical grading criterion.

Documentation

The *documentation portfolio* is a record of student progress that also includes student self-reflection. This is a somewhat more structured portfolio. Because it shows progress, however, it is unlikely to be useful for grading, accountability, or curriculum assessment. It contains both qualitative and quantitative data, so teacher judgment is an important aspect in evaluating this type of portfolio.

Evaluation

The *evaluation portfolio* is a standardized collection of products, probably coming from the teacher or the school district. Self-selection may be allowed, but this is a very controversial issue, because the comparability of self-selected assignments is difficult to establish. Reckase (1995) asserts that a portfolio ought to have a graded component reflecting student self-reflection. Grading criteria for this kind of portfolio may consist of high-inference behavior and therefore require rating scales, or it may be low-inference and require checklists or simple observation. The evaluation portfolio seems the only one of the four that can be used for grading, teacher or school accountability, district curriculum evaluation, or statewide assessment. However, there is significant evidence to argue that these uses are questionable until technical and logistical problems are solved (Koretz, Stecher, & Klein, 1994).

Class

The *class portfolio* is a class summary of portfolio achievement that contains (1) summary sheets for each student, (2) teachers' comments, and (3) teachers' curricula and instructional plans for accomplishing the student outcomes of the curricula.

the best to be offered for measurement of student learning, but it loses many important qualities of the ideal portfolio. The *class* portfolio appears to be an administrative shortcut that makes use of the portfolio as an evaluation tool a little more feasible.

One important point is that the evaluation portfolio is probably a little bit more than the collection of performance items featured in Chapters 5 and 6. The lofty intent of a portfolio, embodied in the ideal type, is mostly lost with the evaluation portfolio. The seamless instruction, high instructional quality, student–teacher partnership, low-stakes atmosphere, and other good qualities seem to slip away when accountability enters into the equation, as it does with the evaluation portfolio.

Uses of Portfolios

Given the unique composition of the portfolio, how can it be used? Should the portfolio be used as a friendly formative evaluation, giving students guidance so that in the future they can excel on a performance test that measures, under pressure, what they have learned? Should it be used as a test, as part of the criteria for a student grade? Should schools and school districts—or states—use portfolios for accountability?

We have answered these questions to some extent in the previous section. This answer has to do with the choice of a portfolio. But as Valencia and Calfee (1991) contend, it is hard to see a clear-cut example of each portfolio type in practice. If you design a portfolio for your students and want it to be used consistently and validly, you will have to make careful decisions.

Certainly a portfolio can be used as a formative test, helping students understand what they are learning, how well, and what comes next. This is clearly the intent of the ideal portfolio. It is a type of elaborated criterion performance test, but very loosely designed so that scoring and grading may be difficult and hard to defend. So formative evaluation is a strong possible use of the portfolio.

Using a portfolio for grading purposes presents a serious problem, for two reasons. First, only the evaluation portfolio seems a candidate for this purpose. Externally motivated students will place a high value on the grade, so they might be tempted to cheat, to violate the boundaries set up by the teacher, to copy, or to get help that the teacher did not intend. If there is pressure for high grades, students are likely to bend or break the rules. Another wrinkle in the evaluation portfolio is that students are asked to put their reflections as a sort of "Dear Diary" section. How do you grade this? If you grade it, most students will write whatever you expect them to write, and you will get a dishonest result that panders to the teacher. This issue will be treated more at the end of this chapter.

When we use portfolios for class, school, or state accountability measures, the pressure transfers to teachers and school administrators. High-stakes pressures may cause teachers and other school personnel to bend or break the rules or to use questionable practices to boost standardized achievement test scores without resorting to sound instructional practices, as studies have amply shown (Haladyna, Nolen, & Haas, 1991; Smith, 1991).

We can summarize this section on the use of the portfolio as follows:

Possible Use	Comment about Appropriateness
Formative evaluation	Probably the most appropriate use of portfolio, where results are used to guide instruction and give feedback about student learning but *not* to grade students.
Summative evaluation	May be used to grade students but needs to be applied carefully so as not to promote widespread cheating.
Teacher or school accountability	Probably not a good idea because of the temptation to manipulate results to get a good accountability score.
Curriculum evaluation	A good idea because the data one gets will be richer and more faithful to what the curriculum is trying to accomplish (developing student abilities).
High-stakes accountability	Given the problems we have encountered regarding validity and reliability, this is *not* a good use of a portfolio.

The next two sections deal with strengths and weaknesses, pros and cons, and reasons for and against using portfolios for the many purposes identified in this chapter.

Reasons for Using a Portfolio

Allows for Seamless Instruction

The term *seamless instruction* conveys a smooth transition from teaching to testing, so smooth that both teacher and student hardly notice it.

Historically, the criterion-referenced test movement of the 1960s and 1970s was intended to help teachers match their intended student outcomes to test items. This matching gave students a better understanding of the connection between teaching and testing. The antithesis of this matching is the use of standardized achievement tests, typically consisting of fragmented knowledge that was tested without connection to its ultimate use to develop an ability. A standardized test score reflects in a general way student achievement across the student's lifetime, including home and family influences and mental ability.

Criterion-referenced testing did not go far enough. The integration of knowledge and skills to develop higher level thinking abilities was not a strong feature of this approach to teaching and testing. Other writers treated the integration of teaching and testing as standard and desirable features of classroom tests (Cohen, 1987; Nitko, 1989); but, again, cognitive psychology tells us that mental and physical abilities are the sine qua non of teaching.

Getting back to the idea of seamless instruction, students do not see the performance activity as a test, but in a real sense it is a test. Educational reformers view this lack of discrimination between instruction and testing as desirable. This new version of integrating teaching and testing makes instruction and testing seem virtually indistinguishable, hence the term *seamless instruction*.

Promotes Good Instruction of Worthwhile Learning Outcomes

An important feature is that the tasks that make up the portfolio are often criterion behaviors, things that are important to learn. Thus, assigning of worthwhile, meaningful, and relevant learning activities promotes effective learning and instruction. Both teacher and students see the obvious merit of many tasks found in the portfolio. This idea of good instruction relevant to worthwhile learning outcomes is often contrasted with teaching that involves fragmented knowledge and skills, which in sum may lead to ability development but is not well integrated or clearly relevant to ability development. For instance, worksheet drills in grammatical usage, punctuation, and the like help students develop writing skills, but if they never write, the point of all that tedious drill is lost.

Advocates of portfolio use argue it expands the dimensions of learning. They are referring specifically to the heavy emphasis on process in learning, as opposed to simply achieving lower level outcomes that are suggestive of an ability but not exactly what we are trying to develop.

Somewhat Easy to Design

There are five types of portfolio, but the basic design is simple. The portfolio includes a series of correlated performance tasks that differ with respect to the ability being developed. It also captures the broad spectrum of instructional activities over a long period, say a unit, a grading period, or a semester. Chapters 5A and 6 provide most necessary information on how to design specific items for the portfolio, although the portfolio contains more than just performance on items. Several rules or conditions of performance are integrated into the portfolio to provide a guidance system for students and teacher to follow. These rules pertain mainly to collaboration, consultation, and accountability.

Another feature of the portfolio is its durability and reusability. Once we design the portfolio, it can be used time after time, with enhancements or improvements employed periodically to fine-tune it. Japanese teachers call this "polishing the stone," a phrase that refers to the constant improvement of a lesson, unit, or course. The main idea here is that if you adopt, adapt, or create a worthwhile activity for a portfolio, you then may take years to polish it, using it over and over. Over time, you create a very effective tool for teaching and testing.

Stimulates the Development of New Teaching Abilities

Teachers are mostly locked into traditional modes of instruction and testing. The use of the portfolio stimulates teachers to teach differently, to unlock group instruction methods and use a common core of tasks to let students work continually toward a learning target. Teachers change their professional role from the "sage on the stage" to the "guide on the side." Cicmanec and Viechnicki (1994) claim that this teacher development is an important outcome of portfolio use, but they also admit that many problems exist that are currently unresolved. One problem is that inexperienced teachers are reluctant to use portfolios because of problems they have encountered of extra work and confusion over assignments. As with any innovation, these difficulties are natural and can be alleviated through the use of effective inservice training, constant monitoring, and patience.

Is Directly Observable

Because student portfolios reflect exactly what students are supposed to learn, we consider portfolios to be authentic in the sense that they are real, not indirect, artificial, or contrived. This directness or authenticity is a primary feature of what educational reformers, like Wiggins (1989, 1993), suggest. A criticism of this view, however, is that few school activities are free of the contamination of artificiality that comes with any classroom assignment. What is probably intended by educational reformers is that things that we do and put in a portfolio should be things that are well worth doing in themselves. The merit of each activity should be apparent to students, their parents, and the teacher.

Documents What Has Been Taught (Opportunity-to-Learn)

Accountability in education has been defined as the transfer of information between interested parties to make decisions about policies, programs, or alloca-tion of resources. Students are in the accountability business. They are held responsible for their accomplishments. One of the goals of a portfolio is to develop student self-responsibility. At the same time, teachers are accountable for seeing that students receive instruction at the appropriate developmental point and that sufficient opportunities exist for developing abilities. In the fed-eral government's Goals 2000, one standard receiving considerable attention is known as opportunity-to-learn (Porter, 1995). As a tool for accountability, this standard implies that students must receive instruction on certain content pre-ceding formal testing. Portfolios not only show how certain school-related abili-ties are being developed, but also show the kind of instruction students have received. Thus, the portfolio represents exactly what each teacher has taught. So both teacher and student can be held accountable—the teacher for teaching, and the student for learning.

Increases Communication among Students, Parents, and Teachers

An age-old concern of teachers and parents is effective communication between school and home. The portfolio not only represents something worthwhile to do, but the use of the portfolio may actually increase communication among these three parties (Cicmanec & Viechnicki, 1994). A strong feature of recent books on portfolio assessment is the conferencing that goes on among parents, students, and the teacher (see Glazer & Brown, 1993).

Provides a Developmental Perspective

Another attractive feature of the portfolio is that the teacher/judge can view a stu-dent's development over a long period of time, thus getting snapshots of the child's developing ability. This perspective gives a truer indication of where the student started and where the student is now regarding this developing ability. No single test can give you this perspective because a test occurs at a single point in time in the developmental span.

Promotes Worthwhile Student Learning Outcomes

Much justifiable criticism has been heaped on testing strategies that are tangential or remotely related to worthwhile learning outcomes. For instance, testing for spelling and grammar on a multiple-choice test may be defended as developing several writing skills important to writing, but a main objective of any language arts program is the development of students' descriptive, persuasive, expository, narrative, and imaginative writing abilities (Roid, 1994).

The portfolio can reflect writing ability being developed instead of these micro-skills that may only *predict* how well one writes instead of showing how well one *actually* writes. This is not to say that micro-skills as not important, only to assert that the macro-ability is the reason that the micro-skills are being learned.

Limitations of Portfolios

Now that I have reviewed some claims and supporting rationale for portfolios, I will examine some criticism.

Best Effort or Typical Work

Whose work is this? We encourage consultation and sometimes collaboration both in school and in life. It is hardly believable that anyone does not consult someone else along the way to ask: How am I doing? We encourage students to seek help and learn from others. But eventually, the portfolio must represent the student's own work. Responsibility for the work should rest with the student. How do we draw the fine line between what's "mine" and what's "ours"? There is no easy answer. The portfolio is hardly likely to represent the typical work of students, especially if it is tied to the teacher's grading policy. The question will always arise: Did the student really do this work?

Honesty

We may not want to admit it, but students will cheat at school. The *Arizona Republic* newspaper (Wednesday, March 29, 1995) reports the findings from *Who's Who among American High School Students* survey of 3,177 students, of whom 89 percent say cheating is common in their school and 78 percent say they have cheated, with copying someone else's homework being most common. Of those who cheated, 93 percent were not caught.

Any system of teaching that encourages or promotes cheating is probably not a good system. Competitive normal-curve grading forces the class to compete for grades, which promotes anxiety and prompts students to wish the worst for others because someone else's misfortune is their gain. For the portfolio to work as a teaching and testing device, it has to be an honest effort. If 100 percent of the grade is based on the portfolio, students may be tempted to cheat.

If the school or district is being evaluated on the basis of student performance on the portfolio, will the teacher be honest in presenting student work? Past research and experience suggest that less than honest reporting will result. A study by Haas, Haladyna, and Nolen (1991) reported voluntary comments from nearly four hundred teachers regarding the misuse of test results and nonstandard test preparation practices. Although the teachers hated the misuse of these tests, many reported spending excessive amounts of time preparing their students or taking shortcuts to ensure high scores. Some actually confessed to cheating. If high-stakes accountability is used with portfolios, this same kind of behavior is likely.

Efficiency

Portfolios are very time-consuming to score. There are no shortcuts. The teacher must spend a large amount of nonclassroom time reading the portfolio. Not only must the teacher read the portfolio, but because of the need to score consistently and objectively, another content expert should also read and evaluate the portfolio (and that content expert should be another teacher). Reckase (1995) estimates that the cost of scoring a portfolio, which might be at least twenty-five pages long, ranges from $10.00 to $17.50. This is a significant limitation. Policymakers in states and in school districts need to figure out if the cost is worth the outcome. Teachers are unlikely to take on the burden of scoring portfolios in addition to their present duties. School leaders such as principals also have to figure out ways to make portfolio use and scoring feasible in their school.

Given the many good qualities of portfolios, perhaps the investment of time and effort is worth it. Students will appreciate the attention they receive when their portfolios are read and comments are made regarding their work. Parents appreciate portfolio work as well because it offers a realistic picture of what students are learning, as opposed to test scores, which provide a useful summary but a less clear picture of actual learning.

Storage and Student Records

Student records have always posed a problem. In the old days, the cumulative file followed the student through the elementary grades. You couldn't stuff too many examples of student work in this file without making it too cumbersome and unmanageable. With student portfolios in reading, writing, mathematics, and science, we would need a warehouse for student records.

Fortunately, improvements in personal computers and the expanded storage and retrieval capacities of the newest ones make scanning student work into computer files almost manageable. Software developers have invented systems that record student records and make them instantly available to teachers. Thus, one limitation of portfolios may be reasonably solved, but the availability of such information does not necessarily translate into ease of use by a teacher wishing to review her or his class for the new year. Unless the results of portfolios are summarized, as in a test score, perhaps their usefulness will be limited despite overcoming the storage problem.

Lack of Objectivity (Interrater Consistency)

Objectivity has to do with scoring. If two scorers typically get the same result using the same scoring guides, then we consider the scoring to be objective. Any kind of high-inference scoring is not objective. A good remedy with subjective scoring is to make the scoring guide so clear that two raters (judges) will get about the same result. Another remedy is effective training of scorers with validation. Collectively, consistent scoring leads to more reliable results. Analyses and studies have been reported recently attesting to the inadequacy of scoring in this area (Koretz et al., 1994; Reckase, 1995).

This problem can be overcome by having at least two scorers read every portfolio and having these scorers trained and validated in the use of the scoring system.

Reliability

As just mentioned, reliability depends on consistent, objective scoring, but it also depends on other factors, such as the number of items scored, the variability of results, and the relationship among items. Interitem correlations among scores should be high. Reliability is a property of test scores, not of tests. With the portfolio, the resulting evaluation by a teacher or other content expert is subject to the standard of reliability. In one large study of the Vermont Statewide Assessment using portfolios, many difficulties were encountered, not the least of which was chronic low reliability (Koretz et al., 1994). This is a serious problem with the use of portfolios.

Reckase (1995) maintains that to achieve satisfactory reliability, the portfolio should be scored in sections, using rating scales that range significantly—for instance, a seven-point rating scale. If scoring consistency can be achieved and bias eliminated, reliability of student portfolio scores might be adequate for purposes of accountability and curriculum and instructional evaluation.

Group scores are much more reliable than individual scores. If you are using individual scores for pass/fail decisions, such as for high school graduation, reliability may be too low. But if a class score is developed for evaluation of the program, the class score is likely to be reliable even though the individual scores constituting that class score may be less reliable.

Bias

In Chapter 5B, we learned that scoring bias is a directional error for subgroups of students when we use a rating scale. In other words, some students could be systematically downgraded or upgraded, while other students do not receive the same biased treatment. It all depends on who scores your portfolio. Other forms of bias exist and weaken scoring. Chapter 5B discussed these biases. Because a portfolio is essentially a battery of performance items supplemented with evidence of student reflection, it is subject to the same threats as the performance items discussed in Chapter 5B.

Summary

Given this discussion of the strengths and limitations of portfolio, you can see that you must carefully evaluate the pros and cons of the portfolio before embarking on their use, because it is a major commitment. Given the strong arguments in favor of the portfolio, it seems that the use of portfolios is favored over discrete assignments and traditional types of testing. But a teacher has to be very judicious in not letting the portfolio become so important that it impels students to tamper with its integrity. When it comes to accountability at the class, school, or state levels, enough questions have been raised and left unanswered regarding validity and reliability, that it seems unwise to use a portfolio for anything *but* formative student evaluation and as one of the criteria for grading. Therefore, the portfolio will be an increasingly important teaching and evaluation tool in the classroom, but it should be used very cautiously for high-stakes testing.

How to Design a Portfolio for the Classroom

This section focuses on designing the student portfolio. In view of the discussion of types of portfolios earlier in this chapter, I will focus on the evaluation portfolio. Because writing portfolios are the most often used, best developed, and familiar, we will work through the development of a writing portfolio. Experts on portfolios may desire more unstructured portfolios. As Wolf (1989) bluntly puts it: "Portfolios are messy" (p. 37). But in the context of designing test items to reflect student learning, I take the position that a structured approach will lead to a more satisfactory result that will stand up to rigorous standards for validity and reliability. The evaluation portfolio must have the same common elements as any test; it should not be "messy."

The Design of an Ideal Evaluation Portfolio

The steps for designing an ideal evaluation portfolio are familiar to readers of previous chapters:

1. Identify the learner outcomes desired. Generally speaking, this will be a student ability, such as reading, writing, or mathematical problem solving. You might identify where along the continuum the student is and where you want the student to go. Roid (1994) identifies five types of writing activities: descriptive, persuasive, expository, narrative, and imaginative. You might identify six analytic traits of concern in the development of writing ability: ideas, organization, voice, word choice, sentence fluency, and conventions (e.g., spelling, grammar, capitalization, punctuation). You also might identify the developmental level of the student, as Purves (1993) did using three levels: basic, proficient, and advanced.

2. Determine the content areas to be covered. From this three-dimensional array above (five types of writing, six analytical traits, and three developmental levels), you can specify what the portfolio is supposed to accomplish. This might resemble a test blueprint and look like Table 7.4.

3. Provide a place for student self-reflection, analysis, and growth. This is a critical part of the portfolio contents. Students are acting as autobiographers, describing how they have improved, their insights into learning, where they are going. A good self-reflection should be something like a good Barbara Walters' interview: It should contain specific questions to help students reflect. This is a rare opportunity for students to express their personal views about learning. Remember that you need to gain students' confidence and trust to express their true feelings about learning. Thus, grading the self-reflection is a questionable practice. The next section deals with an acceptable way to score this part, if you want to do so.

4. Provide a schedule for completion. Students need to have a specific timeline and deadline for the portfolio. A good idea is to have a timeline for the completion of specific aspects. Procrastinators will let everything slide until the end. Checkpoints in the timeline allow teachers and parents glimpses into the process, but without appearing too heavy-handed or interfering. Deadlines should be estab-

TABLE 7.4
A Blueprint for a Student Evaluation Portfolio

	IDEAS	ORGANIZATION	VOICE	WORD CHOICE	CONVENTIONS
Descriptive	4	3	2	4	3
Persuasive	10	3	2	4	3
Expository	4	3	2	4	3
Narrative	6	3	6	4	3
Imaginative	8	3	6	4	3

lished; but if a mastery approach is used, then flexibility is needed with respect to any deadline, as students should have extra time for revision and polishing.

5. *Provide for choices in assignments.* This is a controversial issue in testing. With choice come differences in performance that may happen because a student chose an easy or a hard assignment (Roid, 1994). Testing experts will recommend against choice among items or activities (Wainer, Wang, & Thissen, 1994), but curriculum and instruction experts will insist on it (Wiggins, 1993). You will have to decide to use a structured, unmessy approach and lose some of the advantage in student selection, or to use a more unstructured approach and follow Wolf's predilection for a more collegial and collaborative arrangement between student and teacher.

6. *State how the portfolio should be created.* Should a table of contents be provided? Yes, because it provides an advance organizer for the teacher/evaluator. Yes, because it also provides a good overview for the student of what the portfolio is trying to accomplish.

Table 7.5 provides a template for designing an evaluation portfolio that might be used by the teacher, with a more detailed version given to the student. Chronic scoring problems occur with poor interrater consistency, bias, and reliability in scoring performance tests and portfolios. Templates for high-inference and low-inference items can be found in Tables 5A.2 and 6.3. These templates can help you design specific items for the evaluation portfolio.

TABLE 7.5
A Template for Designing a Student Evaluation Portfolio

Table of contents:	This is a one-page listing of the products included.
Student's reflective letter:	This section contains the student's autobiographical reflections on learning, frustrations, successes, motivations, and other insights. Indicate a maximum length for this letter.
Specific tasks to be included:	This section contains the products to be evaluated in the order listed in the table of contents. Determine if students choose examples or if you have a specific list of what you expect. Refer to Tables 5A2 and 6.3 for specific advice on items requiring high and low inferences.
Limit for number of pages:	How many pages long is this portfolio?
Consultation:	Were students allowed or encouraged to consult with others?
Collaboration:	Was editorial assistance obtained? Is this O.K.?
Appendix:	Is an appendix required that may contain ancillary material, such as preliminary drafts?
Grading criteria:	Ratings scales and/or checklists are included for each object, with the point value applied to the student grade. This section should inform the student of exactly how the portfolio connects to the student grade, specifying, if points are assigned, how every student performance is evaluated in terms of points. Refer to Table 5B.6 for information on systematically constructing rating scales.

Scoring the Evaluation Portfolio

This section is problematic because the technology for scoring portfolios is so new and experimental. Recent experiences in Kentucky and Vermont with statewide testing programs featuring portfolios have provided some negative results with scoring. With the Vermont portfolio, Koretz et al. (1994) reported low reliability. Kentucky's experiments with statewide portfolios found local teacher bias to be considerable in scoring. External auditors scored the same portfolios and discovered systematic discrepancies indicating leniency on the teachers' part. Because of this bias, the state reevaluated its portfolio scoring process and eliminated intradistrict scoring.

In part, these problems were due to the inexperience of the teachers involved in this project. Public accountability was also a factor, as was discussed earlier in this chapter. If teachers know they are going to be evaluated, then their judgments are likely to be influenced by this fact. These statewide assessments have told us that schools and teachers mostly favor using portfolios, but the scoring process is still fraught with hazards that limit the usefulness of results thus far.

You need to develop a strategy to overcome these limitations. You know that scoring will be time-consuming and expensive and that teachers and other judges will need to be well trained and experienced. To ignore these technical problems invites trouble. If test scores are used to make decisions affecting students, such as pass/fail, or affecting teachers' future employment, litigation may be initiated and school personnel may be in an indefensible position with respect to how the portfolio results were used.

We will review several basic approaches to scoring portfolios, and then focus on one method that is best suited for measuring student behavior while still providing some dependability.

Holistic Scoring

A holistic rating scale has not been substantially supported in this book as a sound basis for scoring performance tests, with the portfolio being considered a special case of a performance test. Thus, the holistic rating scale is not recommended here. The primary reason is that if a single rating scale is used to score a portfolio, the limited range of scores is not likely to be very dependable (Reckase, 1995). Another problem is that a holistic rating scale is used with student products that may vary according to personal choice; the rating scale does not automatically standardize results. Some students may choose more challenging material or tasks than other students do. Although this is true with other approaches, too, it is less of a problem there. The sole argument favoring a holistic scale is that you may be concerned with the wholeness of writing or some similar ability. Given the preponderance of arguments against the holistic scale, it is easy to see why it can't be recommended here.

Analytical Scoring

Recalling from Chapter 5B, the analytical scales provide a profile of important characteristics of performance. For instance, if we were scoring writing samples, we might be interested in analytic traits, as shown in Table 5B.3. Analytical scoring has the advantage of producing more variation in scores and, more likely, higher reliability. Thus, you can have more confidence in the student result and have a more defensible result. Another advantage is that the analytical traits provide a diagnosis of strengths and weaknesses in the ability being tested.

Reliability

Reckase (1995) provides a thoughtful and useful analysis of reliability of portfolio scores. To get a sufficient reliability level (.80 on a scale from .00 to 1.00), he estimates that roughly seven scorable categories are needed. If the quality of scoring is very high, the number of scorable categories might be reduced to five. As mentioned earlier in this chapter, the cost of such a lengthy scoring process is likely to be very high, between $10 and $20 per test. But as also mentioned earlier, if the portfolio is viewed as a significant achievement of each student and if the use of the portfolio results is important for placement, future instruction, and grading, then this cost and effort may be justified.

A Scoring Guide

Table 7.6 presents a scoring guide that organizes the aspects of the evaluation portfolio in summary form. The total portfolio is worth 100 points, and the 100 points can be used as part of the criteria in a grading policy. The first two items in the scoring guide contain essential elements that are nongraded, although points are assigned for their completion. The same is true for the appendix. You simply want the information, but it is nongraded. Six generic items are provided, following Reckase's recommendation for scorable units. A minimum of six items, together with the three observations (table of contents, self-reflection, and appendix), should constitute enough scoring categories to provide a reliable index of achievement. The analytical rating scales might contain five points and reflect the developmental levels desired in teaching abilities, such as writing. The most confusing part of the scoring is that the five-point rating scales do not conveniently transform into points assigned, because you are likely to vary the weight assigned to each item, and the weights are not multiples of five.

The self-reflection section is not evaluated but is merely acknowledged. Students are not required to write a "good" reflection but to take the opportunity to reflect on their learning style and strategy and what they did to succeed. If they complete the reflection, this hypothetical scoring system provides student point credit toward a grade. The premium is on doing the self-reflection, not on the quality of the effort.

The scoring guide in Table 7.6 is consistent with good measurement practice and gives you the opportunity to structure the portfolio so that a student can produce a high-quality effort of work consistent with your standards. The scoring is objective with respect to the table of contents, self-reflection, and appendix, but will require extensive work with respect to the six items.

TABLE 7.6
Hypothetical Scoring Guide for Writing Portfolio

ACTIVITY/ ASSIGNMENT	POSSIBLE POINTS	RATING[a] OR CHECKLIST	POINTS EARNED
Table of contents	10	Yes ☐ No ☐	
Self-reflection	10	Yes ☐ No ☐	
Item 1	12	1 . . . 5	
Item 2	22	1 . . . 5	
Item 3	8	1 . . . 5	
Item 4	20	1 . . . 5	
Item 5	8	1 . . . 5	
Item 6	5	1 . . . 5	
Appendix: Showing rough drafts	5	Yes ☐ No ☐	
	100		

[a]Based on a series of five-point analytical rating scales designed for each of the six specific tasks. Refer to Chapter 5B for information on the design of these scales. The value of each rating-scale point should be converted to the points possible in a consistent manner. For instance, a five-point rating scale to judge item 2 would require that each rating-scale point be worth 4.2 points. This straightforward arithmetic conversion reflects that fact that each item has a different weight, as determined by you, the teacher.

0	1	2	3	4	5
0	4.4	8.8	13.2	17.6	22

Students should always know the value of each item. In fact, they should have the scoring guide when they receive their portfolio assignment.

Summary

In this chapter you have read about the five types of portfolio and how portfolio results should and should not be used. The strengths and limitations of the portfolio were discussed. Although using the portfolio poses many problems, it may be the most significant and controversial aspect of teaching and testing today. For the many reasons given in Chapters 5 and 6 and in this chapter, the portfolio is likely to be a mainstay in classrooms at all levels, including professional, business, and military training. Portfolio design can reach a high level of expertise, and with fine tuning we can expect to use a portfolio design repeatedly over many years. The template in Table 7.5 helps you design a portfolio, but considerable creativity is also needed. There are major problems in scoring the results of a portfolio. Not only do we face problems with interrater consistency, but there is bias as well. The cost of scoring portfolios may be higher than sponsors want to support, and short-cuts lead to low reliability and undependable results that cannot be used for high-stakes purposes. The most realistic position to take here is to evaluate the importance of the portfolio versus its cost. If it is done correctly, it can be used to drive instruction appropriately, provide evidence of opportunity to learn, and pro-vide scores that are dependable enough to assign grades, place students for instruction, evaluate curriculum, evaluate the instructional program, evaluate teaching, and give state or national policymakers information about how the pub-lic's resources are being spent to educate students. Table 7.6 provides a hypotheti-cal scoring guide. The portfolio should continue to increase in use, but at the same time teachers will improve their knowledge, skills, and ability to design and use portfolios to address more effectively the development of school-based abilities.

References

Belanoff, P., & Dickson, M. (Eds.) (1991). *Portfolios: Process and product.* Portsmouth, NH: Boynton/Cook.

Cicmanec, K. M., & Viechnicki, K. J. (1994). Assessing mathematical skills through portfo-lios: Validating the claims from existing literature. *Educational Assessment, 1,* 167–178.

Cohen, S. A. (1987). Instructional alignment: Searching for the magic bullet. *Educational Researcher, 16,* 16–20.

Gearhart, M., & Herman, J. (1995). Portfolio assessment: Whose work is it? Issues in the use of classroom assignments for accountability. *Evaluation Comment.* Los Angeles: UCLA's Center for the Study of Evaluation and The National Center for Research on Evaluation, Standards, and Student Testing.

Glazer, S. M., & Brown, P. D. (1993). *Portfolios and beyond: Collaborative assessment in reading and writing.* Norwood, MA: Christopher-Gordon.

Haas, N. S., Haladyna, T. M., & Nolen, S. B. (1991). *War stories from the trenches.* Phoenix: Arizona State University West.

Haladyna, T. M., Nolen, S. B., & Haas, N. S. (1991). Raising standardized achievement test scores and the origins of test score pollution. *Educational Researcher, 20,* 2–7.

Koretz, D., Stecher, B. M., & Klein, S. P. (1994). The Vermont Portfolio Assessment Project: Findings and implications. *Educational Measurement: Issues and Practices, 13,* 5–6.

Nitko, A. J. (1989). Designing tests that are integrated with instruction. In R. L. Linn (Ed.), *Educational Measurement* (3rd ed., pp. 447–474).

Nolen, S. B., Haladyna, T. M., & Haas, N. S. (1992). Uses and abuses of achievement test scores. *Educational Measurement: Issues and Practices, 11,* 9–15.

Porter, A. (1995). The use and misuse of opportunity-to-learn standards. *Educational Researcher, 24*, 21–27.

Purves, A. (1993). Setting standards in the language arts and literature classroom and the implications for portfolio assessment. *Educational Assessment, 1*, 175–200.

Reckase, M. D. (1995). Portfolio assessment: A theoretical estimate of score reliability. *Educational Measurement: Issues and Practices, 14*, 12–14, 31.

Roid, G. H. (1994). Patterns of writing skills derived from cluster analysis of direct-writing assessment. *Applied Measurement in Education, 7*, 159–170.

Smith, M. L. (1991). Put to the test: The effects of external testing on teachers. *Educational Researcher, 20*, 8–11.

Tierney, R. J., Carter, M. A., & Desai, L. E. (1991). *Portfolio assessment in the reading–writing classroom.* Norwood, MA: Christopher-Gordon.

Valencia, S., & Calfee, R. (1991). The development and use of literacy portfolios for students. *Applied Measurement in Education, 4*, 333–346.

Wainer, H., Wang, X.-B., & Thissen, D. (1994). How well can we compare scores on test forms that are constructed by examinee choice? *Journal of Educational Measurement, 31*, 183–199.

Wiggins, G. (1989). Teaching to the (authentic) test. *Educational Leadership, 76*, 41–47.

Wiggins, G. (1993). *Assessing student performance: Exploring the purpose and limits of testing.* San Francisco: Jossey-Bass.

Wolf, D. (1989). Portfolio assessment: Sampling student work. *Educational Leadership, 46*, 35–39.

8 Affective Survey Formats

THIS CHAPTER CONCENTRATES ON THE DEVELOPMENT AND USE OF TEST items for surveys of affective aspects of schooling. Many worthwhile affective student outcomes are being developed in the schools, including attitude toward school and subject matters, perceived importance or relevance of each subject matter, fatalism (locus of control), self-esteem, and class and school climate (learning environment). Not only are those outcomes important in themselves, but they also contribute to making learning more effective. But we seldom survey students systematically to learn about the affective goals we hope they achieve. In this chapter we will study the following:

- What a student survey is
- A framework for understanding affective outcomes
- Types of affective outcomes you may want your students to develop
- Questioning strategies and item formats
- Response formats
- Ways of scoring and reporting results

What Is a Student Survey?

The student survey is a periodic assessment to determine affective conditions in a class, school, or school district. It is anonymous, nongraded, and nonthreatening to students. Yet it can provide useful information about the progress a class, school, or district is making toward affective goals or on the presence of factors that affect the achievement of cognitive and psychomotor goals. In some instances, this survey can assess factors that may affect still other factors that affect student learning, such as the quality of instruction. This survey often takes only a few minutes yet can provide dependable information about the entire class, school, or district.

Therefore, I recommend that, as a class, school, or district policy, such surveys be given annually or several times a year and that the data from these surveys be used to evaluate instruction programs and how students are doing with respect to the affective goals you have established. For instance, if you believe that attitudes toward social studies are not good, then a school or district goal might be to improve these attitudes. The student survey can document whether attitude has really improved collectively for a class or school.

A Framework for Understanding Affective Outcomes

Educational theorists and other educational thinkers and researchers have developed frameworks (working models) that suggest ways to organize schools for learning. Start with outcomes, what you want students to do when you are finished with them, and with causes, the forces that affect these outcomes. You can conceptualize schooling as consisting of these three entities:

What cognitive, affective, and psychomotor outcomes do you expect of students as a result of schooling?	What factors exist in schools that cause students to achieve these outcomes? These are factors over which teachers and administrators have control.	What factors exist outside of school that influence student attainment? These are factors over which teachers have no control.

Table 8.1 provides a framework of the causes of cognitive, affective, and psychomotor outcomes. This framework may seem simplistic and may overlook many other causes that you can identify. But the framework identifies the main factors that I think influence the cognitive, affective, and psychomotor outcomes of schooling. Any assessment of what is happening in the school should consider the role that external as well as internal forces play in how well schools succeed in terms of student outcomes. These external forces may provide advantages or pose handicaps to achieving these cognitive, affective, and psychomotor outcomes.

The two sources mentioned are mental ability and social capital. Mental ability (intelligence) is a primary predictor of test performance in our schools. Much has been written about the dominance of this factor in developing student abilities. Students' rate of success is greatly affected by mental ability. This is not to make excuses for teachers and students, but to recognize that the road is steeper for some students and expectations should be geared appropriately. The second source is the concept introduced by James Coleman, a renowned sociologist, who describes the material and social influence of home, family, and neighborhood on student development. Coleman believes that social capital is declining in the United States and that, if social capital is too low, no amount of schooling will make a difference. These factors exist before a student comes to school and represent either an asset or a liability to learning. Teachers have an opportunity to understand these powerful forces that influence student achievement and to place their efforts to teach in this context.

For example, consider the softball coach in the film *The Bad News Bears*, who inherits a fumbling group of unmotivated softball players. Should the coach be

TABLE 8.1
A Framework for Thinking about the Role of Affective Goals in Teaching

STUDENT OUTCOMES	INTERNAL INFLUENCES	EXTERNAL INFLUENCES
Cognitive		
Knowledge	Attitude	Social capital
Skills	Importance	Mental ability
Abilities	Locus of control/fatalism	
	Self-esteem	
	Self-confidence	
	Class climate	
	Quality of teaching	
	Quantity of teaching	
Affective		
Attitude	Attitude	Social capital
Importance of subject matters	Importance	Mental ability
Locus of control (fatalism)	Locus of control/fatalism	
Self-confidence	Self-esteem	
	Self-confidence	
	Class climate	
	Quality of teaching	
	Quantity of teaching	
Psychomotor		
Good nutritional practices	Attitude	Social capital
Good health habits	Self-concept	Mental ability
Physical skills and abilities	Self-confidence	
Physical well-being/wellness	Motivation	
	Class climate	
	Quality of teaching	
	Quantity of teaching	

evaluated in terms of the team's success in relation to other teams or in terms of the talent at the start? Should students be measured against the rest or in terms of their own potential, given the raw material with which they have to work?

A presumption here is that you must always consider the context in which you work when you measure success. In a small class of children with severe mental handicaps, an effective teacher may succeed in teaching only a few life skills in an entire year, while another equally skilled teacher may take a group of academically talented students through considerable achievement milestones. Neither teacher should be compared to the other in terms of student outcomes because one has a tremendous natural advantage over the other.

This chapter focuses on several affective outcomes and on class climate. As noted in the framework in Table 8.1, the affective outcomes are desirable in themselves but also are internal forces that affect cognitive and psychomotor outcomes. In Chapter 1, I said that cognitive student outcomes were the paramount concern of schools, but I also realize the potency of affective student outcomes. This chapter focuses on developing student surveys that measure affective behaviors.

Who and What Get Surveyed?

This chapter is aimed mainly at surveys of students. Of course, you can ask teachers the same questions or similar ones. Parents can be surveyed, too. Most school districts like to survey everyone involved, because the information gathered may help school board members and other decision makers make good policies and allocate resources wisely. Thus, although this entire chapter is devoted to surveying students, the techniques discussed apply to surveys of teachers and parents as well.

Positive Affective Outcomes to Develop or Maintain

This section assumes that you are interested in developing and measuring the following affective traits in your students:

- Attitude toward school and its subject matters
- Importance of school and its subject matters
- Fatalism/locus of control
- Self-esteem
- Class climate (learning environment)

There are other affective constructs to consider as well. But, as discussed in Chapter 2 with cognitive abilities and other types of higher level thinking, some affective traits are not well defined, researched, or measured. I will forgo these and will concentrate on those mentioned in this chapter simply because they have been measured successfully.

School and Subject-Matter Attitudes

Attitude is an emotional disposition toward or against an object or person. In his classic monograph on student attitude, Robert Mager (1968) stated that the likelihood of a student putting knowledge, skills, and abilities to work in the future depends on her or his attitude toward that subject. While Mager's observation may be too simplistic (because some students succeed despite a poor attitude), most teachers believe in developing positive student attitudes. Certainly the development of negative attitudes should not be tolerated.

This simple definition of *attitude* is applied to school and its subject matters: language arts (reading, writing, speaking, listening); mathematics; science; social studies (history, political science, psychology, anthropology); physical education; and the visual and performing arts. But it could apply to other subject matters found in high school, college, or specialized training. Attitude toward the school itself can also be surveyed. Studies of student attitude can show interesting patterns that inform schools and teachers about their success. For example, Figure 8.1 shows some of the trends we observed in a large survey for an entire state that revealed very interesting patterns (Haladyna & Thomas, 1979b). Class or school level analyses can be done to track how a group of students are doing relative to a large population. The idea is to develop targets for schools or districts and to assess periodically to determine if attitude is improving or not. Systematic surveys of student attitude can show to some extent how a district, school, or class is achieving a goal to improve student attitude. Boy–girl differences were found at many levels, trends were observed across grade levels, and differences were observed among subject matters. Moreover, attitudes toward specific subject matters were generally higher than attitude toward the institution of school itself. In other words, something within schools created an unfavorable attitude toward "school," while students still rated the school's subject matters consistently higher than the school attitude.

Through the use of the questioning strategies illustrated in this chapter, attitudes can be reliably and inexpensively measured and can be used to evaluate class, school, and school district effectiveness with validity.

Importance of School and Its Subject Matters

Another dimension to consider in a systematic survey of students on a periodic basis is the importance of a subject matter. Generally speaking, a single question with a series of five graded categories is sufficient:

FIGURE 8.1

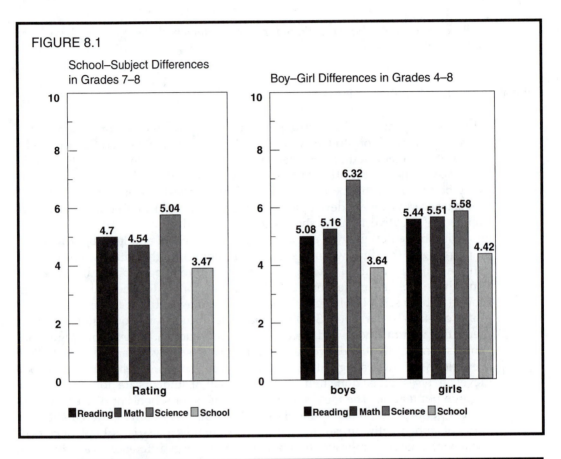

School–Subject Differences
in Grades 7–8

Boy–Girl Differences in Grades 4–8

How important is _____ in your future work?
How important is _____ after you graduate from school?

   a. Very important
   b. Important
   c. Neither important nor unimportant
   d. Unimportant
   e. Very unimportant

OR

You might use the rating scale: strongly agree . . . strongly disagree

_____ is an important school subject.
_____ has no usefulness in life.
_____ will help me in life when I have finished school.
_____ is a worthwhile and necessary subject.

Referring again to Mager (1968), who cited noted educational psychologist Jerome Bruner (1960), learning is for the future. What students learn should be important (relevant) for their future. Through their home and school experiences, students form impressions about the importance of various subject matters. The routine use of student surveys can find out how *important, useful,* or *relevant* each subject matter is to the student. To the extent that teachers try to help students to develop various abilities, such surveys provide indicators about their success. Getting information about the relative importance of what you teach is another element in this affective domain.

For example, we found that student attitude toward social studies was very negative and declined at the higher grade levels. Very few classrooms surveyed had positive perceptions of the value of social studies. Thus, teachers might focus on ways to make social studies more relevant to students, and thereby earn higher ratings on these student surveys.

Locus of Control (Fatalism)

The term *locus of control* comes from psychology and is less familiar to educators. This dimension of student behavior addresses the extent to which each student controls her or his life. Low locus of control refers to children who think that they have little control or influence over events in their life. In an effective school or classroom, students feel that whatever happens, they are responsible for their own success or failure.

The term *fatalism* captures a sense of futility, the feeling that "no matter what I do, I will fail." Successful teachers engender the opposite of fatalism. In other words, the student, not the teacher, should determine each student's success or failure in school. We have found fatalism to be a powerful factor in the affective domain and in our studies of elementary school children (Haladyna, Olsen, & Shaughnessy, 1982, 1983; Haladyna, Shaughnessy, & Redsun, 1982). Teachers and schools can do much to affect how students feel about their ability to affect their futures. The current term used to describe this feeling is *empowerment*. In the ideal classroom situation, students develop self-responsibility. The measurement of locus of control/fatalism is suggested in items like the following:

I am not the type to do well in _____. (−)
Luck determines how well I do in _____. (−)
No matter what I do, I get the same grade in this class. (−)
Most students are luckier than me in _____. (−)
I know what I can do to be successful in _____. (+)
I usually do well in _____ when I try. (+)
In this class, we can do as well as we want to. (+)
I am in control of my destiny in this class. (+)

Items should be balanced positively and negatively, like these. These items should be mixed with other items to make the measurement of each trait less obvious to the students.

As teachers improve the learning environment, provide more options and opportunities for students to succeed, and are sharper in their instruction and testing, class fatalism should decline over a school year. Because fatalism can be reliably measured, your design of a fatalism variable can be very helpful in tracking how your teaching results in a change in the class's or school's perception of control over student outcomes.

Academic Self-Esteem

Academic self-esteem is a general predisposition toward oneself and affects how students view themselves in the context of school. One of the most widely used standardized measures of self-esteem, developed by Coopersmith (1967), consists of such aspects as (1) student initiative, (2) social attention, (3) success/failure, (4) social attraction, and (5) self-confidence.

A general hypothesis is that students with positive self-esteem will do better in school. To the extent that you can increase a student's self-esteem, that student will work harder, interact appropriately with others, deal with success and failure in school, accept criticism well, have positive interactions with other students, and be willing to share work and learn confidently. Even though critics of self-esteem building make many valid points, they do admit the existence of an association between self-esteem and school achievement (Kohn, 1994).

What are the criticisms of self-esteem? A major criticism is that educators overemphasize self-esteem to the point of public ridicule. Another criticism is that self-esteem, like many desirable outcomes in education, is not well defined. Another criticism is that some parents, particularly those with strong political or religious beliefs, feel that measuring self-esteem is intrusive and inappropriate. Teachers in some districts will need to be cautious about collecting these kinds of data in the classroom. In many locales, special permission must be obtained through a human subjects committee that determines if such data gathering is proper.

In general, the systematic surveying of student self-esteem at the class, grade, or school level seems appropri-

> I can get good grades in . . . (+)
>
> . . . doesn't scare me at all. (+)
>
> I am sure I can learn . . . (+)
>
> I do as much work as possible in . . . (+)
>
> The other kids like what I say in . . . (+)
>
> Teacher likes the work I do in . . . (+)
>
> Other students will talk to me in . . . (+)
>
> When the teacher criticizes me, it helps me learn. (+)
>
> I work well with other students. (+)
>
> I like to work with other students. (+)
>
> I have good ideas in . . . (+)

ate. Successful instructional programs should either improve self-esteem or, at least, not damage self-esteem. You can use a standardized instrument, like the Coopersmith, or you can create a home-grown version. The items on the previous page try to capture some elements of self-esteem. These items refer to a specific subject matter. All of the items are positively worded but could be revised to be negative. Remember to keep a balance between positively and negatively worded items in a survey.

Class Climate

Several well-developed environment scales are commercially available, including the Learning Environment Inventory (Fraser, Anderson, & Walberg, 1982) and the Classroom Environment Scales (Moos & Trickett, 1974). If you want to design your own scales, you can either use some of the dimensions discussed in this section and adopt or adapt items suggested, or develop your own scales and items (see Table 8.2).

Two dimensions of class climate that you might consider are *social/psychological* and *management/organization*. Each will be briefly discussed, and the aspects of each will be identified and described. Then items will be suggested in a single table. You might try to write four items for each scale, two positively worded and two negatively worded.

Social Psychological
This dimension of climate has to do with the affective state of the classroom. We have several aspects to discuss.

1. *Cohesiveness:* This scale refers to the degree to which class members "hang out" together socially. Are class members friendly and respectful to one another? Cooperative learning promotes cohesiveness, where a team approach often exists and where students are willing to help one another.
2. *Physical environment:* This scale discusses the physical appearance of the classroom, school, and school grounds.
3. *Friction between students and the teacher:* In some classrooms, friction exists between the teacher and the students. Such classes have a negative learning environment that inhibits effective student efforts. This rare situation is serious enough to warrant intervention.
4. *Friction among students:* If students are in conflict with one another, this may interfere with orderly progress in a classroom. It should be avoided, particularly if gangs are involved.
5. *Favoritism:* Bias is a natural tendency in all of us. In the classroom, it can be a negative influence. If some students are favored over others, students will feel like either winners or losers.

TABLE 8.2
Class Climate Dimensions

Social/Psychological

Cohesiveness

A student has a chance to get to know the student in this class. (+)
Students know each other very well. (+)
Students don't know each other very well in our class. (−)
Everybody goes their own way in this class. (−)

Environment

We are proud of our classroom. (+)
Our classroom is a nice place to study. (+)
Our room is not very nice. (−)
This school is old and crummy. (−)

Friction (between Student and Teacher)

The teacher and the students seem to get along well. (+)
Students like their teacher in this class. (+)
The teacher argues with students in our class. (−)
Students and our teacher don't always get along. (−)

Friction (among Students)

Students respect one another in our class. (+)
We students get along with one another in this class. (+)
Some students in this class have no respect for other students. (−)
Some students interfere with class activities. (−)

Favoritism

All students are treated the same in this class. (+)
The teacher is fair to all students. (+)
Some kids in class get all the breaks. (−)
Some students get breaks in this class. (−)

Cliques

We are all equal in this class. (+)
No group in our class gets special treatment. (+)
We have special groups of students. (−)
A few students run this class. (−)

Apathy

Students really like _____. (+)
We have a lot of enthusiasm for _____. (+)
Most kids don't seem to care about _____. (−)
We don't like _____. (−)

Continued

Table 8.2   *Continued*

Management/Organization

Formality

We have a lot of rules in this class to follow. (+)
There is a set of rules to follow in this class (+)
The class is rather informal. Few rules are used. (–)
The teacher in this class does not have lots of rules. (–)

Speed (Pace of Instruction)

We have plenty of time to finish our work. (+)
We seem to have enough time to complete our work. (+)
We never seem to have enough time to finish our work. (–)
We are always behind in our work. (–)

Goal Direction

Students in this class know what we are supposed to do. (+)
We get to work right away in this class. (+)
In this class, many students don't know what they are supposed to do. (–)
Most students in this class don't seem to know what to do. (–)

Satisfaction with Schoolwork

Most students are happy about their schoolwork. (+)
I like the things I do in this class. (+)
Most kids never feel like they are doing good work in this class (–)
I am not happy with what I am learning in this class. (–)

Organization

We use our time very well in class each day. (+)
The teacher is well organized each day. (+)
We are not very well organized. (–)
The teacher does not know what we are going to do each day. (–)

Difficulty

Most students find this class easy. (+)
This class is easy. (+)
Many students in this class struggle with _____. (–)
This class is hard. (–)

6. *Cliques:* A classroom may have a core of talented, popular students who maintain social control over almost everything that happens. This lack of democracy can be demoralizing to other class members.

7. *Apathy:* In some classrooms, especially in junior high schools and high schools, apathy may set in that is class-specific. An apathy scale might capture this lack of enthusiasm for the subject matter.

Management/Organization

This dimension of climate deals with the teacher's efforts to create a system of teaching that has the following desirable characteristics:

1. Formality: Some classes may be highly structured, with many rules and strict enforcement. Other classes may represent the other extreme, with only a few rules. Without making value judgment about which is better, you may want to know how a class stands compared to others and which type of class is optimal for learning. Generally, a more structured approach is favored for achieving clearly stated goals, but this may be related to the type of students you have.

2. Speed (pace of instruction): Students are very mindful of how fast the teacher goes. A delicate balance exists within any heterogeneous class; the teacher probably goes too fast for some students and too slow for others. If students complain about class activities going too fast or too slow, this may be a signal to change the pace of instruction and aim for a happy medium.

3. Goal direction: Effective schools research tells us that students should be aware of teacher's goals and should be working to achieve some worthwhile end, assuming that the two are the same. From observation, such classrooms have students who know what to do and are working toward a goal. A survey could reveal if students think that they have enough goal direction or lack this important guidance.

4. Satisfaction with schoolwork: This category recognizes that students may be happy with what they are doing in a class or may be dissatisfied. This scale may be correlated with other scales, such as attitude toward the subject or importance, but the main issue here is the extent to which each student and the class collectively is making satisfactory progress toward some end.

5. Organization: Organization deals with the issue of teacher preparation for class and how students spend their time. Is the teacher well organized, or is he or she scrambling to get through the day's activities? Is there a plan? Is there a lot of leisure time in class, or are students usually busy?

6. Difficulty: Some subjects are harder than others, but that is not the issue here. The issue is the rigor of the class compared to others in the same subject. Are the demands in this class high, average, or low compared to those in other comparable classes?

Summary

This section has tried to give you an idea of the richness of the climate of the school or classroom. Student surveys can provide glimpses into the class or school climate that are not easily obtained from casual observation. The survey of class climate is assumed to be schoolwide, systematic, and useful for guiding teaching and improving student learning.

Questioning Strategies/Item Formats

The student survey should be brief and simple. It should contain items and response options, much like those on a multiple-choice test. The items are questions or statements requiring a student response. Generally, the responses can be coded on a scannable answer sheet so that data processing can be done quickly. The response options are any of the graded category rating scales introduced in Chapter 5B, or you may want to invent a scale. An example follows:

How do you feel about the new writing program in which you must use a computer?

A. Very good   B. Good   C. Fair   D. Poor   E. Very poor

The appendix at the end of this chapter contains a mixture of items for student, parent, and teacher surveys. These items were written by parents, teachers, and other educators for local school evaluation projects. You might adopt or adapt these items, or write your own.

Item Formats

This section focuses on four specific item formats: (1) generic item sets, (2) statement, (3) question, and (4) pair comparison. The first of these four formats is recommended because of its ease of production and systematic nature, which results in very predictable and useful data. The statement is a standard type of item format. The question is recommended over the statement. The fourth type, pair comparison, is useful for ordering objects or persons but is *not* recommended.

Generic Item Sets

This is one of the most effective methods for surveying students. In elementary school, we have used generic item sets to repetitively ask the same question, trying to get students to answer in a way that consistently reflects their attitude toward school or a subject matter. A good example of a generic set follows:

What face do you wear . . .

    1. when it is time to go to school?
    2. during school time?
    3. when it is time to go home?
    4. when vacation ends?
    5. if you never had to go to school again?

Students select one of the three face options given in the next section in Figure 8.2. on page 215. There are happy, neutral, and sad faces. Generic item sets can be very accurate and reliable. They give excellent results in a very short time period. Item sets are easy to develop and, when written, can generate items for a variety of similar topics. For instance, the generic item set for attitude toward school has been modified for language arts (reading, writing, speaking, listening), mathematics, science, social studies, physical education, art, and music. Any subject matter or type of class or program can be substituted in the example. Students tend to respond consistently at every grade level from first grade up. Even high school students have responded with consistency, although the tendency there is not to use the pictorial response options but to use words instead.

Statement

The statement type format is just like a completion item in multiple-choice. With each statement, you write companion response options that reflect how the student feels relative to the item stem. Statements are easy to write, which makes them a popular choice for student surveys.

We do interesting things each day in reading.
_____

We do the same things in reading each day.
_____

My reading class work is pretty hard.
_____

Question

The question format is recommended over the statement format because the relationship between question and answer is natural and logical, whereas the statement-and-choices relationship is less direct. The question-and-answer format is what students are used to, and the question usually leads to an honest answer when appropriate response categories are given.

Pair Comparison

Although this technique is not recommended, it is presented here because it is good for forcing a consensus about the ranking of some objects you might be evaluating. For instance, if I was comparing three reading series and I asked students which one they liked and wanted a clear cut-winner, I would use a pair comparison technique that would force each student to choose among the pairs, as follows:

For the next three items, choose either (A) or (B).

Which reading program do you like better:

1. (A) Reading for Fun or (B) Lima Bean Stories
2. (A) Lima Bean Stories or (B) Telephone Book
3. (A) Telephone Book or (B) Reading for Fun

Notice that each pair of the three reading programs are matched and the student is asked to choose between (A) and (B). Notice that each program is mentioned first once and second once to achieve balance and not bias or lead the student in responding. The pair comparison method will always force one choice to stand out above others.

Response Formats

This section deals with types of response formats that can be paired with items. Whether you use generic item sets, statements, or questions, the response format influences the quality of responses. This section provides some basic advice on how to construct or adapt rating scales presented in Table 5B.1.

Graded Categories

As suggested in Chapter 5B, a rating scale requires choices among ordered categories. In the student survey, we use the graded category rating scales listed in Table 5B.1. You may want to develop your own graded categories to fit your specific item.

The first issue is how many rating-scale categories to allow students to choose and how these categories range semantically. Do not use more than seven categories. Use seven choices whenever possible. With most elementary school children, using five choices is more reasonable. With younger children, three choices is a reasonable number. With fewer choices, reliability may suffer somewhat.

The second issue is how to range the categories. Compare the two sets of categories for the item: How often during the week do you go to the library?

Desirable	Undesirable
Often	Always
Occasionally	Sometimes
Hardly ever	Never

The column on the left offers reasonable choices that students can select. The choices on the right include extremes that may force most students to choose the middle category. If that happens, in effect, you force students into a central tendency error because two of the three choices are so extreme. A good rule of thumb is to create categories that reflect the range of feeling without getting too extreme.

For a set of graded categories, there are two main types of response. Table 5B.1 offered words as choices. This is the mainstay of affective student surveys. You can also use faces or other pictorial choices. The faces in Figure 8.2 were used by us in a number of studies (Haladyna & Thomas, 1979a, 1979b; Haladyna, Olsen, & Shaughnessy, 1982, 1983). The results of these studies in a technical sense as well as from the standpoint of users and students were very successful. Faces are friendly. They are easy to mark. And they are very versatile for a number of purposes. We have limited the use of faces to students from grades 1 through 8, but even high school students have responded to items using the choice of faces.

Pair Comparison
While not recommended, if you decide to use this technique, we will show how to score results. The reason you may want to use it is that it is quick, inexpensive, and simple.

Figure 8.3 provides an example from Haladyna and Shaughnessy (1982). In this experiment, we asked students to choose among subjects. Because we had five subjects (reading, mathematics, physical education, art, and music), we had 10 possible pairs. In Figure 8.3 these pairs were mixed sufficiently and counterbalanced so that all subjects do not always appear first or second. The student marks an X on the choice. The scores are tallied by the teacher to give a vote on preference. For a class, the result can be very revealing about which subjects are doing well.

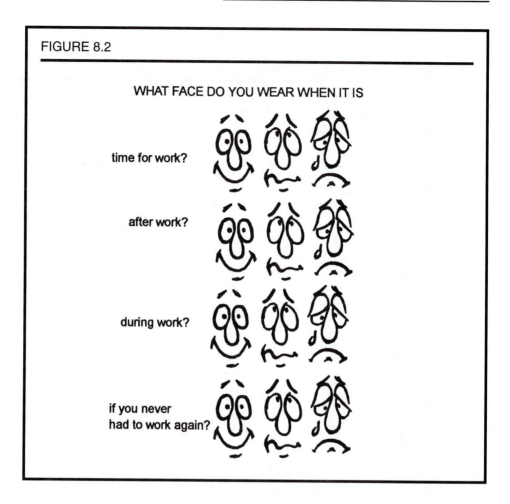

FIGURE 8.2

WHAT FACE DO YOU WEAR WHEN IT IS

time for work?

after work?

during work?

if you never
had to work again?

Unfortunately, pair comparison is a competitive measure. If many school subjects were doing well or poorly, pair comparison would not reflect this condition. Another limitation of pair comparison is that if you compare more than five objects, the number of possible pairs expands considerably:

Objects	5	6	7	8
Items/Pairs	10	15	21	28

FIGURE 8.3
Which Would You Rather Do?

Check the grade:
   ☐ 4   ☐ 5   ☐ 6   ☐ 7   ☐ 8

Check the gender:
   ☐ girl   ☐ boy

PRACTICE

Which would you rather do?

| Watch TV | ☐ | OR | Clean your room | ☐ |
| Eat lima beans | ☐ | OR | Play with friends | ☐ |

FOR REAL

Which class do you prefer?

Music	☐	OR	PE	☐
Math	☐	OR	Music	☐
PE	☐	OR	Reading	☐
Reading	☐	OR	Math	☐
PE	☐	OR	Math	☐
Math	☐	OR	Art	☐
Art	☐	OR	PE	☐
Reading	☐	OR	Art	☐
Music	☐	OR	Reading	☐
Art	☐	OR	Music	☐

If you want to make pair comparisons among seven objects, for example, then 21 pair comparison items are needed. This can get out of hand quickly.

The introductory information on grade level, age, gender, and other demographic variables can be used for research purposes or omitted. The two items marked A and B are practice items so that younger students can get the idea of how to mark. (If the student picks "clean your room," you might want to eliminate or otherwise question the validity of the student's participation in this exercise.) Although most students cooperate and are truthful and consistent in marking, a few confused, uninterested, or idiosyncratic students can mess up your survey. You should toss any papers that seem to fit into any of these three categories.

Scoring and Reporting

Scoring the results of these affective student surveys is technical. Hand scoring is feasible but tedious. Computerized scoring is recommended if you have access to research services or data processing. Student responses can be scanned by a elec-tronic optical scanner and then computer-analyzed using a computer program, as discussed in Chapter 10. In this section, I will provide a simple example and use hand scoring to show the process used to correctly score a set of student responses. Let's work from a simple example with a four-item survey:

A. □ *Agree*   **B.** □ *Not Sure*   **C.** □ *Disagree*

   1. I really like lima beans. (+)
   2. Lima beans are yummy. (+)
   3. Lima beans are yucky. (−)
   4. Only a sick person would like lima beans. (−)

Following is a response form for a single student:

Ratings——>	Agree	Not Sure	Disagree	Points
Item 1 (+)	x			3
Item 2 (+)	x			3
Item 3 (−)		x		2
Item 4 (−)			x	3

Items 1 and 2 are written positively so an "Agree" gets 3 points, "Not Sure" 2 points, and "Disagree" 1 point. Items 3 and 4 are negative, so the scoring key is reversed: "Agree" gets 1 point, "Not Sure" again gets 2 points, and "Disagree" gets 1 point. The maximum score for the scale is 12, and the minimum is 4. The mid-point is 8. So if an entire class had an average of, say, 10.4, you might conclude that the school cafeteria could serve lima beans without provoking a riot or a food fight. But if the class average was 4.2, you might conclude that lima beans would get you into trouble. You can also compare classes or school on these averages.

This simple example shows you how to score a four-item scale designed to measure an attitude or other affective trait. Hand scoring takes time, but if you have research and evaluation services, such surveys can be done using automated methods.

Summary

Most educators appreciate the importance of developing positive attitudes, self-esteem, and the like in students. Positive affective traits help students stay in school and attend to learning. The attainment of these affective traits is important in itself, also, without considering how they affect learning. The school or class climate is also important in relation to learning as well as for itself. A positive learning environment fosters effective learning. The first part of this chapter built a rationale for affective surveys of students. Table 8.1 provides a good overview of the framework for thinking about the role of affective traits. Table 8.2 provides a list of affective traits and sample items, written by various educators. Appendix 8A provides a potpourri of such items written for student, teacher, and parent surveys. Other parts of this chapter focused on item and response formats you can use and on methods for scoring results.

References

Bruner, J. (1960). *The process of education.* Cambridge: Harvard University Press.

Coopersmith, S. (1967). *The antecedents of self-esteem.* San Francisco: Freeman.

Fraser, B. J., Anderson, G. J., Walberg, H. J. (1982). *Learning environment inventory.* Curtin: Western Australia Institute of Technology.

Haladyna, T. M., & Thomas, G. P. (1979a). The affective reporting system. *Journal of Educational Measurement, 16,* 49–54.

Haladyna, T. M., & Thomas, G. P. (1979b). The attitudes of elementary school children toward school and subject matters. *Journal of Experimental Education, 48,* 18–23. Reprinted in W. R. Borg (Ed.). (1981). *Applying educational research: A practical guide for teachers.* New York: Longman.

Haladyna, T. M., Olsen, R. M., & Shaughnessy, J. M. (1982). Relations of student, teacher and learning environment variables to attitude toward science. *Science Education, 66,* 547–563.

Haladyna, T. M., Olsen, R. M., & Shaughnessy, J. M. (1983). Correlates of class attitude toward science. *Journal of Research for Science Teaching, 20,* 311–324.

Haladyna, T. M., & Shaughnessy, J. M. (1982). *A manual for the affective inventory of attractive aspects of schooling.* Monmouth, OR: Teaching Research.

Haladyna, T. M., Shaughnessy, J. M., & Redsun, A. (1982). Relations of student, teacher and learning environment variables to attitude toward social studies. *Journal of Social Studies Research, 6,* 36–44.

Kohn, A. (1994). The truth about self-esteem. *Phi Delta Kappan, 16,* 272–283.

Mager, R. F. (1968). *Developing attitude toward learning.* Palo Alto, CA: Fearon Press.

Moos, R. H., & Trickett, E. J. (1974). *Classroom environment scales.* Palo Alto, CA: Consulting Psychologist Press.

Appendix: A Potpourri of Teacher-Authored Affective Items[a]

Student Items

My classroom is too crowded.

This school is a safe place to be.

Kids like this school.

The teachers in this school seem to like what they are doing.

Kids in my class are well behaved.

The teacher treats us fairly.

I would like to learn to speak Spanish.

Someday I will graduate from high school.

Someday I will go to college.

Working hard in school pays off later.

My teacher keeps me busy.

My school work is pretty hard.

My teacher gives me help when I need it.

We often work with other kids in teams to do our class work.

My teacher likes science.

Parent Items

My child enjoys school.

My child enjoys [subject matter].

We have a good drug education program.

My school is a safe place to be.

Teachers return my calls.

School spirit is good.

My child gets enough homework.

My child will graduate from high school.

I like the idea of my child staying with the same teacher for more than one year.

I feel welcome when I visit school.

I like attending parent–teacher conferences.

Continued

I like the idea of a homework hotline.

The school is a safe place for my child.

Parents are adequately involved in decision making in the school.

Teachers seek parents' opinions on important school issues.

Teacher Items

I feel that the district office is supportive of teachers.

I feel that the school's mission is used as a basis for making school-level decisions about instructional programs.

I receive regular communications about what is happening in school.

I believe there are few discipline problems in our school.

My colleagues are cooperative and supportive.

I believe that the climate in this school supports learning.

I believe that the school's facilities are conducive to learning.

I believe that opportunities are provided to reward students for academic achievement.

I believe that the principal is accessible to discuss matters dealing with instruction.

We have strong instructional leadership.

My instructional resources are adequate.

My classes are too large to be taught effectively.

Expectations for appropriate student behavior are clear.

This school has clear and consistent rules for students.

Teachers are involved in important decision making regarding instruction.

[a]These items are public domain. They were authored by teachers and other educators for local evaluation projects where the affective domain was an important aspect of their evaluation. These items can be adopted or adapted. No copyright is intended on any of these items.

Part Three
Evaluating Test
Items

This last part contains only two complementary chapters. Chapter 9 deals with a series of integrated reviews that are necessary to transform the first draft of any item into a polished item worthy of tryout with a class of students. Some of these reviews are crucial to measuring the content and cognitive ability desired. Chapter 10 is necessarily statistical and deals with analyzing and evaluating item responses to determine if students are responding to items in desirable ways. Classroom teachers probably will not be heavily engaged in all of these processes because of limitations of time and other resources. But participation in any of these will enhance the overall quality of items used to test student learning.

9 Reviewing Test Items

TEST ITEM WRITING IS HARDLY A SCIENCE. EVEN THE MOST HIGHLY motivated and able item writers find that a surprising number of their test items fail to work as intended. This chapter presents an *ideal* set of procedures for polishing and improving test items once they have been written. You probably do not have enough time to perform all of the suggested reviews. Keep in mind that each test item will probably be used and reused in future years of teaching the same course or grade level. This means that your items will become highly polished over a longer period than a single semester or year. Because these review procedures are complementary, it is a good idea to get the full perspective and then invest your time wisely in doing the reviews you think are feasible or desirable. The objective of this chapter is to help you use your time wisely to improve your items. An implicit theme is that good test items are like a comedian's best jokes. Save them, and use them repeatedly. Saving good test items is no joke.

If a test development project is being conducted by an organization or team of developers, as might be found in a school district, then this chapter offers a series of integrated reviews that should produce highly effective test items.

Introduction

These item review activities are as follows:

- Quality appraisal
- Content verification
- Classification of mental behavior
- Key verification
- Adherence to item-writing advice
- Editorial review
- Bias/sensitivity review

Each activity can be performed by a single person, but ideally a team of people with complementary skills is needed. For example, the first four activities require content experts, like you, the teacher. *Adherence to item-writing rules* requires some knowledge of item-writing advice, as is found in Chapters 4 through 8. *Editing* requires a skilled editor or an English teacher. *Bias/sensitivity review* requires a team of persons who have had sensitivity training and can spot items that may insult, inflame, irritate, or disgruntle various subgroups of test-takers. As stated at the outset of this chapter, although most of these activities are not feasible for classroom testing, these procedures represent an ideal, a goal that you would pursue if you had more resources or time. Many test items can be used and reused over many years. With constant polish on each item using the procedures presented here, each item may mature and produce the kind of results you are looking for: high-level, complex student performance. Bad items, on the other hand, may confuse students to the extent that they cannot perform as expected, or they may become frustrated and angry. The premature use of complex performance items can have negative effects on students and teachers, so writing good performance items and conducting all of these reviews is desirable. Another consequence of poorly written test items is a low opinion of your testing program and a lack of respect for you as the teacher. A common complaint among undergraduate teachers-in-training is that they endure poor testing practices on the part of their instructors, so the problem may be endemic.

Quality Appraisal

First, does the test item represent something worthwhile to teach and test? This is a subjective judgment, but past practices and initiatives for reform in teaching provide lots of guidance. In this book, I have taken the position that memory is O.K. to test if you can justify it as part of the knowledge the student needs to learn a skill and eventually to develop an ability. You should emphasize higher level thinking, including abilities like critical thinking, problem solving, and creative thinking. Understanding is a good low-level outcome, somewhere between memory and these higher level abilities. Quality appraisal usually comes from a second opinion and can follow a rating scale, such as:

Excellent . . . Very good . . . Fair . . . Poor . . . Very Poor

Who should offer a quality appraisal? Fellow teachers, curriculum directors, and (don't forget) the students. In many aspects of item writing, the best source of expert feedback can be the students, who can tell what was taught and not taught. In the process of discovering good items and weeding out bad items, students can give you an impression of what they believe they have learned and how well you have tested their learning, especially if you have encouraged them to be self-reflective and to talk or write about what they are learning.

In summary, your main concern in this category of item review is to answer a question:

> Does this item represent something worthwhile I have taught or want to teach?

In other sections of this chapter, I will discuss what that "something" is. But you already know that it involves critical thinking, problem solving, and creative thinking or the development of an ability of lifelong importance, such as reading, writing, speaking, or listening.

Content Verification

Chapter 2 stated that content of any item reflects either a fact, concept, principle, or procedure. Chapters 4 through 8 emphasized the use of a template to design each item, and one of the first steps was to identify which of four types of content were being tested. A test item can also be so complex that it involves combinations of use of the facts, concepts, principles, and procedures. Standard subject matter disciplines make up the school curriculum. These subject matters help us organize our thinking regarding content, deriving from curriculum.

This review seeks some agreement or consensus that the type of content being tested is exactly what the item writer thought was being tested. Generally, this review is very simple. Another reviewer or two will code the item using the four content categories. We expect agreement or consensus among reviewers.

Classification of Mental Behavior Required

Chapter 2 also described five types of mental behavior: memorizing, understanding, critical thinking, problem solving, and creative behavior. Classifying test items for memorizing and understanding is easy. Questions can ask students for *verbatim* reproductions of facts, concepts, principles, and procedures. Questions also can ask students to identify or produce paraphrased definitions of facts, concepts, principles, or procedures. These questions demonstrate *understanding*. Or you can give students characteristics or examples of these facts, concepts, principles, or procedures and ask them to choose between characteristics and noncharacteristics, examples and nonexamples. These types of items for students, discussed in Chapter 2, provide evidence of what you are teaching and trying to accomplish. *Critical thinking* may involve predicting, evaluating, or the familiar inductive or deductive forms of logic. *Problem solving* is seldom represented by a single item but is better tested by a series of items, following the steps in problem solving. The item set introduced in Chapter 3 and illustrated in Chapter 4 is an excellent approach to measuring problem solving with a multiple-choice format, although certainly an open-ended approach could be used as well. Some items simply ask for the solution to a problem without concern for the process. This is right/wrong scoring, discussed in Chapter 6. Creative thinking or production is difficult to develop and test, but if it is done with an open-ended item such as shown in Chapter 5A or 6, it would involve a response that might be unique. In other words, there is no right answer in this instance, but there may be a variety of appropriate responses.

As with content verification, an effective review gets two or three other content experts to read items and classify each item with respect to the type of mental behavior being exhibited by the student when she or he responds to the item (Table 9.1). Again, we expect a high degree of agreement among the content experts.

Key Verification

Whether an item is multiple-choice or high-inference or low-inference performance, we normally have a correct student response in mind. This right answer must be correct, and wrong answers must be absolutely incorrect. In some instances, there might be multiple right answers, perhaps—in problem solving, creative thinking, or production. In this case, we need to be prepared to defend our choice of appropriate versus inappropriate answers. Perhaps the most controversial and difficult area in which to judge a student response is creative thinking or

---

TABLE 9.1
Item Classification

Item number _____   Quality rating: _____   Quality rating:_____
                            Rater 1   Rater 2

TYPE OF CONTENT		TYPE OF MENTAL BEHAVIOR		TEACHING TARGET	
Fact	☐	Recall	☐	Knowledge	☐
Concept	☐	Understanding	☐	Mental skill/ability	☐
Principle	☐	Critical thinking	☐	Physical skill/ability	☐
Procedure	☐	Problem solving	☐		
		Creative	☐		

creative production. If your intent is to judge creative behavior, you will need to proceed cautiously, with considerable clarity about what constitutes appropriate and inappropriate behavior.

One of the best ways to verify an answer is to get a second opinion from a fellow teacher or curriculum specialist. Especially with high-inference items where teacher judgment plays an important role, the correct response or the class of correct responses should be delineated as clearly as possible, so that all teachers of the same material agree.

Another way to verify the key is by student agreement. This should be tempered by each student's depth of learning. An outstanding student can give you new insights into your questioning. A less able student may give you insights into how low-achieving students are thinking when they take your test items. Willingness to obtain options from students is brave because we invest so much of ourselves and our egos in writing our test items. Still, the extra effort and eventual criticism will only improve your items.

A final message: You will be surprised at how often your keyed response is wrong. This is true in professional licensure and certification testing, for which the nation's leading experts in a profession write items. These experts will sit around a table debating the merits of one expert's right answer versus another expert's other right answer. Who's right?

It is also true for classroom teachers. Everyone's knowledge about any subject is partial. Therefore, we occasionally trip over the key of our own item. Key verification is a crucial phase in avoiding the embarrassment of public exposure or, worse, a student pointing out our error. Don't I know this?

Adherence to Item-Writing Advice

Chapters 4 through 8 provide some collective wisdom on how to write items. Although many rules are not well supported by research, as a test item developer, you will need to apply what you know and what you believe about what you are teaching to find out if items conform to standard beliefs about how items should be written. You have tremendous flexibility in the rules you choose to follow, but you should be consistent. Writing items is like creating a recipe—it should be clear to all involved in the cooking process. A bond between teacher and students regarding learning and testing is created with the test item. Following sensible item-writing advice should lead you to develop better items, which will help you teach and help students learn and eventually test well. Chapter 4 provides good guidance in phrasing stems and options of multiple-choice items. Chapters 5A and 6 provide item-writing templates to guide you in performance testing that often involves complex cognitive skills and abilities. Chapter 7 gives you guidance about portfolio development. Each of these chapters has a template to help you check items against some criteria. In the end, you have your common sense to guide you though this review.

Editorial Review

Ideally, you will want a professional editor to edit your items—you know, that English major who always knows where the hyphen goes, who can spot bad grammar, and who tells you "it ain't gud to right like dat." This editor always knows the difference between *effect* and *affect*. Editors actually enjoy doing this. Professional editors are specially trained in technical writing or a similar field and have a sharp editorial (that's *editorial*, not *evil*) eye for lack of clarity, poor grammar, misspelling, and punctuation and capitalization errors. Editors are *not* supposed to tamper with the content of the item, but they can and should tamper with the wording to effect (not *affect*) a clear, well-written item.

If you lack that kind of assistance, than the responsibility falls on you. It is easy to ignore editing and, in the rush to produce a test item and test, to let the editorial responsibility slide. This is not a good idea.

First, poorly edited items reflect on you, the teacher. They send a message to students that you don't care, or worse, that you are incapable of writing clearly and correctly.

Second, test anxiety is real. Poorly written items increase student test anxiety.

Third, poorly edited items often cause confusion among students, leading to poor performance. If the students have learned what you are teaching, then give them a chance to perform by offering them well-edited items.

How to Do the Editorial Review

Clarity

The most important aspect of writing the item, once you have determined the content and mental behavior to be demonstrated, is to make certain that the student knows what to do. Clarity is difficult to accomplish. How often I remember writing a wonderful item only to have the entire class tell me they didn't have the slightest idea what I was asking. There is a message here: Clarity is an elusive concept. Typically, clarity refers to the use of the canons of English composition, but clarity also reflects your state of mind and your clarity of purpose in teaching. If you have some confusion about what you are teaching, it is likely to creep into your items. To match the item with your instructional intent is critical here, but the editorial review allows us to examine the clarity of the item. Thus, you need to focus on what you are trying to test and to obtain a second or third opinion from others, preferably students. If students tell you that an item has a major problem, then they are probably right.

Spelling

Spelling is an ability that is improved over time. Correct spelling is taught throughout the school career and is expected at later stages. If missspellings creep into your writing, they leave a bad impression with students. They send the message that spelling is not important. Missspelling also can confuse students who are test-anxious. (Did you notice that *misspelling* was missspelled? Did it distract you?) We need to ensure that our spelling is impeccable. One good way to effect good spelling is through the computer's word-processing spell checker. This is good because you can build a specialized vocabulary that the spell checker will use in checking the words on your test items. However, spell checkers will not check the accuracy of *principle* versus *principal* or *effect* versus *affect*.

Grammar

Always use correct grammar. Incorrect grammar distracts students and may confuse them. Grammatical errors may increase anxiety because the student is thinking more about the teacher's grammar than about how to answer the question. Another reason for using correct grammar, spelling, punctuation, and capitalization is that students may lose respect for the teacher if the test is rife with grammatical and other editorial errors.

Punctuation and Capitalization

For the same reasons offered previously, items should have correct punctuation and capitalization. Some grammar checking software is good for written material, but this software does not work well with test items because they are not complete sentences.

Style

In major testing programs, it is not uncommon to use a style guide that addresses issues of the presentation of items by each format, writing style, and conventions, such as acronyms and abbreviations that are permitted. Although a formal style guide may seem silly for classroom testing, consistency of style goes a long way to engender respect for your tests. For example, acronyms are popular, but what if a student misses an item because she or he doesn't know what the acronym means?

Presentation

One concern of the editor is the appearance of the test item. Modern computers and their text and graphics capabilities offer tremendous opportunities to present items with a very professional look. As technology changes, teachers will learn more about the capabilities of computers and will be more likely to use these capabilities not only to create items but also to store items for future use. Effective presentation of items on the printed page will convey to students the high-quality image of teaching and testing that should be backed up by the substance of your teaching. You can enhance presentation in a very simple way by (1) choosing an attractive type font (like Times Roman or **Helvetica**) and a font size (usually 11 point or 12 point). The appearance of items can be as good-looking as on any professionally developed test with a simple word-processing program such as WordPerfect or Microsoft Word. Graphics can be imported into pages containing items and boxes or outlines. These enhancements are almost routine with today's personal computers, and increasingly teachers have access to computers and software in their classrooms. Not only do the capabilities exist, but today's students have great skill with computers and can help you improve your own computer abilities.

Figure 9.1 shows a page from the Teenage Obedience Academy class on cleaning your room. Notice that the page contains a header and a footer, with page numbers and directions to the students. Two-column printing is used to effect a

---

FIGURE 9.1
Teenage Obedience Academy: Room Cleaning Test

1. Who is responsible for your room?
   A. Mom
   B. Dad
   C. Aliens
   D. Me
2. How often should your room be vacuumed?
   A. Continuously
   B. Every Saturday
   C. Once a month
   D. On February 29th
3. Should you receive compensation?
   A. Yes
   B. No
4. How often should the sheets be changed on the bed?
   A. Every day
   B. Once a week
   C. Once a month
   D. When I see creatures moving
5. Should the room be fumigated?
   A. Only if the number of creatures found there other than friends exceeds 10.
   B. It depends on whether it's a boy's room or a girl's room.
   C. Never, it might affect the occupant.

6. Should food be allowed in the room?
   A. Yes
   B. Maybe
   C. No
7. Should the room be aired out?
   A. Yes, as often as possible.
   B. Yes, once a month.
   C. No, unless there's a fire.
   D. No, never.
8. Should friends be allowed in the room?
   A. Only if they are fumigated.
   B. No
   C. Yes
9. When should the carpets be cleaned?
   A. Depends upon who's living there.
   B. Once a year
   C. Spot cleaning monthly
10. When should the room be dusted?
    A. For fingerprints only and only after a crime is committed.
    B. When you can see the dust thick on something.
    C. About once a week.

more compact look to the items and allow more items to fit on a page. A good editor will ensure that each page looks its best and follows an agreed-on format. As a teacher (editor), you can achieve the same kind of look on your test by using a standard format and then using your computer and its features to enhance everything you print for your students.

Bias and Sensitivity Review

Bias and sensitivity review has two facets: judgment and statistical. The next chapter takes care of the statistical. In this section, I will address some serious issues related to how test items may affect students in undesirable ways.

Generally speaking, with high test anxiety and various other difficulties with testing, you do not want to make references or comments in test items that reflect badly on the school or whomever else you represent. You also do not want to upset students by making insensitive remarks about gender, ethnic background, race, sexuality, or any other personal characteristics. Items may become cold and insensitive if they avoid creating personalities and other touches that would make them realistic. In test items in which a scenario is presented, people are often the focus of the item. For instance, in a test of medical problem solving, a patient will be the object of the question. In many other circumstances, you will weave people into the item stem. As you do this, be mindful of the potential for bias. I will mention a few common but avoidable problems that may creep into item writing.

One of your most important tasks in test development is to scrutinize your items for potentially biased or insensitive references. These references are not made consciously but often creep into tests inadvertently. Sometimes other reviewers can spot such items and advise you to change them. The following are some common areas to investigate.

Gender Stereotyping

References to boys and girls or to men and women should be balanced in a test. Not only should balance in numbers be achieved, but the roles played by a boy or a girl, a man or a woman should not be stereotyped. Stereotypically passive, submissive, weak, or compliant women are found in movies. Try to avoid stereotyping men as brave, strong leaders and women as weak, vacillating followers. Instead, try to achieve more gender balance in the leadership roles of characters in test items.

Ethnic, Racial, Cultural, or Sexuality Stereotyping

References to a person's ethnic, racial, or cultural background are usually irrelevant to our testing purpose. If, however, there is some reason to mention an ethnic group or designation, race, or cultural background, then it should not be done pejoratively. If any person is mentioned, avoid stereotypical depictions. For example, those who are servants or leaders should not be depicted exclusively as members of a particular group. If necessary, distribute the identity of leaders and followers proportionally with respect to gender, ethnic background, and race. I am reminded of a test item on one national licensing examination that depicted a homosexual couple as poor, despondent, and emotionally troubled. In this case, homosexuality simply was not a necessary reference in the item.

In summary, if a reference to a character in an item is necessary (and it is often desirable), be careful to make the reference without a derogatory connotation to ethnic, national, or racial origins or a person's sexuality.

Field Testing

Developmental Tryout (Think Aloud)

Cognitive psychologists have used a method of discourse with students while taking a test that gets them to think aloud as they answer questions. By interviewing students during the test, you can learn how they are thinking and addressing your items. This is not practical or realistic in a classroom, but consider it for an extended-performance item, as discussed in Chapters 5A or 6, or the portfolio in Chapter 7. As students progress through an extended performance, you might conduct periodic interviews (informal conversations) to look for any trouble you may have created with your item. Perhaps you can adjust or clarify for the students as they perform, but invariably you will find trouble with a new item. It would be a mistake to let the trouble persist and allow students to struggle with ambiguity, confusion, or lack of clarity.

This informal review process is very sensible and feasible for complex items, but not multiple-choice items. We have other techniques for those types of items to be discussed in another section of this chapter.

Formal Field Test

Don't read this section if you are a classroom teacher. This applies to testing program personnel. Formal field testing is highly recommended for any significant testing program. One aspect of formal field testing is developmental field testing, in which items are administered informally to a group of representative students around a table where open discussion of the item can lead to insights about its success. When a student hesitates or seems confused, you can probe to find out what the difficulty is and take notes.

High-achieving students should answer the item correctly and proceed smoothly and directly from beginning to end. Low-achieving students should commit typical errors associated with students in the early stages of development of the skill or ability being tested. Ideally, your item should identify the typical error that would be committed. Because individual students perform at all developmental levels, testing should pinpoint those levels and help them move along the developmental continuum. In other words, a good item discriminates among these students so that you can intervene early and provide the correct help.

The results of a formal field test inform us about the usability of the item. Is it a go or a no-go? Do we need to revise the item to make it more effective? This is a team decision involving the item development staff.

The formal field test also has statistical aspects that are treated in the next chapter. These statistical considerations for field testing are crucial to the future of any item.

Student Posttest Review

Following a formal test, a debriefing period is useful for both students and teachers. Students need to let off steam after an anxiety-producing test and let the teacher know what was good and bad about test items. Students can have brilliant insights, often pointing out flaws in items or plausible lines of reasoning that led them to choose the wrong answer or to construct an answer you did not anticipate. Asking students for commentary promotes critical thinking about what is taught and what is tested. Students are the best sources for this analysis and criticism. Again, it takes a brave teacher to do this, but the results can be wonderful. Students will respond positively, and you will learn things about teaching and testing that were not apparent to you before.

Here are some areas to probe in this debriefing:

1. Plausible other answers. If you are using multiple choice or a key, as suggested in Chapter 6 with low-inference items, then there might be many possible right answers. You may not have thought of all of them. Having a student suggest a right answer that is plausible reveals higher level thinking that you are actually trying to promote. To be fair, you have to give credit (which is what all students want from a test).

2. Trick items. Trick items were discussed briefly in Chapter 4. Some items can be deceptive to students and can mislead them from giving their best work. If enough of your students complain and their complaints sound valid, then perhaps you should consider throwing the item out of the test. The detection of trick items is not a well-developed science. Human judgment and common sense are the key ingredients. Students' lines of reasoning are critical here.

3. *Instructionally irrelevant items.* When teaching and learning are very focused and precise, students become trained to detect irrelevant material. If you did not teach something and you then tested it, howls of protest will arise. Students will flash their notes, quote from the book, and say the usual "you said . . ." This is an easy call. If you tested something that was instructionally irrelevant, you should *never* hold students accountable. But here is the problem. Some items call for the use or transfer of what was learned to a novel situation. Is this instructionally relevant? If you have been teaching this transfer of learning, then the answer is *yes*. Students are the best judge. You also will notice and be surprised at their study habits or strategies, because when they try to argue a point, they will reveal how they know about the item's worth or status.

4. *Developmentally inappropriate items.* Teachers at the college or professional school level, some high school teachers, and new teachers often make the error of teaching and testing developmentally inappropriate material, material that is either too advanced or too primitive for the student. For example, you would not teach third graders about Einstein's theory of relativity using Stephen Hawking's *A Brief History of Time*. Nor would you teach graduate students how to alphabetize words (well . . . maybe you would!). Occasionally, you will frustrate learners by introducing developmentally inappropriate material. Test results quickly tell you how you messed up. If all or most students miss an item, it may be too soon to test for what the item tested. If all students get an item right, it might be good teaching and learning, or it may be something that is so easy and was learned so long ago that everyone gets it right, and you wasted the students' time testing for it.

5. *Key errors.* Students are quick to spot key errors. If they argue that your key is wrong, this sometimes reveals their failure to learn, which is good for their reflections about learning. The next chapter gives you an excellent method for spotting key errors of a different type, when most class members fail to answer an item. If they think another answer is correct or if they have an equally good answer, listen to them and evaluate what they are saying. They may have a spin on your item that makes their response plausible. If so, give them credit.

6. *Too difficult.* Sometimes an item is more difficult than you intended. Because you probably have a grading standard (e.g., 80%–90% = B), a difficult item penalizes the entire class. It also may signal another problem I discussed, that of inappropriate or irrelevant material. If everyone, including students who you were sure had mastered the knowledge, skill, or ability represented, fails this item, you will need to make accommodations that respond to the problem. Or you might change your standards to recognize the unusual difficulty of your tests.

7. *Ambiguous.* If you believe that a test item is instructionally sound and covers what you had hoped, but all or most of the students missed it, then it is probably ambiguous. A quick student poll will let you know. The most tactical and tactful thing to do is to concede to the students that the item is flawed and give them credit.

8. Instructional failure. Students may miss an item that you thought you covered in class—but you forgot to teach it. What should you do? Don't penalize students for your failure. Remove that item from the test and reteach the material.

Answer Justification

This technique merges the quantitative tradition of testing with qualitative inquiry. Invariably, students will want to argue that their answers are good ones. They may want to write an essay or paragraph explaining their position, maybe even fervently. Or they may want to express orally to the class and you why their line of reasoning is correct. Whether you choose the written or oral way of justifying an answer, let your students do this. There are many reasons that this is a good practice:

- The student may have a correct alternative solution, representing a creative and appropriate behavior.
- This process encourages the practice of critical thinking.
- This process encourages persuasive writing and speaking.
- Students will reveal learning difficulties or lack of emphasis in teaching that led to wrong responses.
- The process is therapeutic for students; it gives them a chance to let off some steam.
- If their justification is correct, they will earn additional points, giving a truer representation of their performance on the test. (In our technical testing jargon, this is what validity is all about.)
- Finally, students will be happier and will display a more positive attitude toward school, the subject being tested, and you. The learning environment will be more positive.

I have used answer justification for years, and student involvement, participation, and learning have been highest during this time. Also, students feel good about the process, mostly because they improve their test scores by using their wits. You will learn more about the test and about teaching. Although answer justification takes class time, it is a very worthwhile activity.

An Item Review Template

Because you are used to templates in previous chapters, here is another one. Table 9.2 provides a checklist of procedures presented in this chapter that offer you a systematic way to analyze each item you write. As discussed at the outset of this chapter, these activities are idealized. Given your resources, interest, and other factors, you will decide how much you can do. The more you do, the better off our items will be.

TABLE 9.2
A Template for Item Review

Has each item received a quality appraisal?	Yes ☐	No ☐
Has each item's content been verified?	Yes ☐	No ☐
Have you identified the kind of higher level thinking or skill or ability to be tested for each item?	Yes ☐	No ☐
Has each item been classified?	Yes ☐	No ☐
Has the key (correct answer) been identified or the appropriate response been created for each item?	Yes ☐	No ☐
Have you followed the item-writing advice given?	Yes ☐	No ☐
Have you edited the items?	Yes ☐	No ☐
Have you reviewed the items for bias or insensitivity?	Yes ☐	No ☐
Have you field tested the items?	Yes ☐	No ☐

Summary

Chapter 9 has provided you with advice on how to improve your items once each has been written. Although it is unrealistic to assume that you will have time for all reviews, as much of this kind of reviewing as can be done will go a long way to increase the effectiveness of your items.

For formal testing programs with more personnel involved, such reviews are very desirable. If the stakes are high enough, these kinds of reviews should be mandatory (Downing & Haladyna, in press). When making a crucial decision about a person on the basis of test scores, such reviews go a long way toward building a legally defensible argument about the quality of the tests used to make these decisions.

References

Downing, S. M., & Haladyna, T. M. (In press). Test item development: Validity evidence from quality assurance procedures. *Applied Measurement in Education.*

10 Statistical Analysis of Item Responses

THIS CHAPTER COVERS SOME "SADISTICAL" [SIC] WAYS TO EVALUATE item responses. The methods contained in this chapter apply to a variety of item formats used throughout this book. Unfortunately, most of the theory and research on statistical methods for evaluating item responses relates to the multiple-choice format. Some of this theory and research applies to the use of rating scales as used with high-inference items in Chapter 5A and affective survey items in Chapter 8. The treatment of responses to low-inference items in Chapter 6 and of portfolio results in Chapter 7 is not especially well developed and receives little discussion in this chapter. This chapter does not intend to be statistically sophisticated. But because this is a technical subject, some knowledge of descriptive statistics is required, similar to that received in a graduate beginner statistics course.

The Role of Statistical Analysis in Item Evaluation

Chapters 9 and 10 were described as complementary.

The judgmental item reviews described in Chapter 9 intend to improve test items through analyses by competent persons with special skills. The item reviewers are close to the instruction for which the items are intended.

Chapter 10 intends to do a different kind of job. In this chapter, I emphasize looking for patterns in students' responses to items to help you find out if the item is doing its job, which is to help measure something important you are trying to teach.

> Teachers seldom have the time or interest to analyze test item responses in this way. But if the stakes are high enough or if the tests are used annually or each semester, item analysis might be a good idea and worth the extra effort.

Because each item is like a miniature test, we expect it to correlate with the total test score that results from adding results from all items. That is, a high-achieving person should get a high total score, which means that most items tried by this person should be answered correctly. Also, a low-achieving person should get a low score, which means that most items tried by this person should be answered incorrectly. We don't wish that our students will get low test results or try to manipulate our test so they get low scores, but the existence of low scores tells us something is happening. Your job is to figure out why and correct it.

The word *most* in the previous paragraph is important. Some items will be too hard even for the best achieving students, and some will be too easy even for the lowest achievers. These exceptional items are the object of our attention in item analysis. Generally, students should be exposed to items that reflect all the important things they are supposed to learn. But inconsistent item patterns reflect test items that may be (1) too hard, (2) too easy, (3) nondiscriminating with respect to what the test is supposed to measure, or (4) improperly keyed. Undesirable patterns in item responses could reflect ineffective teaching, inadequate student learning, or poor testing.

The next section starts with multiple-choice item analysis and then progresses to item analysis for rating scales and low-inference testing. The last sections of this chapter deal with special topics in the statistical study of item responses, including practical procedures that can be used in the classroom to diagnose malfunctioning items. Some of these procedures are intended for high-stakes testing where teachers are less directly involved in their development, scoring, and reporting. Nonetheless, these sections of this chapter are intended to help you understand the importance of some kinds of analysis for a school district or state-level testing program in the event that you are involved in these programs. And it is increasingly likely that teachers will have important roles to play in future high-stakes testing programs.

Item Analysis for Multiple-Choice Item Responses

Many school sites now have scanning equipment that makes scoring of multiple-choice responses easy. Item analysis can be done with scanned data. Item analysis is usually done with a computer program on a personal computer after the test item responses are scanned. The computer analysis provides item and test information. This section will draw from the output of a typical computer program. Many such programs are available. ITEMAN, produced by Assessment Systems Corporation (1993), is one that is especially easy to use, quick, and versatile. It also does rating-scale analysis, which we use in high-inference testing (Chapter 5), portfolio testing (Chapter 7), and affective surveys (Chapter 8).

This section will not show how to do an item analysis because computer programs do this extremely well on most personal computers. The purpose of this section is to help you interpret analyses that are available from these computer programs. Along the way, you will learn about item characteristics and how they interact to tell you how well students are learning and how well items are working.

Item Characteristics

When a group of students responds to an item on a test, we can learn a lot about the items and the kinds of students' achievement by looking at the results of an item analysis.

Difficulty Index

This index tells you how hard the item is. Generally, the difficulty index depends on the students taking the item. If the item is appropriate for the students and instruction has been given, you would expect the difficulty index to be 1.00, indicating that all students answered the item correctly. If instruction is not relevant to the item or student learning was not effective as a group, then item performance should be very low. The resulting difficulty index should be in the range of .20 to .60. The cause of the difficulty index of any item is hard to determine from a superficial analysis. A teacher has to know what the item was supposed to measure and the instructional history of the group of students taking the item. With any test, test score average will mirror item difficulty. The more effective the instruction and the more effective the student learning, the easier (less difficult) the item looks.

For instance, take a simple factual item:

How many pounds is two tons?

If your class does not know this answer, multiple-choice item performance with five options may be 20 percent (some guessed correctly). If your class knows this, item difficulty might be 95 percent (1 out of 20 forgot this trivial fact). The point of this example is that instruction has a bearing on item difficulty. If you are teaching well, the item is fair, and student learning is good, then items should appear easy.

Generally, boundary values for item difficulty are based on the number of multiple-choice options, as follows:

Options:	Five	Four	Three	Two
Lower values:	.20	.25	.33	.50

A common belief is that the more options there are for each item, the better it is, because the use of more options minimizes guessing. However, considerable research suggests that you should use only two or three options, because you seldom can find or write a good fourth or fifth option. Further, guessing plays little role in any test of 10 or more items. For instance, the probability of guessing 10 right answers on a four-option multiple-choice test is very close to zero.

Discrimination Index

This index tells you how well each item discriminates among students who vary in their levels of learning. A variety of discrimination indexes exist. The most popular and technically desirable is the point-biserial (PBI) correlation discrimination index. For the rest of this section, I will ignore the other indexes and limit discussion to the PBI. This PBI index actually varies between –1.00 and +1.00, but PBIs for the right answer are intended to be positive. A low index or a negative PBI signals a big problem with the item. A good way to think about PBI is to think of the average performance of the students getting the item right versus the average performance of those getting the item wrong. Such a difference should exist. Three items are shown from a variety of different tests:

Type of Discrimination	Good Item	Fair Item	Poor Item
Average score of right answerers	83%	74%	56%
Average score of wrong answerers	45%	58%	54%

The good item has a nice pattern. Those who picked the right answers got an average score of 83 percent, whereas those who picked any of the wrong answers got an average score of 45 percent. The fair item is a pretty good discriminator, but not as good as the first item. The poor item shows that there is not much difference between those picking the right and wrong answers. This is a nondiscriminating item.

Generally, we examine and modify or replace any item with a low or negative discrimination. A word of warning about discrimination: You should evaluate discrimination very cautiously. If students have overlearned and you have overtaught some material that is multiple-choice tested, then discrimination indexes can be very low. This does not mean that the item failed to discriminate. With everyone doing well on the test, items on this test will *never* have high discriminating PBIs. Again, you must know and understand the classroom processes before interpreting these statistics.

To shed some light on the previous paragraph, consider the following three items also drawn from different tests:

	1	2	3
Average score of right answerers	96%	33%	77%
Average score of wrong answerers	94%	36%	73%

The first item is nondiscriminating and easy for both high- and low-scoring students. Either (1) teaching and learning was very good or (2) the item is so easy that anyone could get it right. The teacher is the best judge of the real value of this item. You must also consider the performance on adjacent items. If these patterns exist with other items, you have good evidence for drawing a conclusion.

The second item is very hard for both high- and low-scoring students. Either (1) teaching did not occur here, (2) teaching did occur and had little effect, or (3) the item is so hard that no one could figure it out except a lucky few. The third item has a moderate amount of difficulty but little significant difference between high- and low-scoring students. This item looks like a nondiscriminator and should be reviewed and probably revised or retired.

Interaction between Difficulty and Discrimination Indexes

With well-designed tests, we like to study the interaction between difficulty and discrimination. If the scores range widely, from high to low, as is normal in most instructional settings, the interaction between difficulty and discrimination is interesting and important. Table 10.1 shows six different possibilities. With each possibility, there is a series of alternative explanations of the cause of the result we are viewing.

Type 1 items are very easy. Is this good or bad? If the item is a giveaway, then that is bad. If you have taught well, that is good. If this is a schoolwide, districtwide, or state-level test, this is probably a bad situation. You really need to know who is tested and what kind of teaching they received.

Type 2 items are most desirable. These items reflect the ideal condition that those who know choose the right option, whereas those who lack knowledge choose one of the wrong options. If I were teaching whatever was represented by this item, I would like the difficulty to be higher, reflecting effective teaching and learning. But if this happened, discrimination probably would decline, which is all right.

Type 3 items are moderately difficult and not very discriminating. These items have questionable value. You will need to look at these closely. Maybe students have some idea why these items do not work.

Type 4 items are very hard but discriminating. This is a problem. These items are not popular with students, but they do work. If your test has many of these items, you may want to lower your grading standards to compensate for your tough tests. Tough tests are all right as long as your grading related to test performance is fair.

Type 5 items are really lousy. Not only are they hard, but they fail to discriminate between high and low achievers. These items should be tossed or revised.

Type 6 items are embarrassing. (How would I know about this?) The analysis tells you that you goofed. Another option looks like the right answer, and the keyed answer looks like a Type 5 item. Type 5 and Type 6 items are very similar. The major difference is that discrimination for Type 6 is negative.

TABLE 10.1
Classification of Items by Performance

TYPE	DIFFICULTY	DISCRIM.	ANALYSIS
1	Higher than .90	Any value	Desirable if instruction has been effective.
2	Between .60 and .90	Above .20	Shows highly discriminating item with moderate difficulty. Typical of good items.
3	Between .60 and .90	Below .20	A nonperforming item. Needs some loving care or maybe it should be weeded out.
4	Below .60	Above .20	Tough but discriminating. If you have high standards, then this item is probably fair.
5	Below .60	Below .20	Tough and nondiscriminating. Throw this item away or fix it up.
6	Key error	Negative	A key error looks like item 5 but has a wrong answer that looks like a type 1 item. These items drive students crazy. Make certain that students have a chance to verify your key. Good students should agree with the teacher's key.

Summary

This section gave information about how to analyze items relevant to your teaching using computerized item analysis. This section is not especially helpful if most student performance in the class or group is very high, as you might expect with very effective teaching and learning. This section will not help you if this test was a pretest, before instruction, because most scores will be low and the items will be nondiscriminating.

Option Characteristics

I have just discussed responses to test items that are marked right or wrong. In this section I concentrate on how each option works. Are some options "wronger" than others? If options do not do much, you should toss them out. But first you need to know what constitutes a good option and a bad option.

To study option characteristics, you can use a variety of statistical techniques. A new method involves graphing student responses on the basis of their test scores. The *trace line* is a picture of student performance on each option. Although you probably will not want to graph each multiple-choice option, this section will show trace lines in an effort to afford clues to why some options work and others fail. Remember that most research on options shows that only two or three (including the right answer) actually work as intended.

Evaluating Options Using Trace Lines

Figure 10.1 shows four trace lines (A, B, C, and D) for four options. The data for the trace lines comes from a table called a *fractile*, which also appears in Figure 10.1. Option A has a trace line for a right answer. Low groups tend not to choose it, whereas high groups do tend to choose it. The line rises from left to right. This is good.

Option B has the trace line of a wrong answer (distractor). It is the reverse of a trace line for a right answer. If a right answer has this kind of trace line, then this result suggests a key error, which is Type 6 in Table 10.1. Option C has a somewhat flat trace line. This distractor is not working. It does not seem to measure anything worth detecting. You could toss this distractor without hurting the item. Option D is a low-response option. If fewer than 5 percent bite for it, it is probably so implausible that it does not work. Replace it. Trace line analysis provides a good picture of option performance, but it is too difficult to construct for each item. You need a handy method that is simpler to obtain, which is forthcoming.

Evaluating Options Statistically

If you do not have access to trace lines but want a simple, effective way to spot nonworking options, you can use the point-biserial discrimination index provided for each option in ITEMAN, the computer program. Table 10.2 provides a segment from ITEMAN for one item. Other item analysis programs provide similar results.

For the seventh item on a test, the item analysis result might give the information contained in Table 10.2. The proportion choosing the right answer (B) is our difficulty index in percent form. The computer program identifies the highest 33 percent and figures out how many choose the option. The computer does the same for the low 33 percent. The difference between these two numbers is a simplified discrimination index. Using Table 10.1, we can see that this item is fairly hard but discriminating between the upper third and the lower third of those taking this test. Our two distractors seem to be working the way they are supposed to work.

Here is the point of this section. Option A has a PBI of –.15. Because this is a trace line like option B in Figure 10.1, then this is a good distractor. Option C has a PBI of –.26. This is even better. So we would be inclined to keep both options A and C as distractors, but the correct option is a little weak for our purposes. This item is borderline in terms of keeping or tossing. If distractors have a low or positive PBI, you will need to study the item, get feedback from students, and revise or toss it.

FIGURE 10.1
Trace Lines for a Four-Option Item

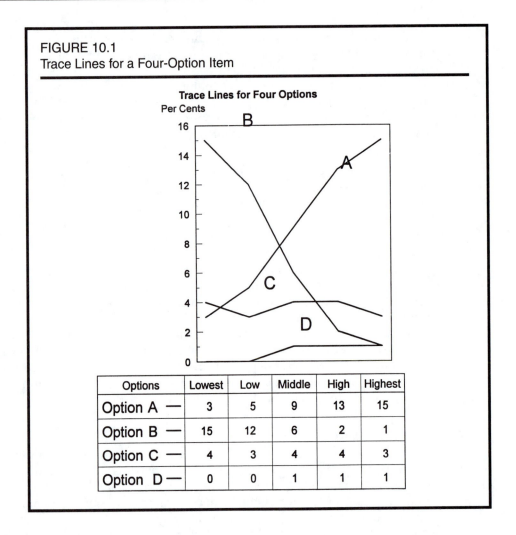

Options	Lowest	Low	Middle	High	Highest
Option A —	3	5	9	13	15
Option B —	15	12	6	2	1
Option C —	4	3	4	4	3
Option D —	0	0	1	1	1

Summary
The analysis of options can be done graphically or statistically. I learned the concept graphically, but I used statistics to study distractors. You can improve items by studying options and revising or removing poorly performing distractors.

Test Characteristics

Generally these computer programs provide descriptive statistics that tell you about the overall performance of the group on the test. Table 10.3 on page 246 contains a listing of typical statistics reported in an item analysis program.

TABLE 10.2
Sample Output from an Item Analysis Computer Program

| | ITEM NUMBER 7 | | |
| | Proportion Choosing Right Answer (B): 58% | | |
Options	A	B*	C
Percent Choosing	18	58	24
High Group	10	76	14
Low Group	17	52	30
Discrimination	−07	24	−16

Average (Mean) of the Group

This is the average score on the test for the group. If instruction has been effective and the group has worked hard to achieve student outcomes, then the average should be very high. A low average would signal a problem: (1) difficult material to be learned, (2) ineffective teaching, (3) poor student effort, or (4) unfairly hard items. Every teacher should explore these possibilities before drawing a conclusion. Another point made previously but worth repeating is that the average should be worked into your grading policy and standards. If the average of your tests is very low, say 60 percent, then adjust your grading policy to deal fairly with the fact that you give hard tests.

The computer printout also gives the median, which is the middle score if you ranked all the scores. Generally, the mean and the median are about the same. If the distribution is badly skewed (lopsided to the right or to the left), then the median is the more representative measure of central tendency for your data.

Standard Deviation/Variance/Range

The standard deviation is an indicator of how scores range. The range is a simpler statistic (maximum minus minimum). The variance is the square of the standard deviation. For your purposes, use the range. With effective teaching, you want the range to be as small as possible coupled with a high average. This would indicate satisfactory group performance. Lower scoring students should receive extra instruction and be retested to reduce this range. In teaching, where a set of scores is available, your goal is to minimize this range of scores, reflecting the condition that all students have scored uniformly high. So, when you see a set of scores with a small standard deviation or range, this is a clue that the distribution is fairly concentrated. If the range is large, then some students have not done as well as you might like.

TABLE 10.3
Summary Statistics from a Forty-Item Multiple-Choice Reading Test

NUMBER OF ITEMS	40	NUMBER OF STUDENTS	233
Mean	25.348	Median	26
Variance	36.939	Standard deviation	6.078
Skew	–0.436	Kurtosis	–.0656
Minimum	11.0	Maximum	37.0
Alpha	.802	SEM	2.705
Mean p	.634	Mean PBI	.277
Maximum score, low group	21	Minimum score, high group	30
N (low group)	63	*N* (high group)	72

Skew and Kurtosis

For readers with some background in statistics, you might remember that a normal distribution (bell-curve) is expected, but sometimes the distribution of test scores may have other shapes. Statisticians have indexes for everything (that's their business). So there are indexes for skewed distributions and kurtosis (which means you could have a peaked distribution or a flat distribution). Figure 10.2 gives you a series of frequency distributions of test scores. Let's analyze each.

The *normal* is what you get with limited instruction and a wide range of student ability. It is hardly ideal or desirable, but realistically, this is what you often get when you test a group of students.

The *left-skewed* distribution shows mostly high scores. This is desirable. The mean is high, but the range might be low. Although this is good for teaching, it is not good for item analysis. This item analysis program shows a negative skew.

The *right-skewed* distribution shows mostly low scores. This is bad. No teacher wants to see this, unless the test is a pretest. If you get this after teaching, you have a serious problem.

The *leptokurtic* distribution shows mostly scores in a very narrow range. Generally, this shows a poor test or a group of students with the same level of learning. You do not want to see this kind of distribution.

The *platykurtic* distribution shows student scores all over the scale. Again, this is not good, because you want a left-skewed distribution.

The *bimodal* distribution shows two lumps, a high group and a low group. This signals that the group tested really is two different groups. You will need to sort through this mess and figure out why you have successful and unsuccessful groups.

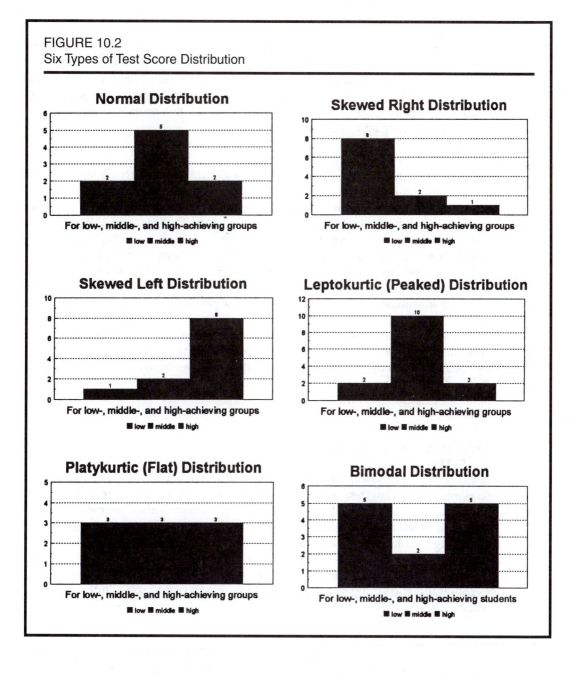

FIGURE 10.2
Six Types of Test Score Distribution

Summary

Studying frequency distributions is very helpful in testing. The six types given in Figure 10.2 provide a basis for analyzing test performance relative to instruction. Only one type of distribution is ideal, one where most kids score high. All others are less than ideal, but often you will see one of them. If you examine distributions and do item analysis, you can usually figure out which items reflect effective and ineffective teaching and learning.

Alpha: Reliability of Test Scores

Generally, this index is not very useful for small groups (fewer than 30), so if you do have a small sample, use caution when interpreting results. Alpha is the name of the reliability index normally used (based on the formula KR-20 or KR-21). This index tells you how much confidence you can have in these scores. However, if instruction has been uniformly good and you get a left-skewed distribution, then reliability will be very low because this index is influenced by the range of scores. So if your reliability index is low, say less than .50, you will have to look at the frequency distribution. A high index is not good either. If you have a wide range of scores, then your scores may be reliable, but the performance of lower scoring students is unsatisfactory.

Reliability strongly rests on a foundation of highly discriminating items. If items are highly discriminating and test scores vary, you can bet that the reliability coefficient will be high. As a teacher, what can you do to ensure high reliability? Use good discriminating items. Use as many items as possible. Avoid filler items that measure nothing or are too hard or too easy. Use Type 2 items described in Table 10.1.

SEM (Standard Error of Measurement)

The SEM is a standard deviation of how much random error (fluff) you can expect in test scores. In this reading test, the SEM is 2.7. This means that if a student's true score on this reading test was 50 percent (20 items right), then her or his actual score might be anywhere plus or minus 2.7 right answers about 68 percent of the time. The SEM is a good reminder that test scores are fallible indicators of some knowledge, skill, or ability. Never make a high-stakes decision about a student on the basis of a single test score, because the SEM is probably so great as to create considerable doubt for students scoring close to an important decision point (such as pass/fail). The saying: "Don't put all your eggs in one basket" applies to using test scores.

Mean p

No, this is not an angry letter p. "Mean p" tells you the average difficulty of your test. As I said earlier, this average should be used to judge the difficulty of your test relative to your grading standards. Hard tests are all right, if your standards are adjusted to match test difficulty. Your objective is to change the mean p upwards to reflect good teaching and student learning.

Mean Item-Total
This is the average of your PBI discrimination indexes. Ignore this statistic if instruction has been especially good and student scores are uniformly high, because this average will be very low. This does not mean that your set of items failed to discriminate. How could any items discriminate if everyone did pretty much the same on the test?

Mean Biser
This is the average of the other discrimination index that you are ignoring.

Summary
We have discussed the list of statistics put out by an item analysis computer program for multiple-choice test items. As you can see, it is pretty daunting. And it could be a lot worse, because testing is pretty complicated sometimes. What I have tried to do here is to take a standard item analysis program and interpret the results. As discussed several times, you can largely ignore these results if instruction has been good and if most students congregate at the upper end of the distribution, showing good learning and teaching. If the scores are scattered throughout, then this item analysis makes good sense.

Frequency Distribution (Histogram)
Another feature of ITEMAN is an actual frequency distribution that shows how the class scores are distributed. Table 10.4 shows a frequency distribution for 233 students on an elementary-level reading test. This graph could be a bar graph, but because these are test scores, we call it a *histogram*. In a previous section, I discussed six types of frequency distribution. What type is Table 10.4? It is pretty normal. Although it is not desirable from a teaching standpoint, this test helps teachers place students for specific kinds of reading instruction in the school district where it is administered.

Item Analysis for Rating Scales

This section deals with the analysis of items where rating scales are used, such as the high-inference item in Chapter 5 and the affective survey items shown in Chapter 8. Fortunately, most of what you learned in the previous section on multiple choice applies here. So this section will be briefer than the previous section and will emphasize distinctive aspects of the item analysis results for rating scales.

Interrater Consistency
Generally, if judges were involved in the rating, you will want to know if the judges were consistent. This is a major league science, well beyond the scope of this chapter and this book. However, you have an index we can compute from a set of judges and items that tells you if your judges were consistent. This index is used

TABLE 10.4
Test Score Distribution

NUMBER CORRECT	FREQUENCY	CUMULATIVE FREQUENCY	PR	PCT	
. . . No examinees below this score . . .					
10	0	0	1	0	+
11	2	2	1	1	#
12	3	5	2	1	#
13	4	9	4	2	##
14	8	17	7	3	###
15	4	21	9	2	+ ##
16	3	24	10	1	#
17	3	27	12	1	#
18	6	33	14	3	###
19	13	46	20	6	######
20	10	56	24	4	+ ####
21	7	63	27	3	###
22	6	69	30	3	###
23	16	85	36	7	#######
24	10	95	41	4	####
25	14	109	47	6	+ ######
26	11	120	52	5	#####
27	16	136	58	7	#######
28	12	148	64	5	#####
29	13	161	69	6	######
30	18	179	77	8	+ ########
31	17	196	84	7	#######
32	11	207	89	5	#####
33	9	216	93	4	####
34	12	228	98	5	#####
35	3	231	99	1	+ #
36	1	232	99	0		
No test-takers above this score					

```
                                        |————+————+————
                                        5    10   15
                                   Percentage of
                                     test-takers
```

for measuring the consistency of judges who are using the kinds of rating scales found in Chapter 5B. Indexes above .80 are usually taken as being acceptable. Interrater consistency is related to reliability. If interrater consistency is low, then it follows that reliability must be low. That is why training is always recommended with the use of raters. To supplement training, task-specific analytical rating scales should be used. A second best choice is the use of generic analytical rating scales. The more specific, crisp, and precise the descriptive categories, the greater the interrater consistency is likely to be.

Item Characteristics

Difficulty

This index generally represents the range of a rating scale. For instance with a five-point rating scale, the scores generally vary between 1 and 5 with a zero assigned for no response or an inappropriate response. The difficulty of an item is the average rating, so it will vary between 0 and 5. A moderate difficulty is 3.0, indicating the center of the rating scale when zero becomes a real performance level.

Discrimination

This index is the correlation between how students were rated on their performance on the item and their total score. Generally, to have a positive index, a high performance on an item is correlated with a high overall performance. A low discrimination would indicate that how students did on the item has nothing to do with the total score. A negative discrimination would signal that low-scorers tended to get the item right and the high scorers tended to get the item wrong. Negative discrimination would be an unfortunate finding.

Here is an example of a use of the interrater consistency index in a performance test using high-inference rating scales in which I was involved.

Cactus County Rollerblading Championship

Judge ——> Skater:	Haladyna	Mayor Meyer	Major Minor	Hal the Computer
Nancy Cardigan	7	4	2	3
Tonya Hardly	8	6	4	5
Tippy Spindizzy	10	9	8	9
KiKiKi Tyler	6	7	6	8
Rose Busch	10	8	4	8

We had five skaters and four judges. The interrater consistency coefficient tells us the extent to which the four judges are in agreement. What do you think it should be if 1.00 is perfect and 0.00 is rotten. The resulting coefficient was a poor .57. So the judges were lousy. About all they agreed on was the skating of Tippi Spindizzy, who is the national champion. Considering that this group knew nothing about rollerblading, what do you expect? Generally, we like coefficients in the .80s or .90s. If you have only one judge, then you cannot compute this coefficient.

This coefficient is very useful. It is *not* a reliability coefficient. That is a different idea. Finally, this coefficient does not consider bias in ratings. Notice that Haladyna gave mostly high ratings and Major Minor gave mostly low ratings. This leniency and harshness are not considered in this coefficient and should be studied separately. Another kind of error not considered occurs when the judge essentially gives all contestants about the same rating (central tendency or flatlining).

We have an emerging science of judge evaluation, using a variety of statistical techniques that would make your head spin like a professional rollerblader. This kind of analysis is frequently done by statisticians who specialize in analyzing and evaluating judge's behavior. Therefore, none of this is applicable to classroom testing.

On the other hand, what principles can we carry forward to classroom evaluation of student performance that involves rating scales and judges?

- Two or more judges are better than one.
- More items are better than fewer items.
- More analytic rating scales per item are better than fewer rating scales.
- Use task-specific analytic rating scale if possible.
- Judges should be consistent with one another.
- Judges should not be biased.

This is an ideal list. You can see that performance testing using rating scales is not inexpensive or easy. To get best results requires some extra effort. But more and more teachers are thinking that it is worth the extra effort because the quality of learning is better.

Reliability

This coefficient is the same one I used for multiple choice. Its technical name is coefficient *alpha*, named after its inventor Lee Cronbach (figure that one out). Like the previous index, alpha ranges from .00 to 1.00. Generally, if this index hits .80 or higher, you should be pretty happy. Why? Because judges are notoriously inconsistent. With multiple-choice tests, you don't have the problem of judge inconsistency to affect reliability. Also, the number of items used in a performance test is usually limited to three to five, so reliability cannot get too high. With a 100-item multiple-choice test, you can expect reliability to surpass .85.

As I said earlier, if you are measuring something that can be tested with either a multiple-choice format or one requiring a rating scale, use multiple choice for its higher reliability. But high-inference performance testing often leaves no alternative other than to use a rating scale. Once you have determined that you need judged ratings, you face the possibility that reliability will be lower than desired.

Remember that low reliability is not a fatal condition. Be careful not to weight a less reliable test score too heavily. For instance, I would not count the results of a low-reliability performance test score too much in a student grade. Instead, I would combine it with other information. When you combine information from a variety of good sources, your result is usually very reliable. That's how you can get good reliability from a high-inference test where rating scales and judges must be used—strength in numbers!

Item Analysis for Checklists and Simple Observation

This is a very brief section. Generally, you would not do item analysis for this kind of testing. Only the simplest and most basic type of learning is evaluated in this way. The results are so easy to see or measure that you do not need to question difficulty or discrimination, or to estimate reliability. Simply note whether the answer is right or wrong, whether the behavior is present or absent, or check the checklist. This kind of testing is very attractive from the standpoints of objectivity, reliability, and avoiding bias. However, as pointed out in Chapter 6, there are few applications of this in testing for complex mental skills and abilities. If you are inventive enough, perhaps you can devise checklists that effectively tap elements of critical thinking, problem solving, or creative thinking or production. Most test item constructors use rating scales in these applications.

Table 10.5 shows a display of results of an extensive performance test given to fifteen new teachers in a local school district on an important professional skill: making coffee in the teacher's lounge. The school district was very concerned that new teachers conform to the high coffee-making standards stated in *Goals 2001*. The performance test analyzed has six main tasks in making coffee in the teachers' lounge. These six tasks were identified by the National Panel on Teacher Competency (Big Government, 1984).

Given the results from Table 10.5, we can draw some conclusions. First, Beth is the best coffee maker. Kim is far behind. Theresa is a pretty lousy coffee maker. Fortunately, she's a really good teacher. However, district policy says that each new teacher will have to show effective coffee making on a performance test to be proved competent!

Let's analyze the tasks and learn about this training program for new teachers. Everyone gets task 1 right, so it must be pretty easy or teaching must be very good. Task 2 shows that high scorers tend to complete it, while low scorers tend not to complete it. So this one looks like a discriminator. Task 3 lacks a pattern for who

---

TABLE 10.5
Summary of Checklist Performances of Ten Teachers on Six Coffee-Making Tasks

TASKS:	1	2	3	4	5	6	
POINTS	16	32	10	24	18	10	TOTAL
Beth	yes	yes	yes	yes	yes	no	90
Kim	yes	yes	no	yes	yes	no	80
Ron	yes	yes	yes	yes	no	no	72
Judy	yes	yes	no	yes	no	no	62
Mark	yes	yes	yes	no	no	yes	58
Tom	yes	yes	yes	no	no	yes	58
Elise	yes	yes	yes	no	no	yes	58
Del	yes	no	no	no	yes	yes	44
Linda	yes	no	yes	no	yes	no	44
Theresa	yes	no	no	no	no	yes	26
Total	10	7	6	4	4	5	

---

gets or doesn't get it. It looks like a nondiscriminator. Task 4 is like task 2, but a lot harder. Are we teaching this enough? Perhaps if more emphasis were given in the training session, performance on task 4 would improve. Task 5 is tough and nondiscriminating. It has no relationship to how teachers do overall. Maybe this is an irrelevant task. The last task looks as though it was incorrectly scored. High scorers got it wrong and low scorers got it right. We might have goofed on this one, or perhaps it is simply a lousy item.

If you haven't guessed it yet, this analysis is very much like the one shown in Table 10.1, where we typify different types of patterns to multiple-choice items. The logic of analysis is the same for checklisted tasks.

The summary table of student performance by tasks gives you a picture of how students are doing and what areas need additional work. Teaching emphasis, new strategies, individual student attention for some weak areas, and changes in tasks are all instructional activities related to improving performance.

Item Analysis for Portfolios

This section is really brief because the previous two sections apply here.

High-Inference Ratings

If you have decided to approach portfolio assessment from the standpoint of high-inference ratings, you will want to refer to the previous section on rating-scale analysis. As Reckase (1995) states, reliability can be a problem with portfolio assessment. He recommends the use of many rating scales and warns that the cost of scoring may be very high relative to other scoring systems.

Checklisted Items

If you have decided to approach portfolio assessment from the standpoint of low-inference analysis, using a checklist, you can refer to the previous section. Your checklist will have point allocations for each observable item you want to see. This system typically does not employ item analysis to evaluate items, but Table 10.5 shows that you can draw conclusions from a chart that shows student performance by task.

Item Analysis for Affective Surveys

Fortunately, much of what you learned in the section on high-inference rating scales applies here. In this section, I will review the same concepts and discuss some strategies that are unique to affective surveys.

The purpose of affective surveys is to learn about student attainment of affective goals for a class, school, or school district. With an affective item and a rating scale, the students become the judges as they reflect on their attitude, self-esteem, or classroom learning climate.

Since Chapter 8 focused on home-grown surveys instead of professionally developed surveys, let us use ITEMAN again to review how we might analyze results. Generally, an affective survey will consist of two or more concepts, such as attitude toward school and attitude toward a specific subject matter like writing.

Coefficient alpha is important to tell us if the items "hang together" as a measure of some affective concept. If the affective concept you are measuring is well defined and clear to students, the patterns of their ratings will be internally consistent. This pattern will show up as a high alpha. Alpha is strongly influenced by (1) the number of items and (2) the number of rating scale points used. Thus, the use of more items and a seven-point rating scale should maximize alpha.

Similarly, item total discriminations have to be very high. Finally, if there is no variation in scores, this might be a design flaw, or might simply mean that student ratings are high, reflecting a positive state of mind. The average (mean) rating gives you a status report relative to the rating scale that you are using. For instance, with a five-point scale, an average score of 4.5 would be interpreted as positive and an average of 1.5 would be interpreted as negative. {This assumes that your rating scale assigned 5 to the most positive adjective and 1 to the most negative adjective.}

Polling the Class

Following any classroom or course test (especially in a law school, where the student will want to argue with the instructor or perhaps even go to court), it is a good idea to conduct an informal class review of test results. In Chapter 9, I referred to this as "student posttest review." Well, this is related. Here we will use some statistical ideas to help us find lousy items.

Polling is an informal way to check with students to see if your test items are giving them trouble. It is cheaper, more effective, and friendlier to the class than an item analysis. It also resolves disputes quickly and makes the class feel better after the test. It also generates more evidence of student learning.

Given your understanding of Table 10.1, you can apply that knowledge to any testing situation. During the posttest student discussion, you might informally ask for a show of hands to indicate if more than half the class missed an item on which you expected a high performance. If the poll indicates more than half, you should investigate, using methods discussed in Chapter 9, and act appropriately. Often you will end up discarding the item so as not to penalize students for a bad item.

Polling is quick and easy. It is friendly and often diffuses anger that might arise when students think that the teacher goofed on an item and will not admit it. By admitting it, you allow students to be treated fairly and lessen the danger of antagonizing a class because some items were faulty. Some items in your tests will be less useful than you expected. So an honest student evaluation goes a long way in building trust between you, the teacher, and your students, and it also gives your students a fair appraisal of their learning.

Differential Item Functioning

This is serious business. You probably will not be doing differential item functioning studies. However, if you are involved in a high-stakes testing program at a district or state level, such studies are now being viewed as highly desirable. A competent attorney representing your school district should insist on such studies if the tests are being used for placement, graduation, or pass/fail decisions. Legal defensibility of high-stakes decisions can rest on whether or not these studies have been done and, if so, what actions were taken. You will need to know a little bit about this and participate in a process that identifies these items and changes or removes them from tests used to make important decisions about your students.

What is the idea behind differential item functioning? If a group of students has a problem with an item and another group of students does not, you may have an item that is performing differentially. If these two groups are boys and girls, different ethnic groups or racial groups, or socioeconomically different groups, then the performance difference is not due to teaching and learning but to something else, which is a form of bias.

Our society has become increasingly aware of items that might unfairly trip up students from a specific subgroup. Statisticians have invented over four hundred ways to study differential item functioning (that's what we do in our spare time). A good reference on this topic is a book edited by Holland and Wainer (1993). I won't review the four hundred methods, but it is important to note that such studies are necessary in high-stakes tests.

What can a classroom teacher do to avoid differentially functioning items?

- Look for patterns in item analysis or polling that favor a subgroup of students, and investigate.
- Conduct a bias and sensitivity review, as suggested in Chapter 9.
- Provide alternative means for students to perform on a test if you suspect a cultural, language-based, gender-based, regional, or other reason for failure to perform.

There are many other reasons that students fail to perform. One of the most prevalent is test anxiety. For example, if a student's culture does not promote or recognize a time limit, then the student is not likely to finish a test. By providing a strict time limit, you may be handicapping someone who is not time-conscious in the classroom. Some students are slow, plodding, but accurate workers. Again, time limits stymie these students and lower their total scores. Is this fair? If a student's command of English is not complete, additional time might be needed for mental translation to a native language and back. Time limits may affect performance in this instance as well. Lack of clarity in instructions and other factors may produce poor performance. Without checking into such possibilities, you may inadvertently handicap some students and undervalue their effort to learn. Such unfair treatment may have aftershocks that affect future learning.

The field of differential item functioning is mainly intended to root out bad items using sophisticated statistical methods. Used informally, however, it can spot other problems of student performance. These problems may not be the result of ineffective learning but, instead, may stem from extraneous factors. You should identify these problems and deal with each as you encounter it to accommodate students and get a fair measure of student learning.

Bias Detection

Some excellent new tools exist to detect rater bias in performance testing, as featured in Chapter 5B, but none of these tools can be used in classroom testing. In this section, I will discuss the value of these tools for school district, state, or national testing programs and give some advice on how to avoid some biases in scoring test results in the classroom. As a classroom teacher, you need to understand how bias can hurt the measurement of student learning and you need to combat bias effectively. First, however, you need to review bias.

Bias Redefined

Bias in testing is directional error that affects a subgroup of students. For instance, if a group of Grateful Dead fans and another group of Beethoven fans were tested on a general music test based only on classical music, we might see some bias in the test scores. Items reflecting Beethoven's work should show this bias.

In Chapter 5B, I reviewed many types of bias in judged performance, such as harshness, leniency, and central tendency. In testing, bias usually results in reduced scores that reflect badly on the student. By using biased tests, you will underestimate students' true knowledge, skill, or ability. Tests should reveal what students know or can do, not underestimate their achievements.

Statistical Methods

One new method uses a complex theory of item responses to identify student scores, identify rater biases, and make adjustments accordingly. Known as the many-faceted Rasch model, this computer program actually adjusts test scores on the basis of the harshness or leniency of judged ratings and also allows you to enter into the programming other factors that might bias ratings (Linacre & Wright, 1993). This promising method works for large samples of students taking rating-judged performance tests (Hess, 1994). This method could not be used in a classroom but could be used in district-level, county-level, or state-level tests.

Summary

This chapter contains a technical discussion of the study of characteristics of student responses. I addressed a variety of topics. The most well developed theories, computer programs, and experience exist for multiple-choice test item responses. With the other kinds of items, there is less theory, fewer computer applications, and little experience to accompany the technical problems we face. Nonetheless, it is important to push ahead, to experiment, and to evaluate with new and perhaps better techniques of teaching and testing. The spirit of this effort is that if we are to make progress in teaching and testing, this type of exploration is unsettling but necessary. This chapter has tried to effect a balance between traditional methods that have served in the past and newer attempts to study item response patterns. The statistical aspects of this chapter are the least likely to be studied or used in the classroom, but some methods were presented here that can be applied in your classroom.

References

Assessment Systems Corporation. (1993). *ITEMAN: Conventional Item Analysis Program* (Computer software).

Haladyna, T. M. (1994). *Developing and validating multiple-choice test items.* Hillsdale, NJ: Lawrence Erlbaum Associates.

Hess, R. (1994, April). *Using the Rasch model to calibrate a district-wide, curriculum-based mathematics assessment.* Paper presented at the annual meeting of the American Educational Research Association, Atlanta, Georgia.

Holland, P. W., & Wainer, H. (Eds.). (1993). *Differential item functioning.* Hillsdale, NJ: Lawrence Erlbaum Associates.

Linacre, J. M., & Wright, B. D. (1993). *FACETS: Computer program for many-faceted Rasch measurement* (Computer software). Chicago: MESA Press.

Reckase, M. D. (1995). Portfolio assessment: A theoretical estimate of score reliability. *Educational Measurement: Issues and Practices, 14,* 12–14, 31.

Index

Subject Index